Choosing Revolution

Choosing Revolution

Chinese Women Soldiers on the Long March

HELEN PRAEGER YOUNG

University of Illinois Press
URBANA AND CHICAGO

∞ This book is printed on acid-free paper.

Library of Congress Cataloging-in-Publication Data
Young, Helen Praeger, 1932–
Choosing revolution : Chinese women soldiers on the long march /
Helen Praeger Young.
      p.   cm.
Includes bibliographical references and index.
ISBN 0-252-02672-1 (alk. paper)
1. China—History—Long March, 1934–1935.
2. Women soldiers—China. I. Title.
DS777.5135.Y68   2001
951.04'2—dc21   2001000827

*This book is dedicated to
the women whose words have made it possible
and to the Chinese children and young people who carry
within themselves the same seeds of the spirit and
will to survive that sustained Chinese women soldiers
on the Long March.*

Contents

Acknowledgments

IT IS A DISTINCT pleasure to acknowledge people who have helped and supported me over the many years this book has been in process. However, I also feel an anxiety arising from the fear that I might have missed someone and the knowledge that I can never adequately thank all those who so generously gave of their time and expertise, knowing that there would be no monetary reward for them from this project, which was undertaken for the benefit of the Chinese Youth and Children's Fund.

By nature, a book based on oral history involves a great many people, not only the interviewees but also the others who have given their support in diverse ways and venues. The interviews in this book involved the help of people in the Beijing Military History Museum, the China International Radio Press, Radio Beijing, China Central Television, and the Soong Ching-Ling Foundation; Peoples' Liberation Army historians in Guangzhou, Nanchang, Nanjing; and staff in museums and foreign affairs offices in many places, including Changsha, Hunan; Zunyi and Bijie, Guizhou; and Kunming, Lijiang, and Zhoudian, Yunnan.

Passages were translated wherever my tape recorder, computer, and a willing Chinese-speaking student, colleague, or friend might be: in my apartment in Beijing, at Columbia University, University of Maryland, Stanford University, my home, and friends' homes in Palo Alto.

The writing itself was helped by those in creative writing classes in Palo Alto Adult School, where I reclaimed my ear for the English language of the 1990s after thirteen years resident in Beijing; two writing groups that worked diligently to help me explore both language and ideas; and the Biographers Seminar at Stanford, which gave greater vision to the project as well as very

basic support. The English department at Beijing Foreign Studies University and the Stanford University Center for East Asian Studies provided an
immeasurable amount of interest and help, as well as access to libraries and
physical space for writing.

People who have earned my deep gratitude include Wen Dongnuan, who
started me on the project; Huang Huichun, Jiang Qingnian, and Yan Jintang,
who helped in many quiet ways to ensure that this piece of Chinese history
would become visible. Wang Weihua, Ge Rui, Chen Jingjun, and Feng Xiao-
ming worked on the interviews. Sally Arteseros believed in the project from
the start; Marilyn Young offered early encouragement; and Isabel Crook,
Chris Gilmartin, and Annette Rubinstein have been involved in reading and
discussing the interviews from early on.

Those who worked with me on the exacting and often exasperating job
of translation include Wang Weihua, Li Yinghong, Hu Chun, Hong Jingyi,
Wang Zhenhua, Qian Meng, Han Pei, Chen Shu, Yi Haining, and Li Yong.

At Stanford, Marilyn Yalom introduced me to the Biographers Seminar,
which was initiated by Diane Middlebrook and Barbara Babcock and sustained by Edie Gelles. The Center for East Asian Studies, in the persons of
Lyman Van Slyke, Peter Duus, Hal Kahn, Jean Oi, Ted Foss, Helen Neves, and
Connie Chin, provided me a home base.

Susan Rigdon, a stalwart supporter who came to the project midway, has
read and commented on the entire manuscript, generously giving untold
hours of meticulous reading, questioning and suggesting; others who have
selflessly done the same for one or more chapters are Hill Gates, Chris Gilmartin, Gail Hershatter, Dorothy Ko, Tobie Meyer-Fong, and Shen Xiaohong.

Those who have devoted time, energy, and imagination to the lengthy process of obtaining photo permissions and translations include Chen Yuzhong,
Huang Bingyin, and Huang Kaimeng. Barry Tao worked into the wee hours
of the morning around other jobs to clarify the maps and make them more
presentable.

In places where I have strayed from an accurate portrayal or allowed mistakes to creep in despite the hard work by all those involved, I take full responsibility.

The two greatest debts I owe—beyond those to the interviewees whose
words are the backbone of the project—are to Wang Weihua and Richard
Young. Weihua gave time, expertise, energy, warmth, dedication, and humor
with a contagious enthusiasm even at the times when she was most pressed
or exhausted. I treasure the memories of student and teacher learning from
each other and from the process itself as we worked together over the years.
My other "without whom this book could not . . ." is my multilingual hus-

band, Richard Young. His great patience with the lengthy project, his insights and attention to detail, and his unflagging support and imaginative approach to research, to say nothing of his wonderful dinners at the end of many an exacting day, have all contributed to making this book a reality.

* * *

Chapter 4 first appeared, in slightly different form, in *Science and Society* 59 (Winter 1995–96): 531–47 and was reprinted in *U.S.-China Review* 20 (Fall 1996): 16–23. Used by permission of the editors of both journals.

Chapter 5 first appeared, in slightly different form, in *Women and War in the 20th Century: Enlisted with and without Consent,* ed. Nicole Dombrowski (New York: Garland, 1999), 92–111. Used by permission of Taylor & Francis/Garland Publishing, <http://www.taylorandfrancis.com>.

Chapter 6 first appeared, with some modification, in *A Soldier and a Woman: Women in the Military up to 1945,* ed. Gerard de Groot and Corinna Peniston-Bird (London: Pearson Education, 2000), 83–99. Used by permission of Pearson Education Limited.

Pronunciation Guide

I HAVE USED the modern standard Pinyin spelling for all Chinese words and names, with the exception of the familiar Sun Yat-sen and Chiang Kai-shek. The Chinese family name—Sun or Chiang, for example—is first and the given name, usually but not always two words, follows.

When spelling was standardized, some letters were used that seem strange in English. Four consonant sounds that are different from normal English pronunciation are *c, q, x,* and *zh:*

c is pronounced like the *ts* in "its"
q is similar to *ch* in "chin" or "cheese"
x is similar to *sh* in "she" or "shoe"
zh is pronounced like the *j* in "jelly"

For example,

Name or Term	Pronunciation
Chen Zongying	CHUN ZOONG YING
Cili	TSEE LEE
He Long	HUH LOONG
He Manqiu	HUH MAN CHEW
Hunan	HOO-NAHN
Jian Xianfo	GEE-EN SHE-EN FOE
Jian Xianren	GEE-EN SHE-EN REN
Jiangxi	GEE-AHNG SHE
Ma Yixiang	MAH EE SHE-AHNG
Ren Bishi	REN BEE SHIRR

Name or Term	Pronunciation
tongyangxi	TOONG YAHNG SHE
Wang Quanyuan	WAHNG CHWAN YU-AN
Xiao Ke	SHE-OW KUH
Xinqiao	SHEEN CHEE-OW
Zhou En-lai	JOE UN LIE

Chronology

1930   First Front Army is founded in the Jiangxi Soviet Base Area

1931   Fourth Front Army is founded in the Hubei-Henan-Anhui Soviet Base Area

1932   Fourth Front Army leaves the Soviet base, moving west to Sichuan; Lin Yueqin believes the Long March begins for her at this time

1933   Political Bureau of the Chinese Communist party moves to the Jiangxi Soviet Base Area

Fourth Front Army establishes Sichuan-Shaanxi Base Area

1934   *August*

Sixth Army Group leaves Hunan-Jiangxi Base Area to join forces with troops in the Eastern Guizhou Base Area; Chen Zongying marks this as the beginning of the Long March for her

October

Sixth and Second Army Groups establish Hunan-Hubei-Sichuan-Guizhou Soviet Base Area

First Front Army leaves the Jiangxi Soviet on the Long March

November/December

First Front fights their way across Jiangxi and Hunan and into Guizhou

1935   *January*

First Front Army reaches Zunyi, Guizhou, holds meeting of the Political Bureau of the Party Central Committee; past military decisions are criticized, opening the way for adoption of Mao Zedong's military strategies and his political leadership

1935   *February*
        First Front Army tries to move north into Sichuan from the Guizhou-
            Sichuan-Yunnan border with severe fighting
        Li Guiying is reassigned to stay behind and work locally with Sichuan
            guerrillas
        March/April
        First Front Army moves south and west into Yunnan province
        Liao Siguang's baby is born
        Fourth Front Army moves to the Sichuan-Sikang border
        Xie Xiaomei is assigned to stay behind and work underground in
            Guizhou
        May
        First Front Army crosses the Jinsha River (upper Yangzi River) and
            the Dadu River at Luding Bridge
        June/July
        First and Fourth Front Armies converge, climb the snow mountains,
            rest, and regroup while leaders meet
        Kang Keqing and Wang Quanyuan are transferred to the Fourth
            Front Army
        August
        Chinese Communist Party officially advocates a United Front with
            the Nationalists to fight the Japanese
        First and Fourth Front Armies cross the grasslands
        September
        First and Fourth Front Army leaders are unable to agree on strate-
            gy; First Front Army goes north to Shaanbei, Fourth turns south
        October
        First Front Army reaches the Base Area at Wuqizhen in northern
            Shaanxi province, ending their Long March
        November
        Second and Sixth Army Groups leave the Hunan-Hubei-Sichuan-
            Guizhou Revolutionary Base Area to begin their Long March
        December
        Mao Zedong first uses the term "25,000 *li* Long March" in a speech
1936   *January*
        Second and Sixth Army Groups reach Guizhou
        February
        Fourth Front Army settles in Ganzi on the Sikang-Tibet border
        March
        Second and Sixth Army Groups reach Guizhou-Yunnan border

April

Second and Sixth Army Groups cross the Jinsha River in northwest Yunnan province

May

Second and Sixth Army Groups move north on separate routes into Sikang

June

Second and Sixth Army Groups meet Fourth Front Army

July

Second and Sixth Army Groups reorganize into the Second Front Army

Fourth Front Army agrees to march north to Shaanbei with Second Front Army

August/September

Second and Fourth Front Armies cross the grasslands; Chen Zong-ying and Jian Xianfo deliver their babies

Second and Fourth Front Armies take separate routes, fighting their way toward Shaanbei

October

First and Fourth Front Armies meet in Huining, Gansu province

First and Second Front Armies meet in Gansu province two weeks later

First, Second, and Fourth Front Armies converge and the Long March ends

November

Western Route Army is formed

Wang Quanyuan commands a regiment of women in Western Route Army

Jian Xianfo decides to leave the Western Route Army and take her baby to Shaanbei

December

Chiang Kai-shek is captured by warlord troops and agrees to form a United Front between Nationalists and the Communists to fight against the Japanese

Choosing Revolution

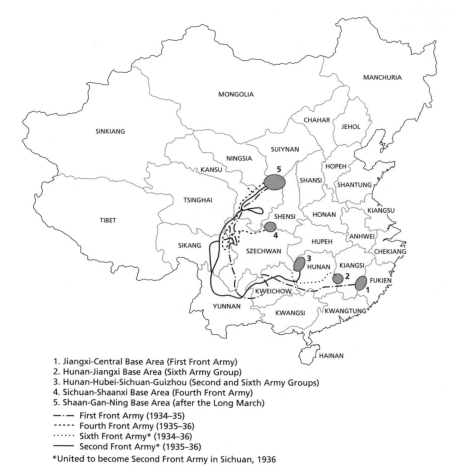

1. Jiangxi-Central Base Area (First Front Army)
2. Hunan-Jiangxi Base Area (Sixth Army Group)
3. Hunan-Hubei-Sichuan-Guizhou (Second and Sixth Army Groups)
4. Sichuan-Shaanxi Base Area (Fourth Front Army)
5. Shaan-Gan-Ning Base Area (after the Long March)

—·— First Front Army (1934–35)
- - - - Fourth Front Army (1935–36)
······ Sixth Front Army* (1934–36)
——— Second Front Army* (1935–36)
*United to become Second Front Army in Sichuan, 1936

China, 1934–36: Routes of the First, Second, and Fourth Front Red Armies, showing Chinese Soviet Base Areas. (Compiled by the author; drafted by Bill Nelson)

Introduction

FORCED BY encircling Nationalist troops to abandon their Base Areas in eastern and central China, the Chinese Red Army struck out across China in the mid-1930s. They strove to move north to join their comrades but were constantly prevented from doing so by enemy forces. The Red Army retreated to the southwestern border of China, finally turning north through the mountains on the edge of the Tibetan plateau into the treacherous grasslands. Starving and in tatters, the decimated First Front Army emerged from the grasslands and fought their way across yet another mountain range to converge with other Red Army troops in northern Shaanxi province. A month later, Mao Zedong told his soldiers,

> For twelve months we were under daily reconnaissance and bombing from the skies by scores of planes, while on land we were encircled and pursued, obstructed and intercepted by a huge force of several hundred thousand men, and we encountered untold difficulties and dangers on the way; yet by using our two legs we swept across a distance of more than twenty thousand *li* [about 6,000 miles] through the length and breadth of eleven provinces. Let us ask, has history every known a long march to equal ours? No, never. The Long March . . . has proclaimed to the world that the Red Army is an army of heroes. . . . The Long March . . . has announced to some 200 million people in eleven provinces that the road of the Red Army is their only road to liberation. . . . In the eleven provinces [the Long March] has sown many seeds which will sprout, leaf, blossom and bear fruit, and will yield a harvest in the future. In a word, the Long March has ended with victory for us and defeat for the enemy.[1]

And in this way, the strategic troop shifts the Red Army made from Chinese Soviet Base Areas under siege by the Nationalists became legendary.[2]

Based as it was on dogged perseverance, almost superhuman endurance, and incredible acts of courage, this odyssey became the symbol of the invincibility of the Red Army. The Chinese Communist party turned the "25,000 *Li* Long March" into a magnificent propaganda tool to amass support for the party and army. Stories about the march quickly spread around the country.

Edgar Snow, an American journalist teaching at Beijing University at the time, upon hearing that the Communists had battled Nationalist armies as they walked across China for a year before settling in Shaanxi province, recognized the historical impact of what had happened. Leaving Beijing ostensibly for Shanghai, Snow slipped into Yan'an, the capital of the Chinese Soviet Base Area. After hours spent interviewing Mao Zedong, he wrote the only authorized biography of the Communist leader and made the incredible exploits of the Red Army during the Long March known to the West.[3] More than thirty years later, underscoring the importance of this event, which marked a distinct turning point in Chinese history, Dick Wilson published the first book-length English-language history of the Long March by a western scholar and journalist.[4] The Long March, considered both a historical watershed in modern Chinese history and the stuff of legendary heroic exploits, became a focal point for Western military and political historians and journalists.[5]

Agnes Smedley, another American journalist who was in Yan'an in the late 1930s, wrote about the Long March in her biography of the Red Army commander in chief, Marshal Zhu De: "Neither facts or figures, or the names of a hundred rivers and mountains, can ever explain the historical significance of the Long March of the Red Army. Nor can they describe the tenacity and determination nor the suffering of the hundred thousand men who took part in it."[6]

At least 2,000 women participated in the Long March. Who were these women who chose to leave their families, join the revolution, and become Red Army soldiers? Of those who recounted the stories that follow, some were teenagers escaping from the abusive "in-law" families they had been sold into, some were avoiding unwanted arranged marriages, others were simply fleeing starvation. Those fortunate enough to go to school became involved in revolutionary activities and sought refuge from Nationalist reprisals. Some were wives, sisters, daughters, or nieces of Communists. All were looking for a family in the Red Army.

Considered as a group, the twenty-two women featured in this book represent a good spectrum of the female participants on the Long March.[7] They were soldiers from the three major contingents of the Red Army, they came from eight different provinces, fourteen were seventeen years old or younger when they chose revolution by joining Chinese Communist Party organizations or the army, eleven of them had been sold or given to other families as infants or small children, twelve were illiterate, and when they began the Long March, their ages ranged from twelve to thirty-two. Their work on the March included decoding telegrams for Headquarters, doing propaganda work in the villages they passed through, carrying stretchers and medicines, caring for the wounded, working in security, doing administrative work for the party, working in a clothing factory, leading the women's working group, and attending school. Some were married to generals, political commissars at various levels, or lesser leaders; others were unmarried or had left their husbands behind when they joined the revolution. Three gave birth to babies on the March.

They were born in the turbulent first quarter of the twentieth century, a time of dramatic political and social change in China. The age-old rule by emperors came to an end in 1911 with the founding of the Republic of China, but the political turmoil in the years immediately after the overthrow of the Qing dynasty had little immediate effect on Chinese people, most of whom lived in remote mountain areas of provinces far from the seat of the national government. Village life continued as it had for centuries while presidents, governors, and warlords struggled to fill the political vacuum.[8]

By the 1920s, change was seeping into provincial capitals and cities through schools established by ardent young teachers who had been influenced by the May Fourth Movement.[9] Electrified by the patriotic and revolutionary fervor of their teachers, future Long March women veterans became student activists. In the 1930s, as the Red Army plied their guerrilla tactics in remote mountainous areas of provincial borders and established Chinese Soviet Base Areas, young peasant women, many facing no good future, joined the revolution through local Communist organizations. They rose within the organizational structures to become leaders, typically in women's departments, and were in the right place when the Red Army began the legendary retreat to victory by the "army of heroes."

*   *   *

Fashioning a historical narrative based on oral interviews is always a time-consuming project. The process grows longer when the material to be written in English is based on interviews in Chinese. Translating words and concepts unfamiliar to readers in Western countries takes additional time. And when the topic is a historical event in a country whose modern history is not well known even to educated people outside the field, it is necessary to present a large amount of background information. It should not be surprising, therefore, that it has been sixteen years since I received the phone call that began the process culminating in this book.

I had been living in Beijing and working at the Beijing Broadcasting Institute since 1979, training undergraduates to be English teachers. I was part of the first wave of Western teachers whom the Chinese government recruited more for our academic training than for political commitment. In May 1985, when every sector of Chinese society was being urged to make a profit, a young Chinese colleague of my husband asked whether I would be interested in helping a Chinese charitable organization earn foreign currency and promote understanding between our two countries. Her mother-in-law was one of the directors of the Chinese Children's Fund. She and others on the board who had also been soldiers on the Long March in the 1930s wanted to know whether I would write up their stories for publication in the West. I immediately agreed, delighted at the opportunity to work on an intriguing topic in modern Chinese history.

With this casual beginning, the project developed in unexpected ways. After I agreed to take it on, the women who initiated the project received permission to pursue it from the highest political level: the secretary general of the Communist Party, Hu Yaobang. However, the group he designated as sponsoring organization for the project did not find it convenient—meaning politically expedient—to support it. Changes in the top leadership in the country were anticipated, although Hu Yaobang was not deposed until a year and a half later.

The women on the board of the Children's Fund were unwilling to be interviewed by a foreigner who had no official sponsoring organization for the project. During the next year, while I was still teaching, I sought a sponsor, enlisting the aid of Huang Huichun, a former colleague at the Broadcasting Institute who then held a high position at China Central Radio. She understood the value of writing the women's history of the Long March and enthusiastically agreed to help.

In December 1985 I met with Yan Jingtang, the historian at the Museum of Military History in Beijing whose area of expertise was the Long March. The director of the museum, General Qin Xinghan, arranged the meeting, thanks to a letter of introduction from the late John Service, a retired U.S. Foreign Service officer who had grown up in China and served in China during World War II.[10] Very much respected by the Chinese government, Service helped Harrison Salisbury make arrangements to retrace the Long March and in 1984 accompanied Charlotte and Harrison Salisbury and General Qin on the trip that culminated in the Salisburys' books.[11]

Although I still did not have a sponsoring organization, the museum people provided maps, background information, and leads to women veterans of the March for me to interview after I found a sponsor. Yan Jingtang explained that historians at the museum had never had time to do research on the women of the Long March and were pleased that I would be unearthing new material. He provided names, dates, numbers, and information about the women's husbands and told us who had given birth to babies on the Long March; he also explained the chronology, geography, and military and political structure of the three contingents of the Red Army that made the Long March.[12]

In June 1986 the China International Radio Press (CHIRP) agreed to sponsor the oral history project as a fund-raising vehicle for the Chinese Children's Fund. Huang Huichun, my colleague from China Central Radio who arranged the sponsorship, knew that studying Chinese for several years in a U.S. university had made me knowledgeable but not fluent. She assigned Wang Weihua, who had been my student for four years at the Beijing Broadcasting Institute and was then working in the English department at Radio Beijing, to assist me as interpreter. Huang Huichun then scheduled an interview with Wang Dingguo, a Long March veteran from the Fourth Front Army. In the CHIRP office on the fourth floor of a building just behind the China Central Radio building, Wang Dingguo began our first interview: "I was born in Yingshan county, Sichuan province. My mother told me I was born in 1913. Actually it was February 1915, 1914 on the lunar calendar."

A few days later, Deng Liujin, the First Front Army veteran who initiated the project, came to my rooms at the Friendship Hotel for our second interview.

* * *

In October 1986, I moved to the campus of the Beijing Foreign Studies University, where I was teaching U.S. social history. In December, three more Fourth Front Army women, He Manqiu, Quan Weihua, and Zhang Wen, came to my apartment for interviews. That same month, just as Hu Yaobang was deposed as general secretary of the Chinese Communist party, the minister of propaganda put his official seal on my proposal to interview women who had been on the Long March and write their stories in English. As soon as the proposal received this official approval, Kang Keqing, widow of the commander-in-chief of the army, Marshal Zhu De, agreed to a televised interview at the China Central Radio building. She was the highest-ranking of the Long March women veterans still alive, healthy, and willing to be interviewed. Her agreement was the endorsement I needed to move ahead. After that, there was no problem finding additional women to interview during my subsequent five years in China.

With a long time to work on the project, I had the leisure to develop con-tacts, reflect on the interview process, do research, and deepen my under-standing of the culture, a luxury most academics doing field work in a for-eign country do not have.

When I first began to interview women who were Long March veterans, I assumed they would give firsthand accounts that would augment the accept-ed military and political history of the Red Army, fleshing out unknown facts and adding to the legends that grow out of national conflict in turbulent times. I had not yet understood how very differently women's stories re-configure the body of knowledge that has been considered history. As the interviews continued, it became clear that I was not just hearing stories of a singular event in Mao's progression to power. The women revealed the Long March as only one of many segments of the revolutionary path they had chosen. In fact, it was not until they heard male leaders talk about the remark-able achievement of the Red Army in making the "25,000 *li* Long March" that they understood the significance the leaders saw in what had seemed to them an ordinary, if arduous and extended, troop movement. What the women spoke about primarily was the work they did and how they adapted to the political, military, physical, and social demands of being soldiers. I began to wonder whether it is the male genius to relate history from the perspective of glorified deeds and to abstract the significance of discrete events in the historical process, whereas it is woman's genius to integrate and absorb un-usual occurrences into their daily lives.

While I was interviewing the Long March women and working on trans-lations of the interviews, I was also developing a graduate course in U.S. so-cial history. My growing understanding of social history, which provides space for the people whose lives contributed to the process that produces political leaders and policies, military leaders and strategies, and other aspects of his-tory, led me to a theoretical basis for organizing the material I was collecting about the Long March. I was also teaching U.S. women's history, fascinated with the way in which a focus on women often changes the way in which history is periodized.[13] And as I integrated women more fully into my U.S. social history course, I understood how truly different history can be when women and their contributions are considered.[14]

Later, I learned to ask questions of historical data that would tell me not to what extent the women were able to do what the men did, but what the women were actually doing. In other words, questions such as "Did the women achieve high political position after the Long March was over?" became "What did the women achieve politically?" And among the many things they accom-plished, they had the first piece of legislation written and ready to be enacted when the Communists came to power in 1949. Drawing on their analyses of conditions for Chinese women before, during, and after the Long March, they presented the Marriage Law, which granted solid rights for women.[15]

The value of interviewing both the educated women who were well-known leaders and the illiterate peasants was also confirmed. It allowed me to present a more balanced picture of life in an earlier time and illuminated those who had previously been invisible in history, helping to end the silence of these "ordinary" people.

Of course, little was ordinary about the women interviewed: The women who chose to join the revolution and later made the Long March were quite extraordinary. Most peasant women did not become leaders in local Communist organizations or leave home to join the Army. Most students did not join the Communist Youth League and take active leadership roles. Most sisters and wives did not follow brothers and husbands into revolutionary work. Most hungry or ill-treated children did not run away to join the Army. The women who did, and who agreed to be interviewed more than fifty years later, had a tenacity and a buoyancy that had led them far beyond the limits of most lives.

* * *

The interviews took place in many venues, usually chosen by the women themselves. The first was held at the CHIRP office, the second in my Friendship Hotel rooms, then at my apartment at Beijing Foreign Studies University, in a reception room at China Central Radio, at the Beijing Museum of Military History, in hotels or guest houses in other cities, and in the interviewees' own homes. Some of the women came alone to the interview, and others brought friends or family members. Army historians joined us when interviews were held at the museum in Beijing and in Jiangxi and Guangdong. Wang Weihua worked with me on every interview, although as she became busier with her career, one or another of her former classmates sat in for her if she was delayed or needed to leave early. My husband, an American of Chinese origin and fluent in three Chinese dialects, was present when time permitted, and once or twice Lao Qi, a retired kindergarten teacher who worked for us, sat down with us.

Having Wang Weihua as co-interviewer and translator with the Long March veterans was a stroke of great luck. During the four years Weihua was my student at the Beijing Broadcasting Institute, I was the principal teacher for her class of seventeen students and became very close to them. Weihua began her career in broadcast journalism before she graduated, and at the time of the first interview she was working for China Central Radio in Beijing. Over the years we worked together, she developed her skills as an investigative journalist and began working on the English-language news broadcasts for China Central Television (CCTV). She became a nationally known TV personality, both as news anchor and as a popular host for CCTV spectaculars.

The women were charmed by Weihua's interest in their stories. They were delighted to have an attentive audience in the person of a TV celebrity who was "born under the red flag" and thus had not experienced the old days before Liberation. Explaining the past to Weihua allowed them to relax in a way they could never have done had I, the foreigner, been the focus of their attention.

Many of the interviewees who asked us to submit questions beforehand were surprised at the nature of the questions. We kept them simple, asking such questions as When and where were you born? Why did you join the army and the party? Can you remember any specific heroic acts by women? They found it strange that we were not seeking information about the military or political history of the Long March but instead wanted to know about their own experiences. Living in a culture that deemphasizes the individual, they were sometimes disconcerted by our interest in their own lives. We also felt limited in the kinds of questions we could ask, constrained both by the culture and by the special stature of the Long March women soldiers. We did not ask questions about sexual relations, nor did we probe into marital relations or feelings among family members.

There is no question that the presence of others at the interview affected narration. They found the frequent interruptions, usually in the form of corrections of a place or date by relatives or a secretary or army historian, quite distracting. Women who were by themselves or with close friends or relatives often went off the record to tell us bits of gossip. On the other hand, several women said frankly in the presence of officials that they were telling us things that they would not want included in a book to be published in China. Inhibiting as secretaries or officials might be, Weihua and I believed the biggest interference to hearing the real truth was not the presence of others but what they might feel compelled to protect from public scrutiny. Almost all the women had been required to write about themselves during the Cultural Revolution, and some were clearly trying to shield themselves from misunderstandings or to clear up circumstances around a charge against them. For example, one spoke in such detail about a dress she had made for herself when she was a teenage underground worker that it seemed evident she was justifying something that had nothing to do with background information for the Long March. Others had something else to hide, such as a name deemed inelegant, questions about parenthood, or past antisocial behavior. In addition, they were all, to one degree or another, eager to communicate the positive side of the party and the army, and to omit the things that in their view might show a dark side.

Because the women usually memorized their stories before they came to the interview, interruptions sometimes caused them to lose the thread of their narrative. In the early interviews we stopped frequently for translation because I was woefully beyond my depth in vocabulary. As I mastered more of the military and political terms and concepts, translations were less imperative and the narratives flowed more freely. With some women it was possible simply to let them talk. With others, we had constantly to ask questions for clarification because of their accents or their muddled narration.

We usually sat around a table, if one was available, with a thermos of hot water and cups for tea at hand. We used two tape recorders, starting one several minutes later than the other, to avoid interrupting the narration to turn or change a tape.

* * *

When we turn our life into a narration, we look for a beginning and an end to the story, highlighting the conflicts and resolutions into a cohesive whole. We choose what we tell, ignoring the bits that do not fit or that detract from the story. The women we interviewed did the same. Sometimes our questions could free them from the memorized construction of their lives to talk about their experiences. This usually happened when they were relating parts of their lives they did not consider important or sensitive. Fortunately, our definitions of what was important were not the same as theirs: We were interested in their childhoods, their reasons for joining the revolution, their nonpolitical relationships with other women, their personal experiences on the Long March, about all of which they spoke freely.

Misremembered verifiable facts such as dates or the names of people are corrected in endnotes. For example, in chapter 7 Wang Quanyuan refers to the woman who made the Long March with bound feet as the wife of the Ninth Army Political Commissar. In the footnote I give the woman's name and her husband's correct position, commander of the Ninth Army.

We handled problems of anachronistic knowledge by stopping their digressions into political and military history with the question, "Did you know this at the time?" What we wanted was their personal history, not their understanding in the 1980s of the official military and political history.

Some of their memories had grown to mythic proportions in constant retelling. When Wang Quanyuan said her eyesight was so good that she could see the light from bullets as the enemy shot at her and could dodge the bullets while sitting in a boat on a river, we accepted it as a bit of harmless exaggeration. Wei Xiuying's description of the meeting where Mao Zedong first made reference to the "25,000 *li* Long March" was so filled with anachronistic phrases and visual descriptions borrowed from movies and revolutionary drama that we felt we must discount it.

Embellished memory was counterbalanced by certain blanks, by details that were entirely missing from their memories. Chen Zongying, for example, had no visual memory of the Nationalist jail in Shanghai where she and her infant daughter spent almost a year. Although we tried to jog her memory in every way we could, she simply did not remember enough to describe it.

Most of the women were unable to give a physical description of the provinces they went through. When asked to describe the mountains they climbed, one First Front Army woman curtly dismissed our request: "A mountain is a mountain—what else?" Deng Liujin, our second interviewee, had so little to tell about the physical terrain that at first I wondered whether she had much actual memory of the Long March and whether she were not telling us what she had heard or read from other accounts. As we interviewed more women and found that most were also unable to describe the scenery of the often beautiful places they passed through, I realized it was not lack of memory we were confronting: They had not noticed their surroundings. The night marches, the physical drain of keeping up a pace of about 120 steps a minute while carrying packs weighing up to 18 pounds, the need to keep their eyes on the difficult mountain paths, and later the hunger, all prevented them from seeing the lovely landscape.

What they did remember was physical, but in a very personal sense. They remembered in great detail their own or others' experiences of childbirth. They remembered the discomfort of menstruation with no sanitary supplies and their embarrassment when male soldiers, misunderstanding the cause of bleeding, thought they were wounded. They remembered when they were sick and their terror of being left behind if they were unable to keep up with the troops. They also remembered nurturing and kindness from other women, especially if it was a leader showing her concern.

* * *

In addition to problems with memory, we also encountered challenges when trying to translate words or concepts. Puzzling to me was what actually constituted marriage in the minds of the women during the Long March, where there was no family to make arrangements and no possibility of keeping records. In chapter 7, Wei Xiuying tells a story about a woman who had gone off with a commander "who took a fancy to her." It helps to explain the difficulty of ascertaining what actually constituted marriage, for in her story she seems to equate a couple sleeping together with marriage. Wang Quanyuan's description of her own marriage to a high-level leader during the Long March, arranged with official sanction although she had left a husband behind in her village, follows Wei's account. I placed the two stories together, hoping their juxtaposition would amplify, although it does not resolve, the question of what was considered marriage.

Birthdates and ages are another example of conceptual differences. In the first sentence of the first interview, Wang Dingguo told us, "My mother told me I was born in 1913. Actually it was February, 1915." Her mother's reckoning was according to the Chinese lunar calendar rather than the Western calendar, which is generally in use now. Moreover, the traditional Chinese concept of a person's age is different from the Western practice. Her mother considered Wang Dingguo one year old during the first year after her birth, rather than becoming one year old at the beginning of the second year, as we do. The reason there is a two-year discrepancy in Wang Dingguo's birthdate is because all births in this collective culture were counted from early in the year on the lunar calendar, rather than on the individual birthday. Because her birthday was near Lunar New Year and she was considered one year old at birth, she became two years old on the day in the New Year when all birthdays are celebrated.

How childhood is understood is also different. There is nothing evident in the women's stories that suggests the modern concept of childhood as a separate, special time of life. After about six years old, Chinese peasant children worked in the house, the store, or the fields, just as adults did. There were many children, called *xiaogui*, or "little devils," who had run away from home, joined the Army, and made the Long March. Wang Dingguo underscored the idea that children were simply considered small adults when she told us that the *xiaogui* carried grain on the Long March just as adults did, although not as much. The adults carried theirs in a bag made from a pantleg, she explained, and the children's bag came from a sleeve.

Some needed clarification arose from concepts embedded in the language itself. In spoken Chinese, the pronoun *ta*, meaning "he, she, it" is not gendered. We had no way of knowing without asking, for example, if the leader of a work group was male or female. It was even more confusing when *ta* had no antecedent or when the subject of a sentence was omitted altogether.

Another problem was the use of the generic word *enemy*. Depending on the situation and location, the enemy could be variously the landlord's men or militia, unaffiliated bandits, warlord troops, Nationalist soldiers, or secret agents. In the text, I tried to indicate to which enemy the speaker referred.

A classical phrase the women, both educated and not, used to describe the status of women in general, and in their families particularly, is one with which I also dealt in context. There is no set phrase in English for *zhongnan qingnu*, which is literally "heavy on boys, light on girls" or, more loosely, "favoring sons while treating daughters lightly." I used various translations that I felt reflected both the speaker and the context in which she used the phrase, specifying that it referred to *zhongnan qingnu*.

The word *jia*, which may be translated as either "home" or "family," carries both the meaning of a group of people with marriage or family ties as well as the house or building where the family members lived. As the party and army became a surrogate family for the revolutionaries, "home" in the sense of a place receded in importance for the women soldiers: They were always on the go, walking from one village to another, running from secret agents or enemy fire, hopping a train, boat, or ship to evade the enemy, begin another phase of work, or leave a child to be raised by their husbands' families. Many of them stated that the party had become their family.

There is another concept inherent in the word *jia*. Because of the coherence of the family group under the head of the family, when Jian Xianfo said, "My family encouraged me to join the Army," or Liu Ying said, "My family didn't approve of educating girls," they were reporting what their fathers, as head of the family, advocated. Thus, Liu Ying could continue her narrative by telling us how her mother had helped her get an education without perceiving any contradiction.

This raises another problem in understanding the words of the women. In Chinese society, although agreement may not be unanimous, it is stated as though it is. "Everybody joined the Communist organizations" may not mean that every person in the village did. It might not even mean that the majority did. What it does mean is that joining the organizations was the desirable norm in the mind of the speaker and that the people who mattered joined.

Deng Liujin spoke about the health examination she and others underwent before leaving with the First Front Army on the Long March. "I was the healthiest!" she exclaimed. When Zhong Yuelin also said she was the healthiest, I wondered how they could both be the healthiest, trying to understand what they were saying from within my own cultural context. Within their context of emphasizing the "we" rather than the "I," what they meant was, "Those of us who were chosen were the healthiest."

A difficulty arose from the terms the women used to describe a spouse: *laotou* for men, *laopo* for women, and the ungendered *laoban*. *Laotou*, especially, is a very common word with at least as many shades of meaning as "guy" has in English. The nearest English equivalent when used to mean "spouse" is "my old man" or "my old lady." However, these terms present problems because the nuances of meaning in English have changed over the years and are not the same for people of different generations. To my generation, "my old man" was used by poor and working-class women in a male-dominant relationship. Because of the changed nature of the term in English, I have substituted the phrase "my old companion" for *laotou, laopo,* and *laoban.* This avoids the problem and reflects the meaning in Chinese but does not convey the class and gender implications.

There are a few terms that are not only culturally embedded but also without an English equivalent. For these, I chose to use the Chinese term. *Dajie* is one. Literally it means "Big sister," but in usage it is a term of respect and often affection for a woman who is older or in a higher position than the speaker. All of the interviewees used the term when speaking to us about other women who made the Long March.

Another term left untranslated is *tongyangxi,* used to describe girls who were given or sold by their birth parents into another family before puberty. *Tongyangxi* is variously translated "child bride," "small daughter-in-law," or "affianced daughter-in-law." Although the status and arrangements for *tongyangxi* varied from place to place and family to family, and the variations often are described by different Chinese words, I have chosen to use *tongyangxi,* which was the expression used by all the interviewees. Some *tongyangxi* were sent to other families in infancy, some after they were six years old. Those we interviewed who were sold as babies generally fared well. They were brought up as part of the family; the ones who went as older children, however, were more often treated—and mistreated—as servants. Only one of the *tongyangxi* we interviewed actually married a son in her "in-law" family. The other *tongyangxi* for whom there was a prospective husband in the family were considered sisters and comrades rather than fiancées by their revolutionary betrothed. For the others, there was no one in the family for them to marry.

* * *

The mechanics of our translation process changed over time. When Wang Weihua and I first began the interviews, we translated the tapes immediately. As her work became more demanding she was often unable to devote the block of time needed to conduct the interviews and translate immediately afterward. She continued the interviews with me, and I enlisted other women, students and colleagues who had grown up in China and generously gave their time to this fund-raising project, to help with translation.

Although the translators changed, the translation process itself did not. Weihua, or another translator, and I listened to the interview tape and she translated sentence by sentence while I entered her words into my computer. It took about six hours to translate one hour of tape. We worked hard to keep the language level the same in English as it was in Chinese, avoiding the use of complicated sentence structures or formal words in English when the Chinese was simple or earthy. I chose to use English words of Anglo-Saxon origin rather than more formal words derived from Latin or Greek for the women who had little or no education because how knowledgeable and sophisticated a person appears can be changed in both reportage and translation. For example, in the English edition of *The Private Life of Chairman Mao*, written by Mao's physician, Chen Zongying is quoted as saying about Mao Zedong, "He has a terrible temper and can turn mercilessly against you at the slightest provocation." The quote came to the translator through the vocabulary and syntax of an educated doctor, and the translation suggests that Chen Zongying was also well educated. A translation from the Chinese text that is truer to her language level is, "Old Mao has a bad temper and can turn his face against anybody any time."[16]

In polishing the raw translations of the interviews, I tried to stay as close to the words of the Dajie as clarity permitted. I eliminated the repetitions that occur in oral speech and moved phrases and sentences around to create a logical flow in English, trying my best to be true to their words and meanings. Because none spoke English, I was unable to discuss the translations with them. I apologize for any distortions of meaning I may have created.

One of our greatest translation problems arose from regional variations in the Chinese language, where local dialects can be incomprehensible from one village to another. The interviewees came from eight different provinces and from different villages or cities within the provinces. They all spoke the standard Chinese known in the west as Mandarin, although many spoke it with strong local accents. Their first language usually was a village dialect of the provincial language. When they spoke of their childhood, their local accents grew heavier and they often lapsed into local idioms. Liu Jian told us that the first girl born in her family had been given away. The second and third children were also daughters. She explained that in those days, poor people had no choice but to put girl babies in the (*unclear word*). It was not until I found a student from Sichuan who could understand her village dialect that we learned she had used the local expression for the urine bucket.

The most challenging translation was that of Wang Quanyuan's interview. The local official who brought her to the interview spoke her village dialect and the Jiangxi provincial dialect. Whenever we were unable to understand what she was saying, we asked his help, and thus the language went from village dialect to provincial dialect to Mandarin, or standard Chinese, and eventually into English. When we translated from the tape, one of my students worked with us. He was from a Jiangxi village near Wang Quanyuan's and was able to understand both her accent and her idioms.

Another issue was what to do with the Communist rhetoric used by all the women. Some colleagues urged me to eliminate it, putting the concept of the words into language more acceptable to the Western reader. I decided to keep to the women's words as they used them, however, for several reasons. In the first place, that was what they said; those were the words they used. In addition, the language of revolution was very much a part of those years in their lives. "Overturn the evil gentry," appears to the Western reader as jargon. To the women, the phrase revealed their social and economic relationship to an absentee landlord who profited from their labor and did not even allow them to have their annual piece of meat at New Year's dinner, for example. Moreover, when the women used revolutionary words in their propaganda work, they were supplying the peasants with language for the feelings their street drama evoked when they acted out a local incident of cruelty by a landlord's men toward a tenant farmer. The rhetoric thus became both shorthand language for emotion as well as a name for the remedy to an intolerable situation. And for the women who did the propaganda work in villages as the Red Army walked across China, using revolutionary language reinforced their feeling of belonging in a group of comrades, of finding a new family to replace the one they had left behind in the village.[17]

When it came time to do the actual writing, my first inclination was to present the women's stories intact. I soon realized I would have to paraphrase much of what the women said, for various reasons. Their stories often needed explanations that could be neither conveniently footnoted nor inserted without interrupting the flow of the story. Some of the less educated women spoke in such simple language that I retold parts of their stories myself, simply to give the reader some variety of language. One of the interviewees came with two of her children, who often chimed in on the stories. Wherever their comments offered necessary clarification, I used them in my own words with attribution to the speaker. Sometimes a story was told more than once, in different language levels and with different supporting details. That happened most often when we had more than one session with our interviewee. I usually chose to retell the story to include all that she had said on the subject.

* * *

The women usually, though not always, began the interview by telling us when and where they were born, chronicling events over time. However, as soon as they began speaking about a topic with related stories, such as childbirth on the Long March, they abandoned the chronology and talked about other childbirths on the March. This was also true when they spoke of such physical subjects such as illness, hunger, and menstruation. When they described things that changed over time—the clothes they wore, the work they did, the food they ate—they also spoke topically rather than chronologically.[18]

Following the example of the women, I have held to a loose historical chronology within the chapters in the book, but the chapter arrangement has more to do with the focus of each particular chapter. The first three chapters all touch on children and childbirth of women in the Second Front Army. Jian Xianren, who brought her infant daughter with her on the Long March, is the main focus of chapter 1, which includes her sister's experience of giving birth in the grasslands and carrying her baby with her until the end of the March. In chapter 2, Chen Zongying's revolutionary activities are intertwined with the nine babies she bore, including one born on the Long March. In chapter 3, Ma Yixiang, who joined the Army at age eleven, tells the story from a child's perspective. Chapter 4 concerns the work and education of a woman in the Fourth Front Army. He Manqiu describes the medical school she attended during the Long March. This chapter, as well as the two that follow, was previously published. Chapters 5 and 6 are topical and have appeared, with added background information, as chapters in books about women and war in general. Chapter 5 examines why the interviewees chose to join the revolution, the Chinese Communist party, and the army. Chapter 6 analyzes the work they did during the March. The childhood and Long March experiences of First Front Army veterans make up a chorus of voices in chapter 7, with the Long March itself, rather than the individual women, the main focus of this chapter. In chapter 8 three women from the First Front Army who did not finish the Long March with the others recount their stories. A short conclusion reflects on ways of thinking about what the narrators have told us.

1. Newborn on the March

JIAN XIANREN and her younger sister, Jian Xianfo, joined the Red Army as a means of self-protection. Jian Xianren's revolutionary commitment had been forged during student days by the exciting ideas she and her brother encountered in the newly established schools they attended during the 1920s, which they passed along to their younger siblings.

Jian Xianren was born in 1909 in Cili, Hunan province, two years before the end of the Qing dynasty and the founding of the Chinese Republic. Her family home was in the eastern edge of the Wuling Mountains. Cili was physically and culturally isolated from the outside world.

Jian Xianren's father came from the more cosmopolitan lake area east of Cili in the floodplain south of the Yangzi River. During one of the more severe floods, his family fled to the mountains and settled in Cili. Her father, whom she characterized as both educated and enlightened, preferred to work at an interesting job rather than pursue a more prestigious career. He chose not to study for the Civil Service examinations, which had become corrupted toward the end of the Qing dynasty, and instead studied handicrafts.[1] When he mastered the secret art of making batik (*laranbu*), he opened a workshop in Cili. As the workshop began to prosper, he took on apprentices and opened several shops selling household goods. He bought farmland "so the family members could eat without going elsewhere for grain," Jian Xianfo said. Both sisters remembered their childhood as comfortable and happy, although Xianren, older by seven years, remembers harder economic times than her sister.

The Jian family had seven living children and other children who did not survive, all born over a period of nearly twenty years. Believing in education for both sons and daughters, the father again departed from tradition and sent his oldest daughter to school. As the family grew in size and the business began to prosper, Xianren's older sister was withdrawn from school as soon as she had learned to read, write, and keep accounts. Because most families functioned as an economic unit, it was quite normal for the eldest daughter to help her mother with housework, child care, and the family business until she married and went to live with her husband's family. According to Jian Xianren's sister, their mother, although illiterate, was very good at housework and managing the family business.

When Jian Xianren and her next-younger brother, Jian Xianwei, were small, their parents were still struggling to make ends meet. The children helped out by doing what work they could in the store and at home. When Xianren was eight and her brother six and family finances improved, the children were sent to school. Xianren explained, "Old Chinese people favored boys over girls, but in our family boys weren't considered more important than girls (*zhongnan qingnu*). They simply thought I was old enough to take care of my younger brother. They let us start school together, since we could read the same books and help each other."

Xianren and Xianwei first attended a traditional private school, studying the Four Books (*Si Shu*) and Five Classics (*Wu Jing*), swaying in rhythm while reciting words they did not understand.[2] After five years spent memorizing the classic texts, the Jian children were sent to new-style, single-sex, upper elementary schools when they were eleven and thirteen. Their teachers, influenced by the May Fourth Movement, were energetic graduates of universities or normal schools. Jian Xianren described how her geography teacher, filled with patriotic enthusiasm, drew a map of China on the blackboard to show the children how it resembled a begonia leaf.[3]

The teacher began to cry when she told her students how China, big and rich in resources as it was, had been invaded by other countries. "We were quite moved by what the teacher said," Xianren explained. "Although we didn't thoroughly understand, we knew it wasn't right that China should become the slave of other countries." She continued, "The May Fourth Movement had a big influence on Chinese young people. Our history teacher told us, 'Don't think that you won't accomplish anything because you are girls. In ancient times, there were women warriors, and women scientists. We have Chinese national heroines like Qiu Jin.'[4] Our teachers taught us to be independent, honest people who worked for the good of society. At that time, we didn't expect to be soldiers."

When Xianren graduated from upper primary school in 1926, she expected to continue her schooling in the Girls' Normal School in Changsha, the provincial capital, training to be a teacher. However, her mother kept Xian-ren home to help care for her ill grandmother. When asked how she felt about the unfairness of being kept home while her brother went on with his studies, she avoided speaking of her own feelings by simply saying, "In those days, we were very obedient. I stayed home."

In 1926 the Chinese Republic was fifteen years old, but the country's government and leadership were fragmented. Sun Yat-sen, father of the Republic, had died the previous year. In an effort to unify the country, the Northern Expeditionary Army (*beifajun*) was formed in Guangzhou. Comprising both Communists and Nationalists under the leadership of Chiang Kai-shek, the army began moving north to consolidate government power over warlord-held areas. "During that year, the Northern Expeditionary Army hadn't affected our area," Jian Xianren explained. "There were only some young students who had secretly learned of Sun Yatsen's fresh, new ideas. I had nothing to do at home, so I read his *San Min Zhu Yi* then."

Dr. Sun Yat-sen is considered the father of the revolution that overthrew the Qing dynasty and established the Chinese Republic in 1911. His work, *San Min Zhu Yi* (*The Three Peoples' Principles*), expounded his ideas on nationalism, democracy, and the livelihood of the people.

While Jian Xianren stayed at home, her brother was in Changsha, drinking in revolutionary ideas as a high school student in a progressive school. He sent revolutionary books and magazines home to his sister, who read articles written by progressives from all over the country in the *Xiangdao Zhoubao*, a Communist journal.[5] She also read *The ABC's of Communism* and *The Communist Party and the Youth League*. She said she did not understand all she read at that time because "I was a young person who had lived in only one place, and was still very ignorant and ill-informed."

When her grandmother died, her brother returned home for the funeral. The two teenagers discussed the progressive ideas in the material he had sent her and decided to put concepts into action. Still too young to join the Chinese Communist Party (CCP), they worked with the Communist Youth League (CYL). In their county, both the Nationalists and the Communists were organizing young people into social action groups. Both parties opposed corrupt officials and worked to stop opium smoking and put an end to the practice of binding women's feet. They also encouraged women with bound feet to unbind them, a process often as painful as the initial binding. The Communists also emphasized the class struggle between rich and poor by physically attacking the wealthier landlords.

As in other revolutionary periods the world over, altering one's hairstyle became a symbol of commitment. When the Qing dynasty, which was Manchu rather than Han Chinese, was established, all men were required to wear their hair in a long pigtail or queue. To cut it off was considered an act of treason against the emperor, punishable by death. When the Qing was overthrown and the Republic of China founded, men cut their hair, eradicating the symbol of submission to the Manchu dynasty. For women, hairstyle signified marital status. Jian Xianren was among the first of the young girls to cut off her long braid, setting a good example as a progressive young woman. After she cut her hair, however, she was afraid to go home, sure that her mother would scold her.

> I'd never done anything before without discussing it with my mother, but this time I hadn't. After I cut my hair, I didn't go home for two days. Mother was getting worried. She came looking for me and found out that I didn't have my braid any more! She got angry.
>
> My little brother put in a good word for me: "All the men used to wear braids, too, but gradually they all cut them off. Mama, you will cut off your braids, too!"

Her father became increasingly concerned about his children's activities. He told Xianren, "The next time you want to do something, you have to tell the family first." He also told her to stop trying to capture the landlords and their employees and to stop shouting slogans. He put an end to her local revolutionary activities, keeping her from going to the county seat for classes and joining in the "intense struggle to oppose the local bandits and grab the evil gentry." Her father asked her, "What do you children understand? Don't follow the others, shouting! If you want to study, I'll teach you."

In 1927, Jian Xianren's parents allowed her to go to Changsha with her brother to study. Her brother, considered a promising "young sprout" for the Communist party, went to the Workers' Movement Institute (WMI) for leadership training in labor unions (*Gongren Yundong Jianxi Suo*).[6] As soon as she and her brother arrived in Changsha, they met the four most celebrated Communist leaders in Hunan, "Mao Zedong, Guo Liang, Li Weihan and Xia Xi. As soon as we got to the provincial capital, we met them. Students called them celebrities but actually, in the country as a whole, there were many who were more celebrated. Those four were the eminent people *we* knew. They were all very good speakers."

Xianren attended a preparatory middle school for teacher training and became active in the student movement.

> There were both boys and girls in my middle school. The girls who entered this school were comparatively advanced and many of the teachers were doing [revolutionary] work. We had to be careful though, because among us were some timid and cowardly girls. When they cried, we told them,

"Crying isn't any use. You can't kill the enemy by crying."

"I'm not crying about anything except the future. If I should die, what will happen to my mother?"

That's the kind of thing those girls were thinking about. At that time, children had a very strong concept of the family. They did what their parents told them to do.

Most of the girls, adopting new ideas, had cut their hair. When the girls encountered a boy from the town, Xianren said, they were likely to hear the rhyme,

> Piaoji po, zao qiang bi,
> Ba ba tou, wan wan sui.
> Nannu xuesheng, yi tong shui
> Sheng qu wawa, jiu chadui.

"*Piaoji*" is a bald chicken. That is what they called our hair style. "*Zao qiang bi*" means you should be executed. "*Ba ba tou*" was one of the current hairstyles. "*Nannu xuesheng, yi tong shui*" means "Coeds sleep together." "*Sheng qu wawa jiu chadui.*" "Their children will be [Communist] pickets." So the rhyme was:

> You bald chickens ought to be shot,
> Babatou hair style is really hot!
> Coeds sleep on the same cot
> Will produce a Communist tot.

Only those of us who experienced these things know about them. You can't read about them in any book.

The students' revolutionary activities intensified in Changsha during the Great Revolution, a time of cooperation between the Nationalists and Communists. The teachers were divided over the issue of the importance of a classroom education versus student activism. Some thought students should be well educated as a prerequisite for becoming revolutionary activists, whereas others wondered how students could possibly continue their studies when they were needed to work in the movement.

As a result, many of the students, including Jian Xianren, did not apply themselves very seriously. She explained, "It was said that I was there for schooling, but actually I was doing propaganda all day long, hanging up slogans, acting in cultural drama, those kinds of things." On the other hand, she worried about wasting her opportunity to gain an education and studied hard when she was not called on to work. "We were afraid that if we had to wait until we finished our studies, the revolution would already be over."

The Great Revolution ended abruptly in Shanghai on April 12, 1927, when the Nationalist troops turned on their Communist allies, beginning what the Communists called the White Terror (*bai si*). Jian Xianren and other student activists were warned that "something was going to happen," but she did not know what form it would take until May 20. On that day, a local holiday called Horse Day, the Nationalist soldiers moved against the Communists and student activists in Changsha in what became known as the Horse Day Incident (*Mari Shibian*).[7]

After the White Terror began in Shanghai, but before the Horse Day Incident, Jian Xianren explained, "Others who knew more than I did said the situation was tense. We all had to be careful because Chiang Kai-shek wanted to be dictator and would try to kill us revolutionaries."

At 9:00 P.M. on May 20, while she and her classmates were studying, they heard gunfire. The Nationalists, bent on disarming the Communists, attacked two of the Communist schools, the WMI and the Peasants' Movement Institute. Students in several of the progressive schools were armed, including those in the WMI, which her brother attended. Xianren, frantic about her brother's safety, was immensely relieved when he arrived at her school just before dawn.

He told the girls that, just after they had gone to bed, the boys in the WMI heard soldiers moving around outside their school. Realizing that the Nationalist soldiers were preparing to attack the school, the drill instructor called the students together. Before long, the institute was surrounded by soldiers who beat on the door and fired into the building. The WMI returned the fire, and in the ensuing fight, several students and teachers were killed or wounded before the school leaders surrendered to the Nationalist soldiers.

When the Nationalists had disarmed the WMI, they questioned the students about their Communist affiliations. The students denied being Communists. Promising to deal with them later, the soldiers confiscated the students' guns, uniforms, quilts, blankets, and clothing, then sent them away, dressed only in shoes and underwear, without detaining any of them.

Jian Xianren found some clothes for her brother, but before he had a chance to rest, one of Xianren's classmates, who was a clerk in the personnel department of the CCP Hunan Provincial Committee, returned to the dorm. She asked Xianwei to run messages for the party, assuring him that he could do it safely without raising suspicion because he was so young.

Xianwei moved into a hostel, posing as a student preparing for exams while actually working for the CCP. He wasn't eating properly because the party had no money and his parents were no longer supporting him. The family had been urging him and his sister to come home after the Horse Day Incident when the White Terror began. The parents feared that their children would be killed because of their political work. "They thought if they didn't give us any money, we'd be so poor that we'd have to go home. They didn't know that we would stay there no matter how poor we were!" Xianren explained. Her brother was subsisting on a couple of *baozi,* meat-filled buns, a day. "One person can eat two or three at one meal, but he ate one for breakfast and one for dinner. He was always hungry when he was carrying messages."

Fortunately for his health, his career as a CCP messenger did not last long. A traitor gave his name to the Nationalists, who sent an agent to his hostel. The owner protected Xianwei by claiming that he was not at home and told the agent Xianwei was not a "hoodlum," as the spy called the Communists, but only a young student preparing for exams. The spy warned the owner that he would be back to take Xianwei away and asked the owner to prevent him from leaving. As soon as the spy left, the owner told Xianwei what had happened and urged him to go into hiding. Jian Xianren said the owner was willing to help her brother get away because the Nationalists, by killing young students, had lost the trust of the local people.

Xianwei went to his sister's dorm to discuss his situation with the classmate who had given him his assignment as messenger. She now urged him to return home to throw the Nationalists off his trail because they were searching for him in Changsha.

Jian Xianren had become a CCP member while she continued to work for the CYL. "I had to accomplish all the work that both organizations gave me and do what each organization told me to do." Xianren's classmate who worked with the Organization Committee of the CCP entrusted her with the list of party member names and addresses. She instructed Xianren to stay in the dorm until she returned from delivering messages outside Changsha. She thought the list—and Xianren—would be safe enough at school and, under the protection of the progressive teachers, would never fall into the wrong hands. "Even if you lose your head, you can't lose the list!" the classmate warned her.

The CCP had gone underground after the Horse Day Incident. "Before that, the CCP and CYL weren't public, but they weren't secret, either."

> What we had done to the landlords was too extreme, but we didn't kill everybody! Chiang Kai-shek [the Nationalists] killed a lot of people. He killed CCP members, killed peasants, killed workers, but we didn't kill very many local tyrants. We didn't commit a crime when we took the food from the landlords and gave it to the poor. There were many Chinese who weren't Communists, only sympathizers, who became implicated and were killed. Although I was only seventeen or eighteen, my determination was great and I wanted to fight. The

worst [possibility] was death. If we died others would continue, so we must do what we can. We saw so many people killed. Everywhere we saw the Communists being killed, mostly young people. That was a great debt of blood!

Jian Xianren heard the stories of what happened to her comrades when the Nationalists caught them. They were tortured to extract information about party organization and membership. After they were executed, girl students' hands and breasts were cut off and their mutilated bodies displayed to discourage people from supporting or joining the Communists.

Jian Xianren was especially upset about the deaths of two close friends, a classmate and her husband.

When the Nationalists killed them, they cut off their heads and put each head between the other's legs. The wife had a baby in her stomach. When she was about to die, she cried a little. Her husband said to her, "Don't cry. There's nothing to cry about. We will die, but there are many other youths who will rise up. We have to overthrow a government like this one."

There were three or four people who were killed at the same time and faced execution bravely. These people were our close friends. When we heard about this, we were very deeply moved. I didn't understand things very well when I first joined the Youth League, but after this I understood clearly. I felt that if I didn't continue my work, I would let down those who had died. I had to carry out my orders and fight to the bitter end. I knew I must carry out the work I was assigned to do.

Her commitment thus crystallized, Jian Xianren left Changsha and went to a commercial area about 100 kilometers up the Li River from her hometown. She continued her underground work while she was an apprentice in a handicraft factory that produced stockings. "I was doing work for the CCP, burying roots and sowing seeds. I was a CCP root, burying myself among the workers, sowing propaganda seeds and recruiting for the Organization."

Jian Xianren and her comrades were young and inexperienced at protecting themselves. The CCP, which had been established in 1921, was also young and inexperienced, she said. Fortunately, she was not betrayed by her short hair because the factory manager encouraged the young women to cut their hair for reasons of cleanliness. Additionally, because many of the young women had cut their hair during the heady days of the Great Revolution the year before, short hair was not yet considered a symbol of Communist leanings. However, the factory manager was alert to underground CCP activity after one of her male comrades, who worked in another part of the factory, was caught and arrested. Her own political stance was exposed when she received "an inspiring letter" from another comrade that was read by the manager, who was from her county.

Then the head of the factory asked me, "Why aren't you in school? You're from a good family. You are the daughter of a workshop owner. Your family has money. Why do you say they won't give you any money?"

"They want me to go back home, but I want to learn a trade so that I will be capable of providing my own food."

He tried to lure me away. "I'll lend you some money so you can go back to school."

"I can't repay it."

He said, "I'll get it back from your family."

"If I borrow money from you, I'll have to get permission from my family. I don't want your money."

"Then you have to write a confession and admit your mistakes."

I argued with him. "I'm not a Communist. Why should I confess?"

"I'll give you twenty-four hours to think it over. We're from the same county and my home is just a couple of *li* from yours. I am your father's generation."

Deaf to the manager's bid for her respect and obedience to a man her father's age, Xianren made plans to leave the factory. She told one of the women she had recruited as a CCP member about her conversation with the manager. While the rest of the workers were eating, she quietly slipped away and ran to Shimen, an adjacent county, where she made contact with the party organization. Her comrades found her a teaching position in a junior high school. It was not unusual in those times before universal schooling for junior high school students to have a teacher with only a junior high education herself.

Some of her former schoolmates were in Shimen, actively "giving the local tyrants and evil gentry a lot of trouble." Because they had come from another area and were unemployed, they needed a cover. Her job provided her with living quarters, and she was able to offer her comrades protection from suspicious authorities and a place for them to rest. "If one of them came to see me, I would say he was my brother, or, if he were older, my uncle. They did their work at night, then came back to my place to sleep." When one of the local "despots" was killed, her room was identified as a hiding place for Communists. She and her comrades were warned that the Nationalists were coming for them and they quickly left.

Now on the list of CCP members wanted by the government, Jian Xianren hid in the mountains with some relatives. She disguised herself as a peasant and let her hair grow long enough to braid. At that time in China, a person's standing in the community and her official identity were both visible and rigid. Changing her student status by living with relatives who were farmers, wearing peasant clothing, and doing farm work provided an excellent disguise for a young student who was part of the intelligentsia. She bided her time until she could again work actively in the revolution.

* * *

In March 1928, General He Long returned to Sangzhi, his home county in western Hunan, to organize the peasants and establish a Soviet Base Area. This remarkable leader had begun his career in illegal, Robin Hood–like activities in western Hunan.[8] He acquired his personal name, *Long,* which means "dragon," when he joined a secret society in his teens. In his twenties he was a bandit, rebel, small warlord, and leader of a peasant army. He amassed large groups of men to fight other warlords, joined the Nationalists during the period of cooperation of the Northern Expedition, then threw his fighting strength to the Communist Army in 1927. He returned to Hunan after a severe defeat that wiped out his army, but within weeks he put together a force of 3,000 men.[9]

Jian Xianwei, Xianren's brother, had been put on the Nationalist wanted list after he fled Changsha. He stayed with his family a short time, then joined He Long's Western Hunan Worker Peasant Red Army (*Xiangxi Gongnong Hongjun*). The next year, 1929, Jian Xianren left her relatives' home in the mountains and joined the army, becoming the first and, for a time, the only woman in He Long's army. She was assigned to a training unit where she taught literacy to other soldiers and studied military affairs. "Compared to university graduates, I can't be considered an intellectual, but at that time I was a petty intellectual," she explained, having had more schooling than most of the other soldiers.

Her life took a different turn when General He Long asked her to teach him to read and write and transferred her to Headquarters. "He said he had been a poor student in school and knew how to write only three words: his name, *He Long,* and my surname, *Jian.*"

> He was 33 years old at the time and in a high position. Although he didn't know how to read and write, he was a good speaker.
> He Long and I had feelings for each other. He wanted to get married so that he could take better care of me, since I was the only woman among 1,000 men.[10]

Jian Xianren was not convinced she should marry this man, who was so very different in temperament, background, and education. Parents traditionally considered similarity of background an essential criterion for marriage whenever possible. In lieu of the family, the party organization assumed the task of encouraging marriages, relying on the interested assistance of those who knew and worked with the couple to make the arrangements. Persuasion often was necessary because many young women, like Jian Xianren, could see no advantage to marriage. She did not mention, as modern young

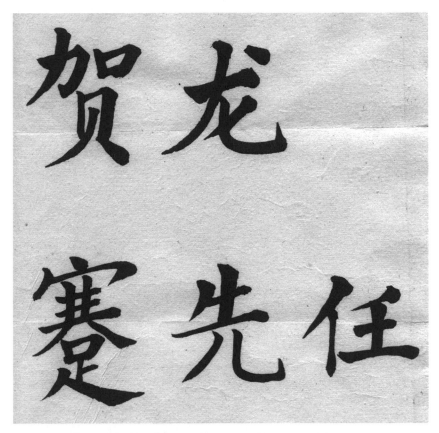

He Long and Jian Xianren calligraphy. (Courtesy of Wang Youqin)

Chinese women often do, a desire to avoid sex and pregnancy. Instead, her explanation was more traditional:

> I wasn't too willing because He Long was a military man and liked to gamble, and I was an intellectual.[11] I was idealistic about my future and he was not my ideal as a partner. My friends criticized me because I wanted to wait and he didn't want to. They reminded me that he came over from the Nationalists to the Communists in face of great Nationalist odds.[12] He was "old military" and should be congratulated.
>
> I said, "Would it be all right if I don't marry anyone at all?" But my colleagues persisted, so I agreed.
>
> At the time we got married we [the army] were surrounded by the enemy. We used boiled hot water, "white tea," to toast our wedding and colleagues made congratulatory speeches.
>
> Two days later we were in battle.

He Long's Second Army Group fought Nationalist troops in Hubei, Hu-nan, and Guizhou over the next few years. He Long's troops were forced to abandon the Base Area they had established in Sangzhi County and move to Guizhou until reinforcements came. The Sixth Army Group, led by General Xiao Ke with Ren Bishi as political commissar, had been sent from Jiangxi to join forces with He Long's Second Army Group. They finally arrived in fall of 1934 after severe losses along the way.

When Xiao Ke was in the vicinity of Cili, he visited Jian Xianren's family. Knowing that two young family members were already in the Red Army, he invited her younger sister, Jian Xianfo, and their younger brother to join the Red Army. Their father, by this time disgusted with Chiang Kai-shek's poli-cy of appeasing the Japanese invaders in northeast China and concerned about the safety of his teenage daughter, Jian Xianfo, encouraged the two to join. Not long after Jian Xianfo and her younger brother entered the army, she and Xiao Ke were married. Xianfo first worked as a copy clerk for the revolutionary committee and later was transferred to the propaganda depart-ment, where she used her art training to craft propaganda posters.

In October the two Red Army Groups, He Long's Second and Xiao Ke's Sixth, established the Hunan-Hubei-Sichuan-Guizhou Soviet Base Area (*Xiange-chuanqian Genjudi*) in Dayong.[13] During the next year, the county seats of the three counties in the center of the base area were taken and retaken six times.[14] The Red Army soldiers successfully fought off the first encirclement campaign by the Nationalist forces, but soon the situation became so critical that the lead-ers decided to break out of the blockade and move west into eastern Guizhou. Jian Xianren describes the strength of the opposing armies:

> The enemy had about 200,000 to 240,000 troops in their army. There were not quite 2,000 people in our 2nd and 6th Army Groups, but our soldiers were highly trained crack troops who had all volunteered to fight.[15]
>
> We were quartered in a Red area and during the year the Nationalists sur-rounded us. They dug trenches and built blockhouses in circles two or three layers deep. [The encirclement] was in a difficult area for the enemy to main-tain, but they found a natural line of defense in water. They flooded a very important [crossing] place in order to stop us, assuming our Red Army couldn't run through mud!
>
> No matter how strong the enemy, how solid the blockhouses or how tight the blockade, they couldn't lock us in. We got out by breaking through the trenches and blockhouses.

General He Long gathered his troops in the town of Lujiaping, administered an oath of allegiance to the Red Army, and began the Long March on No-vember 19, 1935.

* * *

Jian Xianren did not go to Lujiaping to take the oath because she had just given birth to a daughter, He Jiesheng, less than a month before.[16] Concerned for the survival of both child and mother, during the critical first month after birth and later, she and He Long had decided at first to leave the baby behind:

> Many people said that we couldn't take good care of her on the way and we might not survive either, since we would be in battles everyday. At that time my little sister [Jian Xianfo] was doing propaganda work with the Revolutionary Committee. Although she was very busy before we broke out [of the encirclement], whenever she had a little free time she came to hold the baby. Of course, I was sad.
> "Don't hold her," I said. "If she gets used to being held, then she'll cry when no one holds her."
> My sister said, "If the relatives take her away, there's no telling what year we'll see her again." We talked like this and cried because we really didn't want to give her up. We had very contradictory feelings.

He Long's relatives who had agreed to keep the baby asked for a week in which to find a wet nurse for her. When a week passed with no word from the prospective foster parents, He Long sent someone to find them and learned that the same day the relatives agreed to take the baby, they packed up and left. They apparently did not want to be found in a Communist Base Area with the daughter of the Red Army general in their care, fearing reprisals when the Nationalists retook the area vacated by Red Army. Jian Xianren explained,

> We understood they were afraid. If you raise a Communist baby, it is the same as being a Communist; if you don't raise the baby, then you're only a relative.
> We talked it over and He Long said, "Let's bring her along. If it's a hardship, then it's a hardship."
> I was reassigned to the unit for wounded soldiers. The day we left, she was just twenty days old.

Told by her husband to travel on a stretcher when the troops moved out, Jian Xianren tried to rebel on the grounds that she was neither ill nor wounded and was embarrassed to let her comrades carry her. She thought that at 100 *jin* (about 110 pounds) she weighed too much to be carried. Arguing that she was almost at the end of the difficult first month after her child's birth, she suggested that she ride a horse. Her section leader finally persuaded her to go on a stretcher for the next ten days, until the end of the baby's first month, and then change to horseback.

It was like this: we marched along, fell behind, marched along, fell behind. When the airplanes came, we had to hide from them. In the army, only the fighting force was marching one after the other. But in the rear service organizations, when the people in front took one step, the people in the rear had to run several steps to catch up.

On the first day I had my breakfast and lunch in Sangzhi county and arrived the next day at noon in Zhangjiawen, near the Li River.

Jian Xianren interrupted her narrative to illustrate the Red Army's concern for the peasants and their property. A story of this kind often is repeated by women in the Red Army. They tell it in great detail and, although the situation and locale differ greatly, the message is the same: By not stealing from the peasants, the Red Army endeared itself to people in poverty areas, maintaining a "fish in the water" relationship with the peasants. Ma Yixiang, writing for schoolchildren, told about the soldier in He Long's army who left a piece of cloth with her mother in exchange for food. Jian Xianren, in stressing the self-discipline of the hungry soldiers, takes the point one step further.

Now I want to tell you a story.

In Zhangjiawen around lunch time when we were all very hungry and thirsty, the enemy airplanes located us and began strafing. We hid in an orange grove with trees about the same height as a person. We could reach the oranges easily by holding up our hands, but not one person took one orange. The enemy bombs shook the oranges off the trees, but no one picked one up to eat. It might seem all right to pick an orange up off the ground even if we couldn't pick it off the tree, but no one did. Some of the walking wounded soldiers picked up the oranges and put them in a pile under a tree so that the civilians could come and get them. We all did that, although we hadn't had anything to eat for a whole day and night. Our discipline was very strict, although no one used force [to ensure obedience]. Everybody conscientiously observed the Three Main Rules of Discipline and Eight Points of Attention.

After the revolution, I went back [to Zhangjiawen]. People praised us very much and said, "That year when the Red Army went through our orange groves, they didn't touch our oranges at all." They remembered. Now, when I am telling the story today, the scene comes back to my mind as if it had happened yesterday.

This was how it was when we were just started out.

Jian Xianren's unit began to cross the Li River at dawn the next day. In some confusion, they crossed at a ferry landing where the river was too deep to ford. The bridge had been bombed and only a few small boats were available. The logistics team was ordered to cross upstream with the mules and horses while the wounded took the boats. When Jian Xianren got into a boat just after noon, she said,

> My ears are very good, and I heard an airplane coming.
> "Airplane coming! Get on the bank!"
> Some of the people immediately got back on the bank and ran. But I couldn't run, so I didn't. I sat in the boat. The people with me included four who took turns carrying me [on the stretcher] and one who carried my baby. There was also someone who looked after my mule.[17] Another person with us was the head of the Health Department. He's still alive.
> I told him, "I'm not getting out of the boat."
> He said, "If you don't, everyone else will stay. Let's just go. If we're bombed, then we deserve to die! If we're not bombed, then we're across [the river]."
> The airplane turned around and around and bombed the places where they could see crowds of people. After they used up all their bombs, they flew above us and machine gunned us. They weren't very skillful—they didn't hit us.

They embarked from the ferry landing, heading for the landing on the opposite bank. The head of the Health Department poled the boat across the river. He was not a boatman, Jian Xianren said, and was unable to bring them straight across the river. They missed the ferry landing and ended up on a beach where the sand made it very difficult to walk. "It's hard to believe that a woman who had just had a baby twenty days before could do such hard things," Jian Xianren said.

> The beach was thirty or forty meters wide and just going that short distance made all of us terribly tired, even the men comrades. Two stretcher bearers helped me walk. My baby kept crying. The man who carried her said,
> "What are you crying about? If you cry again, I'll put you down on the sand. I'm almost dying, walking on this strange road!"
> The head of the Health Department made some jokes to keep us going. He said,
> "Little girl, what are you crying about? You are full of shit and piss! From yesterday until today, almost two days, you didn't change your diaper. You stink. Twenty years from now, when you will love to be pretty, we will tell you about this! We'll see if you think it's funny." Everyone laughed and kept going.
> Although he said this, those people actually helped us a lot when it was so hard for my daughter and me.

After they left the beach, they found a house where they could stay for the night. By the time Jian Xianren changed the baby's diaper, nursed her, and washed the diaper, it was already getting light. She had neither food nor sleep. "Only during wartime could this kind of thing happen to a woman who had just had a baby," she said.

A soldier arrived from Headquarters with orders for the health department to move out by 10:00 A.M., after digging graves for those killed in the bombing and finding homes where the heavily wounded soldiers could stay with friendly peasants. Jian Xianren decided that by the time the Health Department was ready to move on, the enemy planes would have enough time to target them again. She asked the soldier whether Headquarters had already pulled out and, learning they had not, she asked him to wait for her. She found the groom and they loaded the horse, put her baby into the *beilou* (the basket in which they carried her on their backs), and informed the head of the Health Department she was leaving the unit. He offered her a stretcher, which she refused, assuring him that she would be more comfortable on horseback.

They found Headquarters about a mile away. When she explained to the surprised leaders that the company of wounded soldiers had already been bombed six times,

> Ren Bishi said, "Xianren, you're not using a stretcher. Are you comfortable riding a horse?" Then he asked if I'd eaten yet.
> "My last meal was when we started out from Sangzhi county, and I haven't slept. The last time I slept was the night before we started out."
> He said, "Aiya! You had better come with us. It's less than a month since your baby was born and you will collapse if you don't have enough food and rest."
> The others agreed and He Long said,
> "Before we start out, get some of our food and give Comrade Xianren something to eat."
> The bodyguard gave me a bowl of rice and a cup of water. That was what happened on the second day of the Long March.

At first, it was better for her after she joined Headquarters. She was traveling with people she knew well and with whom she was comfortable. She quickly established a pattern that allowed her food and rest while they were marching. She started her day early, eating with the bodyguards, then traveled with the vanguard to the next camp area. While the soldiers located food and sleeping quarters for Headquarters, she nursed her baby and washed baby clothes. The soldiers took good care of her, seeing to it that she had food, water, and a quiet place to rest.

On the third day after leaving Sangzhi, they began a forced march to the Yuan River, covering 150 *li* through mountainous terrain, she said, without a rest. When they crossed the Yuan into central Hunan, they were in a valley between two rivers. "Our commanders were very smart, very capable and they deployed our forces expediently. They were not only able to maneuver our own troops, they made the enemy troops move, too. Our commanders' strategic plans were quite flexible, but we had only 10,000 or 20,000 people."[18]

In Central Hunan, "we didn't just pass through. We worked there at mass work (*qunzhong gongzuo*), propaganda work (*xuanchuan qunzhong*)."[19] In an effort to lend legitimacy to their activities and counteract Nationalist propaganda that characterized the Communists as "bandits," they told the civilians that they were on a military campaign. They explained their intention to move their army north to fight the Japanese, in opposition to Chiang Kai-shek's policy of delay: "First eliminate the enemy within, then the enemy from outside"(*xian rang nei, hou rang wai*), or in other words, destroy the Chinese Communist Army before fighting against the invading Japanese Army.

To questions about Communist policy toward the rich, Jian Xianren explained the policy as she remembered it, differentiating between the capitalistic businessmen and feudalistic landlords. "We said, 'If you are a businessman, continue doing your business. We won't confiscate it. If the business is done fairly, when we buy your things, we'll pay you a fair price. We won't disturb business. If you are a landlord, we will let you distribute your grain. We will ask for provisions for the army and ask civilians to transport what we can't eat. Only if you are in the business of one of the "Big Four Families" will we confiscate your things.'"[20]

Jian Xianren continued, describing the propaganda work done by women. The political department organized meetings at which they made speeches to groups of people. They investigated the whereabouts of landlords and other "bad elements," tested the strength of Nationalist sympathies in the area, and tracked the enemy troop movements.

> Those were the things that the women comrades could do. I could do this kind of work, too, although I didn't have any official position. If I had time and wanted to do it, I could. I couldn't hold a baby and make a speech, but I could talk individually with the leading women. I told them what kind of people were good and which were bad. That was general mass work.
>
> Women did propaganda because it was light work. Men did it, too. The women had an advantage because it was easier for them to get into contact with the ordinary people. For example, if you are a young man and try to talk with a young girl or a young wife, it wouldn't be acceptable. If you are a woman, you can talk with men or women, young or old.
>
> Other work which both men and women did was recruiting soldiers, expanding the Red Army. Women comrades were good at that work. Within a few days we had recruited more than 3,000 people in Central Hunan. It was a populous area, comparatively rich and culturally developed. The 3,000 people [recruited] from there were all patriotic young people who supported the Red Army. We recruited one woman, Shi Zhi. She's still alive, living in Beijing.

The army, situated as it was between two rivers, was soon encircled by Nationalist troops. This forced a move toward Guizhou province, where the leaders planned to reestablish the base area in eastern Guizhou. Exhausted, Jian Xianren fell ill.

> At that time, I always rode a horse. When I got off, it was bad. I didn't have any strength. I washed the baby and myself, gave the baby something to eat and then put her down to sleep. I lay down, too. The next day I couldn't get up. I had a fever. For the next two or three days, if there were anyone to give me food, I'd eat. If no one came, I'd just sleep. I was in a daze. I was exhausted. When people told me that we were going to start off next day, I got my strength back and could march again. When I wasn't sick, it seemed like I was sick. When I was sick, I was *really* sick.

The army, unable to reestablish the eastern Guizhou base area, moved northwest, to Bijie prefecture in February 1936, three months into the Long March. The Second and Sixth Army Groups benefited from the strict discipline of the First Front Army that had prevented the soldiers from preying on the poor peasants: "A year before, the 1st Front Army had passed through this place. When we arrived there, no one ran away. All the men and women, old and young, beat the drums and gongs and set off firecrackers to welcome the Red Army."

In Bijie, the leaders used a Christian mission for offices, meetings, and sleeping quarters. They established a Guizhou-Yunnan Border Revolutionary Committee, with Zhou Suyuan, a former deputy governor of Guizhou province and a Marxist, as chairman. "In that area, which was under the control of the Nationalists, he openly had Marxist books on his bookshelves. He was the only person we met who was like this," Jian Xianren remarked.

Jian Xianfo, her sister, gave this account of Zhou Suyuan:

> When we got to Bijie, we stayed there as if we were to establish a new base area: doing mass work and holding mass meetings. The local tyrants and evil gentry who were hated by the people and hadn't run away, we caught them. Some of the local tyrants and evil gentry were really horrible, raping women, forcing other people's wives and daughters to be their concubines. Some of them had killed people. The masses settled scores with the landlords, and divided their goods among the people. The people were satisfied and everyone was happy.
>
> It was there that the Red Army recruited a lot of people. The two armies recruited about 5,000. Usually we worked for a couple of days, then rested a couple of days. It was like that. Resting for a couple of days, we never stopped working with the masses. We were very busy there. All of us were very happy.

Our relations with the people were good, especially with one person. His name was Zhou Suyuan. Have you heard of him? He was well-known in Guizhou, a celebrity. Quite a person. He had held important positions in the army and government there. When the Red Army found him, he didn't leave. We saw a lot of books in his house. When the books were opened, there were a lot of circles.[21] Curious. When we found him, we reported it to Wang Zhen, Director of the Political Department and to Xia Xi, the Political Commissar. Xia Xi was a person who really understood Marxism and Leninism. He thought it was strange. He went to his [Zhou Suyuan's] house and had a look. They talked.

"You've read all these books?"

"Yes, I've read them. I have been reading all these books for about ten years. I believe in Marxism. Isn't it true that you, the Red Army and Communist Party, believe in Marxism? When the others left and wanted me to leave, too, I didn't go because I have these ideas."

Comrade Xia Xi and Wang Zhen talked with him about international affairs. He knew everything. He also hated Chiang Kai-shek's policy of non-resistance. They [Xia Xi and Wang Zhen] said,

"Now we are advocating a united front against the Japanese. Will you join us?"[22]

He [Zhou] was almost sixty at that time. After he was mobilized, 1,000 [soldiers] came in. When we had been in Bijie for more than 20 days, the enemy encircled us. Since we didn't want to make a reckless stand, we retreated from Bijie and he went with us. He was not someone who could lead troops—he was a man of letters—so the soldiers were handed over to us. He himself went with the Political Department.

I was in the Propaganda Section of the Political Department. We provided him with a horse and a bodyguard to take care of him. During the march sometimes he was with me. Since he didn't know how to ride a horse, I told him how.

When the enemy planes came over, we hid. When the planes found us, they started bombing and shooting machine guns. He just stood and looked at them.

I told him, "That's not right. Mr. Zhou, you have to get down on the ground." He was wearing a long robe [*changpao*], lying on the ground![23] "You have to find a low place to lie down so that when the bombs explode they can't get you."

At that time the bombs were quite different from now. The technology wasn't very advanced. If you lay down on the ground, you wouldn't be hit.

In Bijie, Jian Xianren began to regain her health. She was treated at a Chinese traditional medical clinic for a blood deficiency disorder and given medication to build up the *yin* and decrease the *yang,* to bring her body into balance. She was also able to have her daughter vaccinated for smallpox: "My baby was quite pretty. If she were pock-marked when she grew up, that would be terrible!" And in that isolated place, she found a true treasure in a jar of Vaseline (*fanshilin*).[24] Unable to change her baby more than once a day while the troops were marching, she had been unable to prevent her from developing a severe diaper rash. The Vaseline protected the inflamed areas and allowed them to heal.

The Second and Sixth Armies left the Bijie area the end of February, "when [the baby's] vaccination had scabbed over." They had intended to stay in Bijie and establish a Guizhou-Yunnan Revolutionary Base Area, Jian Xianren explained, but they had lost a battle and, more importantly, had received a telegram from Headquarters telling them to join the Fourth Front army when the situation permitted and continue north to fight against the Japanese.[25]

> When we got into the mountains, it was the beginning of March. The mountains were very high and the valleys very deep. We were in a minority area. They didn't use the same language. In comparatively flat areas, there were more Han [Chinese]. The roads were rugged and difficult to walk on. We couldn't see the sun and the sky because of the heavy clouds. The local people said that in the winter, all the mountains were covered with ice and snow. Even the birds didn't fly down to these snow-covered mountains. People described how poor the place was by saying:
>
> > There was not three feet of level land,
> > There were never three clear days,
> > There was no man with three pieces of silver.
>
> The few people [living] in this area were under the control of feudal landlords and the minority headmen. They suffered terribly under this feudal slave system.

Surrounded by the Nationalist forces, the Red Army fought in the Wumeng Mountains for the next twenty-three days. Their troop strength had remained steady, for their recruitment efforts at least equaled their losses. The Nationalists, allied with warlord troops, still outnumbered them by more than ten to one. The new recruits received their training during battle, Jian Xianren added.

The army was continually moving west, stealthily marching day and night, maintaining total silence because the enemy was always close by. One of the men in reconnaissance was carrying the baby in a basket on his back, but, Jian Xianren said, "The baby didn't understand. . . . She cried whenever she wanted." Still riding on horseback, she decided to carry the baby herself and fashioned a cloth carrier for the baby, a *budou,* commonly used by mothers in the southern provinces. She positioned the *budou* to allow the baby to nurse at will to prevent her from crying.

They kept to the winding mountain paths, avoiding the main roads. "Riding a horse was hard, but you could do it if you were bold. And you didn't have any choice if you couldn't walk." When the road was impassable, the groom would give her a hand down and lead the horse while she walked. Where the vegetation was dense, she would walk bent over under the low trees, supporting the baby. At times when they broke the encirclement, they would race down the main road at night, the baby on her back.

> Carrying the baby was really hard. She seemed to be sleeping well, but marching like this exhausted me. My chest hurt, my shoulders hurt, my back and legs ached. I thought that this baby was heavier to carry than a machine gun! If I were a man, I would rather carry a gun than a baby. Then I could still fight if the enemy caught up with us. As I said, my health had already broken down before we got into the mountains. In this situation in the mountains, I was exhausted, but I never fell even one step behind the army. In my mind, I had always had faith in my own ideals and I would fight for them. I thought, "Many comrades have been martyred for the country. Those of us who are still alive must persevere, no matter how much we suffer or how tired we are. Our only hope is to keep going." This is how I always kept my spirits up.

Then the baby, He Jiesheng, who was about six months old, became very ill. She ran a high fever and would neither eat nor sleep. Frantic, fearing the baby was about to die, Jian Xianren got word to He Long. Somehow, in the midst of battle, he found time to see his daughter.

> He Long was a bit feudalistic and favored sons over daughters [*zhongnan qingnu*], but when he saw that his daughter was dying, he felt very sad.
> "Even though you are a female, I still love you. You can't just die."
> "You're talking nonsense!" I said.[26]
> "I'm already 40, and I only have you, one daughter. Even though you're not a son, I still love you. If there are no fish in the river, then the shrimp become precious. If you die, then I don't even have any shrimp!"

Jian Xianren found a doctor with one of the army divisions who agreed to examine the baby. He no longer had any medicine, "Not even iodine," she said, but told Jian Xianren about a folk medicine prescription:

> "Try to find an egg and a bit of the burned soil which had been packed around an oven. Grind it up with the egg white and put it on the baby's navel. Wrap a cloth around it and leave it there for a few hours. Then the fever will subside."
> It was just a kind of folk medicine, but it was quite effective and cured my baby. I'm telling you this little detail because not many people know about this very effective Chinese traditional medicine.

They held the Wumeng Mountains for twenty-three days, moving constantly each day. When they broke the encirclement, they moved south along the Guizhou-Yunnan border to Panxian, where the army rested and planned the next stage of their journey. The soldiers got haircuts and wove the straw sandals, which needed constant replacement. While they were fighting in the mountains with no opportunity to weave new sandals, she said, many of the soldiers fought barefoot.

There were discussions among the leaders of the Second and Sixth about the route they would take to the Jinsha (Upper Yangzi) River and how to prepare the army to cross the difficult terrain beyond the river. Although Jian Xianren had access to the few maps available, she did not truly begin to understand what was ahead of them until the commander of the Tenth Division returned from a hurried trip to town with provisions for her. He brought ten cans of condensed milk, baby clothes, and some patterned cloth. She protested against carrying much more than a few diapers and a change of clothes for the baby. The weather was already hot and she thought she would not need anything more. However, the commander explained that they would be going to places even more difficult to transverse than those they had already been through. "I wouldn't advise you take anything not useful," he said, and insisted she ensure that her daughter had food and clothing. She agreed to carry the provisions he had brought.

When they left Panxian, the soldiers began to take off their padded coats in the heat and give them to peasants they met as they marched along. They were told to keep their warm clothing and blankets, but without explanation. "That was a military secret." When the soldiers persisted in ridding themselves of their heavy coats even in the face of punishment, Jian Xianren said, "Orders are orders, notices are notices. They gave away what they had because it was so hot." She persuaded the people with her to pile their things on her horse. When she found she couldn't reach the stirrups if she sat on them, she pushed them forward. Thus, Jian Xianren, with He Jiesheng on her back and a pile of padded coats and blankets in front of her, rode off on a forced march across Yunnan to the Jinsha River. "When we were marching, the enemy tried to wipe us out before we crossed the Jinsha River. The leaders of the army, because of their intelligence, were able to pursue a course where there were the fewest enemies. They made the enemy follow them in a round-about way, leading them astray. Because of the good discipline of the soldiers, they had the support of the people."

Aided by local people who told them where the enemy forces were concentrated, where the local armies were stationed, and where the blockades were, the Red Army successfully passed through the blockaded areas. "While the enemy army was pursuing us, we circled around to the rear of the pursuing army."

When a cavalry force in the van of the Red Army approached a minority area, the soldiers put pieces of red silk made into flowers into their hats in a show of respect for the local customs. The people received them courteously, Jian Xianren said, offered accommodations for the army, and asked about the army needs.

They continued north to Lijiang county, where they were greeted by the Naxi people, who were also openly supportive and helpful.[27]

We had some money when we started, but we didn't have much. We got some from donations and we confiscated money from the local bandits and Nationalist officials, according to [Chinese Communist] policy. When we were in Hunan, we used Hunan local currency. When we were in Bijie, we used the Yunnan local paper money. Sometimes we got some silver coins. When we got to Lijiang, we changed the currency into silver coins. We didn't use the paper currency after that, so it wasn't really a problem.

Our army was a well-disciplined army. When the First Front Army, the Central Army, marched through the area, they used the currencies of the soviet base areas in Jiangxi. This was our own currency, in circulation among the people where we set up our bases. After the Red Army left, the regional government would not recognize this currency. If you used the currency, not only would the currency be taken away, but you would also be fined. People had to hide that currency. When we passed through the same areas, people asked us whether our army was the same family as the army that had passed through last year.

We said, "Yes. We're the same family. They're the Central Army." They asked if they could use the currency they had hidden. Our soldiers weren't quite sure, so they took the question to the leaders, He Long, Xiao Ke and Ren Bishi. Their answer was that they would convert the Soviet Base Area currency to silver coins. One piece of paper money would convert equally to one silver coin.

The people were very supportive of the army, since the army was so good to them. They served as guides and did some reconnaissance, some intelligence work, for us. The local officials were our interpreters and we could communicate with the people through them. They joined the army by the thousands.

Now, I've added another example of the good policy of the Red Army, in connection with the money.

They quickly passed through Lijiang, on their forced march to the Jinsha River, the upper Yangzi River, about thirty miles from the Lijiang county seat. It was imperative that they cross the river before the enemy troops arrived. When they reached Shigu, a cliffside town just above the first bend of the Jinsha River, they were dismayed to find that most of the available boats had been secreted away, at the instigation of the local Nationalists.

When the army arrived, people fled. The local reactionary forces had told the people to hide their boats from the Red Army, and had told the boatmen to run away. He Long was good at telling local people that the Red Army was the kind of army that would not harm them. He sent a letter to let the people know that all the army needed was boats, and he hoped they could find boats for the army. After the head of the township got He Long's letter, he sent four boatmen who brought a boat to help us cross the river. We picked up more boats along the river. The 2nd Army found it very difficult to find the boats because they were camouflaged, but the local people were kind and helped us search for boats. In the end we found eight boats.

Some of the blacksmiths and tree cutters came to our help. We needed them because we wanted them to help us make bamboo and timber rafts. The blacksmiths hammered out the hooks to link the bamboo or timber together to make the rafts. We could use them to transport both people as well as donkeys and horses. However, they weren't very safe because of the fast current, so we mainly relied on boats. Because speed was crucial, everything was very well organized. He Long, the Commander of the 2nd Army Group and the Commander of the 6th Army Group, Xiao Ke, were both there. The first batch of thirty or forty people lined up and got on the boat in an organized way. The size of the boats varied and some could take forty people.

The airplanes were still searching for us, but by the time they found us we had already crossed the river. We had moved very quickly [across Yunnan province], and they couldn't find us. It was a very big area and they weren't sure where we would cross the river. Originally, they thought we would cross where the 1st Front Army crossed. Actually, we sent a small group of people to that harbor to mislead the enemy. They probably knew generally where we were, but they didn't know where we would cross.

They reached Shigu the night of April 25. "The river wasn't very wide there, but it was very deep and the current was very fast."[28] The army, which maintained original strength through recruitment, took a day and a night to cross the river, about one half hour each trip. They found places to cross at various ferrying points between Shigu north to Judian, where Ma Yixiang's group crossed. The ferry landings were quite primitive. There were no real piers and "no ropes you could use to pull the boats over," Jian Xianren explained, because the water rose and fell dramatically with the runoff from the snows.

While boats were being fashioned or found, the rest of the troops rested and ate.[29] The first to go over were the combat forces. Jian Xianren, who crossed with Headquarters in the last groups, spent the waiting time talking with women in town.

> The people treated us very well. When people, especially women, saw me carrying the baby, they all gathered around. I did some propaganda work. I told them why we came here and why we wanted to go to Sikang.[30] Of course, it was to fight Chiang Kai-shek and the Japanese. They were very sympathetic to me,

a woman with a child on such a long, strenuous march. The baby was just half a year old. They offered to hold her, and invited me into their homes. Actually, I was in a hurry. I was a bit worried because I wanted to get across the river, but everyone wanted me to come to their home. Finally a Han woman who was carrying the baby said,

"Just come on to my house, since I have the baby."

So I followed her. When she took off the baby's diaper and saw how soiled she was, she washed her. I washed the baby's clothes, although they wanted to do it for me. I had a bath, too, and we dried off in the sun, but we had to leave before the clothes were dry. They wanted to see me off and went all the way back to headquarters [with me]. I invited them in and asked them to sit on the door which we had taken down to sit on.

When He [Long] saw that I had come back, he made a joke: "*Houniang,* you're back!"

Why did he call me Madame Monkey? Because when we were traveling along and saw a lot of small monkeys, a political commissar asked me,

"Don't you think you are like a monkey?"

"No!" Everyone laughed. I wouldn't agree to this comparison.

So when He Long made that kind of joke, the women called me Madame Monkey because *Houniang* was easier to remember than my name.

They gave me some hot pepper to protect me from the cold and a kind of stimulant to keep me from getting dizzy. And they kept calling me "Madame Monkey." I didn't want to tell them that my name wasn't really Madame Monkey, that it was just a joke. But I didn't want to answer to Madame Monkey, either! After the women left, He said,

"When I called you Madame Monkey, you refused to accept it. But now that everyone calls you that, you have to accept it. You answered to it, so from now on we'll call you Madame Monkey. Your name isn't easy to remember."

Even though the march was very intense, we still had jokes, which made our lives a little lighter. Because we held lofty ideals in front of us, we weren't weighed down by the hardships. Life was still good, in spite of the difficult conditions.

After the 20,000-strong army safely crossed the Jinsha River before the Nationalists caught up with them, they moved north toward Sikang, now part of Sichuan province, inside the *V* created by the first bend of the river. They could see their next ordeal, less than a day's march away, looming above them in the form of a snow-covered mountain range, the first of several snow mountains they would have to cross. The soldiers began to understand why they had been ordered not to discard their warm clothing in the heat of eastern Yunnan.

We arrived in Shigu on [April] the 25th, finished crossing on the 26th, and climbed the snow mountain on the 27th. It was all right when we began climbing. The wind was cool. That was the first ten *li*. Then after another ten *li*, you

The first bend of the Yangzi (Jinsha) River, near where Jian Xianren crossed with her baby. (Author's photo, June 1997)

felt that autumn had come. You could see some snow, but some had melted. But by 30 *li,* you felt that winter had begun. You just looked around and found that there was very heavy fog. And you felt really cold. You put on your padded coat and those who followed also put on their padded coats.

The mountain was high, covered with white snow far and wide as far as we could see. The air was very thin because of the altitude and you couldn't stop. You had to keep going because if you sat down, you couldn't get up again. We climbed over the mountain and came down and came to a flat place for a few miles and then went down some more. Going up the snow mountain, the distance was about 60 *li* but coming down it's only 40 *li,* so in one day we covered almost 100 *li.*

On the mountain, the man who was helping me with the baby mainly carried her in the basket on his back. His name was Yun. He's retired now, back in his hometown. It was too hard to climb holding the baby, and besides, it would be too cold for her. Before we started off, we put a padded coat on her and then we wrapped her up in a quilt. We propped up a piece of black cloth with a stick and put the stick on the basket so the cloth could shade her. I couldn't carry her. I was on a horse—a big donkey—since I couldn't really walk.

We were very thirsty, but we were told not to eat the snow because it was poisonous. We didn't really see anyone drink it, but someone said he saw a dead man just sitting and holding a cup of water. He was dead because he had drunk the water.

After crossing the snow mountain, they reached Zhongdian, on a high plateau 8,000–10,000 feet above sea level, in the northernmost part of Yunnan province. They had left the Naxi minority area and were now in a predominantly Tibetan town. They stayed three days, replenishing their grain supplies and buying tents and "some kind of pepper, some kind of stimulant," although the silver coins they had changed before they crossed the river were not enough to buy all that was needed. They were able to communicate through the local Han officials, who acted as interpreters. The women, as usual, were doing propaganda.

We put up notices showing the purpose of the Army when we passed through this area:

"We are the army of the people, the sons and daughters of the people; we protect people's interest."

We also put up some other notices as to the disciplines according to which we bought things and paid for them. We buy things and we will pay. At that time a lot of people didn't know this and they ran away. After we put up these notices, they came back. Of course, some of them were opposed to us because of the propaganda of the ruling class, the serf-owners. Those were the reactionary upper strata, the ruling class. Other people were generally all right. But in general, people were kind to us. They gave their yaks to us voluntarily. The yaks were draft animals, and their meat was also good for food. They were an important means of transportation. So actually, out of their own initiative, they sent their yaks to carry those who had fallen behind, the wounded soldiers, the sick soldiers. They also offered their tea made with rancid butter and their rice cakes and brown sugar for us to buy. But that still couldn't solve the supply problem of food and daily necessities for the 20,000 soldiers.

While they were in Zhongdian, He Long and Xiao Ke went to the lamasery, the largest outside of Tibet, to negotiate with the lamas for safe passage through the territory administered by the lamas in Zhongdian. The Second and Sixth Armies agreed to follow different routes, a necessity if they were to find enough provisions. The Second Army left Zhongdian and crossed a wide meadow, northwest of the town. The Sixth Army went through the pass to the northeast of Zhongdian. Both army groups still had several snow mountain ranges to cross before they reached the Fourth Front Army.

Before the Second Army was out of Yunnan, they were ambushed by local troops near the Sikang border, and two of the regimental level political commissars were killed. "You could never tell when you reached a certain place if you might be killed by a sniper. They hid in the woods and when you got there they would try to kill you, but you would never see them. Whenever you shouted out they would answer you, saying that you couldn't pass unless you surrendered your guns and bullets."

* * *

In the rugged mountain area on the eastern border of present-day Tibet, between the present Yunnan-Sichuan border and Aba in northwestern Sichuan, where the Fourth Front Army was camped, there are deep river valleys and ravines. When Jian Xianren crossed with the Second Army, they used narrow paths cut into the side of the mountain. If part of the path had washed away, and if hostile locals had removed the wooden boards placed across the washout, the army became easy targets for the snipers. There was also a problem finding water, for local people often dismantled the bamboo pipes bringing water to the mountain villages. "Going on foot in this area was not easy," she said in grim understatement.

In June, the Second and Sixth Armies reached Ganzi in the Aba region, where they met the Fourth Front Army. The Fourth Front soldiers, in a demonstration of "warm welcome" and "deep friendship," had spun yarn and knit woolen vests and socks for the tattered newcomers. Jian Xianren found what she observed of the large number of women soldiers in the welcoming Fourth Army quite interesting:

What I saw were women who were involved in political work, propaganda work, and those who were engaged in health care. They were all laboring women, mostly from Sichuan. Some of the women comrades who hadn't received much education were very capable. Those mainly engaged with propaganda work not only made speeches but sang songs and put on plays in order to enliven the life of the army. When they encountered the enemies in battle, they were very brave on the battlefield. They carried the wounded on stretchers. They carried the medicine kits. They dug trenches and carried grain. Both men and women who worked in the kitchen carried very big, heavy copper or bronze cooking pots. Zhang Qinqiu was the commander of the Women's [Independent] Regiment which later on was expanded into a division. She became the commander as well as the political commissar of the women's regiment. I didn't actually see the women's unit because they had set off ahead of me.

I did see some women comrades holding babies. Wang Weizhou's wife, Ma Huixian—she's still alive and I see her now and then; she's not too articulate, but her mind still works—I saw her sitting on horseback and holding a baby. Her husband was one of the commanders from Sichuan, a veteran CCP member since the time of the Great Revolution. Another woman was Army Commander Cai's wife. He had already died a martyr. She sat on a horse with her baby in a basket on one side of the horse and food in a basket on the other side. It wasn't easy for her to follow the army. Of course, when we were marching, it was hard for us to talk to each other.

In early July, the Second and Sixth Armies were consolidated into the Second Front Army, with He Long designated as commander, Xiao Ke deputy commander, and Ren Bishi political commissar of the Second Front Army. By this time, the toll taken on the health of leaders had become so apparent that Jian Xianren gave them the precious cans of milk she had carried across Yunnan and over the snow mountain ranges. She had probably not fed the milk to her daughter because she was still nursing, or perhaps she was reluctant to give her the canned milk because many Chinese people lack an enzyme needed to digest cow's milk.

It was during this time that Jian Xianren was reunited with her sister. "My sister was in Xiao Ke's [Sixth] army. We had few opportunities to meet after we left Sangzhi, where we started out. We weren't together when we marched because we took different routes. When we stopped to rest, we were never together except in Bijie. Our husbands often met because they had to discuss battle plans, marching routes, but we didn't see each other again until we reached Ganzi."

Jian Xianfo: We stayed in Bijie for more than twenty days and I met my older sister there. She knew I was pregnant.[31] [In Ganzi] it was very difficult to see her. Qi Dajie[32] told me a little [about childbirth]. I prepared a few things, some small clothes, some pieces of cloth. [My sister] had prepared some things for me, little aprons.

Jian Xianren: When we got to Ganzi, she was very close to giving birth to her baby. We were in Ganzi only about ten days. I stayed with my work unit and she stayed with hers, but we met and knew how the other was getting on. I was very worried. Of the four of us who had left home, I now had only my sister, since both my brothers had already died.[33] I didn't dare tell her about our younger brother's death. When I saw my younger sister, I asked her when she was going to have the baby. She answered that the baby was due right then. I hoped that she wouldn't have it in the grasslands.

On July 11 the 2nd Front Army, the two Front Armies [the Second and the Fourth], set out and entered the vast grasslands. It took us more than a month to cross—about forty-five days. I'll tell you something about the grasslands. It stretched as far as our eyes could see. We couldn't see a single house, but there were cow dung and goat droppings. From that I could tell it was grazing land [*mu chang*]. The herdsmen had already herded the cattle away and all we saw were the animal droppings. It was really huge and the weather could change drastically. Within a range of 500 meters, [there might be] clouds and hailstones and rain. Those who had horses galloped ahead and tried to pass to the other end [of the storm]. If it wasn't raining, it was very, very hot.

Jian Xianfo: While we were walking, my stomach was uncomfortable, it hurt, and I wanted to urinate. I didn't understand. My water broke, but I didn't realize it. I kept on walking in a stupor, until afternoon. I didn't know, I had no experience. I walked from the morning until three or four in the afternoon. It was about three or five in the afternoon that my sister caught up with me. She had been looking for me everywhere in the grasslands. When she found me, things weren't all right. She felt badly.

Jian Xianren: We were in the rear of the 4th Front Army. We marched in several columns, so there were people everywhere. One afternoon—it was not raining—I saw my sister on a donkey. I whipped my donkey forward and caught up with her. She said she was in labor and I saw that she was perspiring all over her face. We were on a vast plain with no shelter. It was hard enough for women even to urinate—they had to ask other women comrades to make a circle around them[34]—to say nothing of giving birth to a child. I noticed a broken stronghold with no roof, a kind of a round structure made of earth. [Where we were] was really something like a desert, with very little grass on it—just patches of grass with earth underneath. Those patches of grass, one on top of each other, had been placed to make an earth fortification.

Jian Xianfo: When she helped me off the horse, we saw a dirt fortification about this high, built when our vanguard fought Tibetan headmen and their cavalry. Even though there was no enemy harassment, the reactionary headmen were influenced by the Nationalists and the English imperialism. She persuaded me to go there.

Jian Xianren: [I decided] it was the place to give birth to the child, so we stopped at this stronghold. I took a quilt and an oiled cloth and spread it on the ground so my sister could lie on it. Her water had already broken. That could have been dangerous and the delivery might have been very difficult, but she was quite strong. We aren't laboring women, but we had been having quite a lot of exercise on the march. I laid my baby down beside us, but she cried.

Jian Xianfo: Her baby was quite small, under a year. We didn't know why she was crying. [She was] just like a little mud figure [*xiao ni ren*], on the ground.

Jian Xianren: We had left our horses outside. Xiao Ke came along with He Long and asked why we had stopped where there was practically no water, when we were only about 10 *li* from the place we would make camp. When Xianfo heard him, she told him that we couldn't go any further. She was having the baby. Xiao Ke said he would take care of her during her labor because it would be dangerous if we were left behind and bandits or the enemy came.

Jian Xianfo: It was in July and so very hot sweat was running down my face. It was painful. I'd already suffered a lot. I couldn't lie down on the ground, so we piled up our bundles. I sat on the bundles and put some of them under my back. My husband was supporting my back and the baby was born. My sister cut the cord.

Jian Xianren: Although I was the mother of two children, it was the first time I helped in the delivery of a baby.[35] I managed to deliver the baby according to the procedure I had been told. There was no water, so I cut the umbilicus, wrapped up the baby without bathing it and put him on her stomach.

Jian Xianfo: After the baby was born, a boy, it had already gotten dark and it started raining hard and the wind was blowing. There was a violent storm. We had a small tent and we covered ourselves with everything we had. I held the baby in my arms. Everything was wet. The baby was very healthy.

Jian Xianren: That night Xiao Ke was with us, so there were five of us: two babies and three adults. The baby was a boy. Later we named him "Baosheng."[36] I just wrapped him with the old baby clothes I had with me. After he was born, we had to be on our way the next day.

Jian Xianfo: The following day we started off again as usual. During the storm, my horse disappeared. That was really difficult. The health department sent several stretcher carriers over. At that time, everybody was having troubles. My sister and Lao Xiao [Xiao Ke] gave their food to the stretcher carriers. It was really hard for them [to carry the stretcher].

That same night Li Bozhao had just heard that I'd had the baby.[37] The two of us did work that was complementary: I watched her dramas and she saw my pictures. Through this grew a closeness, a friendship. She left her food, about two *jin* of rice, and didn't tell me. At that time, food was life. Later on I learned that she was really short of food. I felt very sad when I found out that she had been eating grass, had fainted and someone rescued her. I felt so sorry when I heard that. . . .

We marched for three days on a stretcher. In that place, it was hard for everyone. They found me a horse from the supply department. I rode the horse and the groom led the horse and helped me. Then they found me a basket for my back. The person who helped Comrade Xiao Ke carry his books and documents put all the things on the back of his horse and then was sent to help me. The two men helped me carry the baby out of the grasslands.

Jian Xianren: She went through all the hardships. My sister was seven years younger than me. I was 27 at that time. After three days of lying on the stretcher, she went on her way on horseback and let someone carry the baby in the basket. We went on together, both of us sisters, on this grassland.

After ten days or so, she went back to her own work unit, the political section of the army. This is a brief account of how we passed the grassland.

The Second Front Army spent a month and a half crossing the wet and the dry grasslands. Whenever they found villages, they stopped to rest and replenish supplies. Cow dung was their fuel source, and they were on a constant lookout for anything they could use for kindling to get a fire started.

It was near Aba that Chen Zongying gave birth to her baby, Ren Yuanzheng. Jian Xianren said, "Her child was born in a house, in a much better place than my sister had." However, because they were short of food, the two generals tried to find some fish for her. "She wasn't in good shape. She's short and not very strong. That's the way she is."

After they left Aba, they were in the wet grasslands, a vast, flat treeless marsh covered with shallow water. "If you had any wounds on your feet, they would get infected and the skin would rot [*lan*] because the water was poisonous." Finding a high spot to camp became a problem, for possible campsites always seemed either too close or too far for a day's march.

Another problem was the treacherous earth itself, which in some places was like quicksand, sucking soldiers and animals into the depths and covering them. Jian Xianren, describing the quicksand, said,

It was soft ground, yellow in color. When you stepped on it, you felt that it would give and at the same time bounce you up. If you walked along the edge of the yellow color and went a little bit into the center you came to some soil that was darker than yellow, more brown, like soy sauce. If you were trapped in it, you couldn't get out. At the beginning, when I walked on it, I thought it was fascinating until someone told me not to walk on it. We found a donkey that was trapped. We couldn't pull it out because the more we pulled, the deeper it sank.

The land they were marching through was cut deeply by rivers. The Second Front Army camped on the high ground near a river where trees could provide cover, but the cover protected their enemies as well. Because the Headquarters unit was traveling at the rear of the army, it was an easy target, Jian Xianren explained.

> After we crossed a mountain, we usually found some streams on the other side. [That side of the mountain] was covered with thick forests. The [Second Front] Army by the battalions, by the companies, by the combat armies, was marching in front of us. The enemy came out from the forest on the opposite side and we didn't see them. Just behind us there was a narrow tributary, about three meters wide.
>
> The enemy came along the stream and we were right there. He Long was fishing in the stream. I was resting and feeding my baby. With us was a bugler, a 14- or 15-year-old boy. Those who were quick to notice shouted, "Enemy's coming!" He Long immediately pulled out his fishing line and came away. He ordered, "Fight them!" He didn't really have an army—what he had were stragglers who didn't even have rifles with them. I was quite nervous. Some combat troops were ahead of us and those behind hadn't caught up with us yet. The enemy were reactionary cavalry, local chieftains, and soldiers [serving] the Tibetan upper-class.
>
> By that time everyone was nervous, but no one wanted to run away. We didn't move. We just watched them. There were hundreds of enemy on horseback. Hundreds of them were charging us—five hundred meters, four hundred meters, three hundred meters. All we had was a boy, the bugler, about my height.
>
> [I said] "Why don't you blow the bugle when we're about to have a battle?"
>
> The boy asked me if he could blow the call to mobilize the troops—not a marching call, but a call to bring in the troops in the rear. After he blew the bugle, about a hundred [Red Army soldiers] responded to our call. The enemy, caught by surprise, were frightened. They turned around and rode away. [The bugler] was quite intelligent to choose that bugle call.

More dangerous than human enemies was the natural environment. Jian Xianfo explained that after crossing the Jinsha River, "We fought against the enemy, against the heavens and against the earth." On the grasslands, the Second Front Army was subject not only to sudden and violent weather changes but also to hunger and disease. They had used up all their grain. Their medicines had run out months before, when they were in the Wumeng Mountains in western Guizhou. The Fourth Front Army was in front of them, and Jian Xianren saw many unburied corpses as they marched, for the living were too weak to bury the dead. "We saw their dead soldiers, covered with flies, smelling. We were very sad to see them, to see revolutionaries in that situation." The pace of their march became slower and slower as exhaustion and hunger intensified.

When we started out from Aba we had prepared grain for several days. We predicted how far we could go before we could buy grain again. I knew I had to control myself because I had to have food for my baby. I'd eat only so much and then I'd drink some boiled water. Every day I drank only so much water. Why did I eat so little? Everybody had a ration but I had to save some of my grain and give it to the person who carried my baby. I was still breast feeding the baby.

Some comrades were too hungry to control themselves. We each had a long bag for carrying grain, so some people kept eating a bit of grain as they walked along, eating more than their daily ration. If they had followed the ration strictly, they wouldn't have been starved like that. Sometimes I ran out of food too, but just for a meal or two. When that happened, I would get some wild plants and sprinkle some highland barley [qingke] flour on the plants.[38] I was carrying the baby and sometimes several of us would eat together. I offered my baby some, telling her, "You should try some of this, too," but she refused. She was only eight or nine months old. You could see a frown on her face, and she kept shaking her head and wouldn't eat it.

He Long said, "The troops in front of us are also searching for grain, just like combing the hair. We also need grain but we can only get what the comb has left. The army walking ahead of us has to eat a lot of the grass that grows along the path. We also have to eat grass, but we have to go a distance from the path to get our grass, so our hardships are greater."

The man who carried my baby said to her, "You also have suffered with us, you also have suffered the hardships of climbing the snow mountains and crossing the wet grasslands." Everyone was looking at this miserable child.

Actually, I didn't have much milk for the baby. One time when we got to a lamasery where we could camp, the baby kept crying, crying very hard, but not very loudly, because she didn't have enough strength. She was so hungry.

He Long said, "Maybe there's something wrong with the baby."

I said, "There's nothing wrong."

I didn't want to say that she cried because she was so hungry—everyone was hungry—so I just said that she wanted me to hold her.

He said, "Let me hold her." When he took her, the baby started looking for his breasts.

He said, "If you want to eat, Mama has the breasts. Baba doesn't have any. Are you hungry? Of course you're hungry." The baby couldn't talk, she could only cry. He sent for the bodyguard and asked him for something to give the baby. When the bodyguard told him that we had no food, He said, "Why don't we have anything? I thought we had enough for tomorrow."

The bodyguard said, "When you saw some sick soldiers, [you said] that it doesn't matter if we don't have anything to eat tomorrow, so we shared the grain with them. Now we don't have any left."

"Then bring Xianren's bag. There should be something in her bag we can give to Jiesheng."

The bodyguard said, "Her bag is empty, too. When I passed her in the wet grasslands, she was boiling water and eating wild plants."

He Long asked him to bring the empty food bag.

The bodyguard was surprised. "What's the use of bringing the empty bag?"

He Long took the open end of the empty bag, held it shut and shook the bag. He told the bodyguard to hold out a cup and shook the chaff into the cup. The bodyguard boiled it for the baby to eat.

Before the baby finished eating, He Long said, "Keep some for her to eat tomorrow. Tomorrow at noon we'll reach a place where we can get more grain."

We didn't run out of food very often. Some people said that they ate leather shoes, leather belts, leather hats, but I didn't. I saw other people eating leather shoes. Not like the kind of shoes you wear. Those shoes were made of raw leather from yaks. Actually it was only a cover to protect the feet. It was pieces of leather laced together to protect the feet. When they couldn't find wild plants, they put the leather shoes in a basin, boiled it and drank the soup. Some also ate the leather.

When the Army reached Hadapu, a Chinese Muslim town in Gansu province, they were able to find more familiar provisions and potable water. They rested there for about ten days before continuing to Jiangtaibao, Hongxian, where they met the First Front Army in October 1936. "When we met the 1st Front Army we knew we had accomplished our task. Now our Long March had come to an end," Jian Xianren said.

For Jian Xianfo, however, the March was still unfinished. General Xiao Ke was sent to replace the general commanding the Thirty-first Army, the main force of the Fourth Front Army. Because she had already been detached from her own unit, she felt she had no alternative other than to follow her husband. While they were still in Hadapu, the sympathetic women there had offered to keep the children for the women soldiers, but leaving the baby behind had never occurred to her as a viable choice. They were not far from the Central Soviet Base Area, where she felt sure life would be more orderly.

As commander of the Thirty-first Army, Xiao Ke was in the front lines, whereas Jian Xianfo was in the rear with the mess unit. When she had been with the political department before the baby was born, Xiao Ke kept her informed of the situation with the enemy and of the Second Army's plans. Now, she said, she had no way of anticipating when they would be in battle or of knowing in advance how dangerous a situation might be. In addition, the Fourth Front Army soldiers did not know who she was and were neither supportive of nor sympathetic toward a woman with a baby in combat.

Jian Xianfo: I remember one night when we were marching. It was so cold, and we didn't have enough [warm] clothes. In front of us was a 4th Front Army company. There were some people resting in a house, so I went in, too. It was a pretty big house. When I came in, the baby was crying and one of them said,

"Here is someone who is still so backward! Who are you? Get out!"

I said, "You can rest in this house. I can, too! You are in the Red Army, and I am, too! I can't go away. It's too cold. I need to rest here."

He was formidable. "Chase her away!" He was probably a bodyguard.

I stood up and said, "I dare you! I tell you, you are unreasonable. No one in the Red Army chases away another Red Army person, especially when the situation is tough. The Party Central advocates a United Front line to fight the Japanese. If you can't put up with your own comrades, how can you even talk about the United Front line?"[39]

Then he said, "If you don't leave, I'll leave."

I said, "If you want to go, then go on. I myself . . ."

He didn't leave and that was the end of it.

The Army dodged planes and skirmished with the troops of Ma Buqing and Ma Bufang, Muslim warlord brothers from Xinjiang who were aligned with the Nationalists. Jian Xianfo explained the situation as she understood it more than fifty years later:

Three armies of the 4th Front Army crossed the river and went west of the Yellow River. Our army was defeated. Our whole army was wiped out. The 9th, the 5th, and the 30th Army Groups of the Fourth Front Army had all crossed the river. Some who had fallen behind, the wounded and the sick, all crossed to the west side of the Yellow River into Ningxia. I was very anxious. I followed those people and I didn't know what the enemy situation was, that [the Nationalists] had gathered to annihilate us.

[When Xiao Ke] found me, he said,

"Comrade Xianfo, follow us. We'll cross the river together. Let's cross fast before the enemy planes come."

I said, "You go ahead. I'll follow you," but I couldn't go on. After they crossed the river, the troops were wiped out. Almost all of them died.

I turned back and walked to the crossroads late at night. There were three of us—four, including my baby. The road was so rough, full of bumps and holes, and sometimes you thought there was no road in front of you and you felt like you were suspended in air. It was so dark. How could I keep going?

I stopped and said, "Wait a minute, let's see what's happening with our troops."

We waited and listened. Then we heard footsteps. When the sounds came closer and closer, I heard Xiao Ke's voice. That was the most welcome sound I had ever heard in my life!

We marched for another day or two and fought a battle at Tianshuipu. The 31st and the 4th armies blocked the enemy in a mountainous place where the blockhouse warfare they organized was to their advantage. That battle was well-fought. They not only shot down the enemy planes, but also killed and wounded the enemy, taking the edge off of their spirit. We really demoralized them! The enemy wouldn't dare pursue the Red Army to the death.

That was in 1936, before the Xi'an Incident.[40] Probably in November, 1936.

Jian Xianfo decided there was no good reason to stay with the army after that battle and decided to go straight to Bao'an, where the Central Army Headquarters was based. Xiao Ke reluctantly agreed to let her go. She got her papers from the Thirty-first Army political department and left with her two male helpers and the baby, Xiao Baosheng.

The first day they met soldiers from the First Front Army who were on their way from Bao'an to join forces with Xiao Ke's troops. Although they had no map, they told her where enemies were located and which road she should follow.

Jian Xianfo: I just followed their directions. I didn't have any money or any field rations, but wherever we went, the ordinary people were so good to us. They were all poor peasants in a sparsely populated part of our base area.

We didn't know how far we'd have to walk. We walked in the gullies, back and forth. We couldn't find any water to drink because the water was brackish.

We carried the baby, and carried three guns and a stick. We didn't meet any enemy soldiers or landlord's militia, but there were a lot of wolves in that area. Wherever we went, the local people, who had been influenced by the Red Army, were very nice to us. They would take the baby in their arms, and would boil water for us. We stayed in their homes at night. I didn't have any money to give them.

They walked seventy or eighty *li* a day for eight days. When they reached Bao'an, Jian Xianfo reported to the political department. After checking her documents and hearing her story, they gave her a party registration form to fill in, telling her that she had already proved herself to be a strong Red Army soldier. They also encouraged her to attend classes. At one of the first classes, she heard a lecture that impressed her greatly, and she learned that Mao Zedong was the lecturer. Although she had heard about him, she had never met him.

Jian Xianfo: It was at night, we took small stools. He didn't sit on a stool. He stood there, talking.

"Oh, that was Chairman Mao?" I thought to myself, I must go see him. At that time, there was no concept of differences among the ranks. Now, it wouldn't be all right. I asked where Chairman Mao was living and someone pointed casually at a slope and said,

"In that cave."

I went there and his bodyguard asked me whom I was looking for and who I was.

Chairman Mao was inside and when he heard that I was from the 2nd Front Army, he came out and invited me inside.

He greeted me warmly and asked about the situation at the front. I told him everything I knew.

"I've heard that you brought a baby with you," he said, and called his [wife] He Zizhen, and told her to bring their [new] baby out for me to see.

"It has been very hard for both of you." Very warm. He really impressed me.

After the Central Army moved Headquarters to Yan'an, Jian Xianfo was assigned to underground work in Xi'an. Learning that the place where her parents were living in Hunan was peaceful again, Jian Xianfo decided to send her baby to Hunan for her own parents to raise. The child lived until he was six or seven, when, she believed, he became a victim of Japanese germ warfare.[41] Jian Xianfo had been reluctant to talk with us because her memories of bearing her son in the grasslands and then losing him before he reached adulthood were so painful. Her husband and sister finally persuaded her that it would be good for her to talk about the painful times, but she broke down and cried when she told us,

> I made such an effort to carry this baby through the grasslands. . . . I don't know why it happened. . . . So many people died.
>
> If he had stayed with me [in Xi'an], probably nothing would have happened to him. You know, women should have self-respect. If you have enough self-respect, you don't have to listen to what people say: "You girls are backward. Carrying a baby." . . . I wasn't willing. . . . I myself wanted to do more work. I wanted to leave the baby and devote myself to my work. So, the baby died like this. Afterwards, I wouldn't talk about him.

Jian Xianfo and Xiao Ke had another son several years after Baosheng was born. Their second son, his wife, and two sons were living with them in the western part of Beijing, where we interviewed her in 1988. She held increasingly responsible posts within the Communist party, retiring in a party position as deputy department head in the hydroelectric industry.

In 1982 she joined Jian Xianren on the Commission for Inspecting Discipline under the CCP Central Committee and was a member of the Standing Committee of the Chinese People's Political Consultative Council

Sisters Jian Xianren and Jian Xianfo during the 1930s, probably in Yan'an (*top*) and in Beijing in the mid-1980s (*bottom*). (Courtesy of Women of China Publishing House)

(*Zhongguo Renmin Zhengzhi Xieshang Huiyi*).[42] The Chinese People's Polit- ical Consultative Council (CPPCC) is an advisory body made up of both Communist party members and members of other Chinese political parties. The CPPCC (*Zhengxie*) acts as an advisory group to the Chinese government. Most of the members, who are well past retirement age, meet regularly and take their responsibilities seriously.

* * *

After Jian Xianren reached Shaanbei and the Central Army Headquarters moved to Yan'an, she took year-old He Jiesheng to He Long's home village in Hunan province to keep her safe. She left her in the care of a woman whom the author visited in June 1997. She was living in a one-room stone cottage with unfinished walls and a dirt floor, furnished with her bed, her coffin, and a couple of stools around a fire pit in the floor. Her memories of Jian Xian- ren and He Jiesheng were dimmed by age and her impoverished condition.

He Long, like many of the Red Army leaders, requested a divorce and re- married. Even though divorce was becoming more prevalent and more ac-

Jian Xianren and her baby,
He Jiesheng, in Yan'an af-
ter the Long March, 1937.
(Courtesy of Jiefangjun
Chubanshe [PLA Publish-
ing House], Beijing)

ceptable in China in the 1980s, women of Jian Xianren's generation still were not comfortable discussing their own experience with divorce. When questioned about it, she asked to go off the record.

Jian Xianren continued her work for the CCP, studying at the Anti-Japanese Military and Political College (*Kangri Junzheng Daxue*) in Shaanbei, where she stayed on as a political teacher. She studied further in the Soviet Union, then returned to China and held political posts in the northeast during the War Against Japan. After the defeat of Japan, when her workplace was surrounded by Nationalists troops, she led soldiers and cadres to cut a bloody path through the encirclement. After the founding of the People's Republic of China, she held posts in the city of Wuhan, and in 1978 she was in Beijing as a member of the Commission for Inspecting Discipline under the CCP Central Committee, and a member of the Standing Committee of the CPPCC.

Jian Xianren retired in 1985, when she was seventy-six years old. In 1988, when she came to my apartment for her interview, she reported that her small companion on the Long March, her daughter, He Jiesheng, was working as an editor in Beijing.

2. Revolutionary, Mother

CHEN ZONGYING and I stand side by side. The top of her head does not quite reach my shoulder, although she is stretching tall on her abnormally small feet. Even knowing the resilience of Chinese country people, I find it hard to believe that this fragile woman in her mid-eighties had spent her childbearing years as an underground Communist activist and a Red Army soldier during twenty-five years of civil war and the War Against Japan. During the Long March, she climbed the rugged snow mountains of Yunnan province a few weeks before her seventh child was born. Before she was forty years old, she had borne nine children; she grieved the loss of her warm and loving husband when she was not yet fifty.

Chen Zongying and two of her surviving children came to talk with me at my apartment in the foreign teachers' quarters at the Beijing Foreign Studies University. Many of the Long March soldiers chose to be interviewed in my apartment, which seemed ample, even luxurious, in comparison to apartments where many Chinese people lived in the mid-1980s. Six of us sat around the outsized dining table, tape recorders in the middle, thermos on the floor, notepaper, maps and lidded cups of tea in front of us: Wang Weihua, my former student and co-interviewer; my husband, Richard Young, who is fluent in several Chinese dialects; Chen Zongying, her children, Ren Yuanyuan and Ren Yuanzhi, and me.

Chen Zongying's daughter, Ren Yuanzhi, had been plagued with health problems that prevented her from working at a regular job since her release from jail in 1972. At the time of the interview, she was attending art classes for retirees at an army school for advanced learning. Her harsh imprison-

Chen Zongying with two
of her children, Ren Yuanzhi and Ren Yuanyuan,
in front of the author's
apartment building, Bei-
jing Foreign Studies Uni-
versity, June 1987. (Au-
thor's photo)

ment during the Cultural Revolution was a tragic echo of her babyhood: She
spent the first year of her life in a Nationalist prison with her mother in 1931.

Ren Yuanyuan, Chen Zongying's son, born in Yan'an in 1940, bore a star-
tling resemblance to pictures of his father at about the same age. His father,
Ren Bishi, was a Communist leader from the early 1920s until his untimely
death in 1950. Researching and writing his father's biography was the son's
life work. He had even played the part of his father in a documentary movie.

Chen Zongying, Ren Yuanzhi, and Ren Yuanyuan all participated in the
interview, telling Chen Zongying's experiences as if they had all been together
on the Long March. The children added details and explanations, prompted
their mother when her memory faded, and took up her story themselves
when she became tired. Their mutual respect and tenderness with each other when explaining feelings or finishing each other's sentences made it clear
that theirs was an unusually close and loving family, exemplary in any soci-

ety. The Ren family were especially remarkable in the Chinese context, where outward expressions of familial feelings outside the home are not common and family relationships may appear by Western standards to be undemonstrative to the point of uncaring.

Both Ren Yuanyuan and Ren Yuanzhi worked with their mother to craft the stories about her childhood, her years of underground work for the Communists, and her experiences on the Long March. Their joint preparation gave a coherence to her stories, which were all framed within a well-researched, verifiable historical narrative. They did not argue about facts, although they occasionally corrected each other. Chen Zongying, for example, remembered acquiring her revolutionary beliefs at an earlier age than her daughter thought she had. For the most part, however, it was hard to know whether individual thoughts were being expressed when one of them was talking, so closely did the children reflect their mother's voice in the often-told family vignettes. What Chen Zongying and her children told us, garnered from historical facts and the collective memory of their family and society, is their truth.

* * *

Chen Zongying came from Hunan, an inland province in south China. Hunan played a crucial role in Chinese political and military history because of its strategic position on waterways linking the ancient capitals in the north with Guangzhou (Canton) in the south. In modern times, Hunan is renowned as the birthplace of Mao Zedong and of the Peoples' Liberation Army. Famous for its emphasis on education, Changsha, the provincial capital, became a breeding ground for young socialists and communists in the early twentieth century. Chinese people say the Hunanese have tempers as hot as the peppery food they eat, are strong willed to the point of stubbornness, and so openminded they will accept any new idea. It is not surprising that many of the early Communist leaders, Chen Zongying's husband among them, came from Hunan.

On January 5, 1903, ten years after Mao Zedong's birth, Chen Zongying was born to a poor family in Xinqiao, Hunan.[1] Before she was a year old, her mother died. Her father worked as a private tutor of Chinese classics in Beijing, some 800 miles to the north. Although her father's family was also poor, apparently her grandparents had enough resources to do without her father's labor while he studied.

Chen Zongying's family wanted her to have the three-inch feet of the "golden lotus." It has been thought that Chinese women bound their feet because tiny, crippled feet were considered erotic and the resultant swaying walk enticing, but modern scholars are seeing more practical aspects of the centuries-old practice, which continued well into the twentieth century, long after it became illegal. A daughter with bound feet suggested respectability and carried the hope that she might marry into a wealthier family. There was also the reassurance for husbands that their wives could not stray far. Women in Zongying's family bent her toes under the soles of her feet and bound them tightly with cloth, probably when she was about six, the usual age. However, she cut off her own bindings before her feet were too badly crippled to walk comfortably. "But," she told us nearly eighty years later, "my feet were already a little bit crooked." In taking off her bindings, Zongying became part of the new modernism—a "foot reformer," she laughed.[2]

Hunan is known for producing educated people, but in the first decade of the century, "educated people" usually meant "educated males." Like most little Chinese girls in provincial towns, Zongying did not go to school. "My brothers went to high school. They could read but I couldn't. I stayed at home, swept the floor, washed the clothes, took care of their kids."

With no mother and an absentee father, Zongying was moved from family to family, not unusual for a Chinese child of that era who had lost a parent. She was brought up by an uncle's wife until she was eight or nine. Then her sister-in-law took care of her and, she said, mistreated her. Although she was unwilling to elaborate, we can surmise that she may well have become the family scapegoat: beaten, ill-fed, overworked. She mentioned in another context that her sister-in-law left the Chen family and returned to her own parents' home. A women returning to her natal family was a rare action meriting social disapproval.

At twelve, Chen Zongying was sent to yet another family—the Ren family, to which she had been promised as a baby. In many parts of China at the time, families unable to raise all of their children often sold or sent their daughters to other families as *tongyangxi*. Sometimes this happened in infancy, sometimes when a girl was older. In the worst cases, the little girls were virtually slaves. At best, they were the lowest-ranked members of the family. Chen Zongying's father had made arrangements with the head of the Ren family for her to be affianced to one of the sons. She came into the family almost as a relative, for previous marriage links made the families close enough for courtesy: The Rens, she said, did not call her *tongyangxi*.

While Zongying was still at home in her sister-in-law's care, Ren Bishi often came to visit. A year or two younger than she, he sometimes hid on the roof, hoping to see her and talk with her while she hung out the laundry. This began the close and sympathetic relationship that continued throughout their lives. Chen Zongying did not know then that he was the son in the Ren family she would marry. It was not the practice for parents to explain arrange-

ments they made for their children. Parents simply expected obedience because children's marriages were a family matter, involving as they did the
welfare of the entire family.

The Rens, an educated, professional family of teachers, were having their
own financial problems in the troubled warlord times after overthrow of the
Qing dynasty. Chinese family fortunes could change dramatically within a
few generations for a number of reasons other than political. Natural disasters, a changing economic situation in the area, and large families with many
sons but no tradition of primogeniture could sap the family finances. All the
sons traditionally stayed with their parents and shared in the distribution of
land and wealth. Unless each son was able to increase his share, the extended family could easily become impoverished within a generation or two.

Chen Zongying lived with the Ren family about a year, until her father died.
Knowing how poor the Rens were and not wanting to be a financial burden,
she felt she must leave. She could not return to her natal Chen family because
her sister-in-law was no longer there. She decided to go to Changsha to find
work. She described this unusual show of independence as "just wanting to
earn my own bowl of rice," adding that no one influenced her decision. She
was fourteen.

In Changsha, she became friendly with a family in the business of making stockings. She persuaded them to allow her to work with them, promising part of her wages in lieu of the usual apprentice fee. Her job in the small
stocking factory was sewing up the toes of socks.

At the same time, Ren Bishi was attending the high school attached to the
First Normal School in Changsha, where Mao Zedong had studied. He heard
Mao lecture at that time, became politicized, and joined the revolution. Perhaps some understanding had been reached about her betrothal to Ren Bishi
while she was living with the Ren family, for she helped to pay his school fees
from her meager earnings. Her explanation for giving him money: "I had
some feelings for him." Even though they were in the same city, they were
often too busy with school and work to see each other. Occasionally, they were
able to meet at a paper shop owned by Zongying's cousin, an important place
for them later in their lives after they became underground Communists.

Zongying continued to support her future husband when he attended the
Foreign Language Institute in Shanghai, studying Russian. She also provid-
ed money for him when he was sent to study in the Oriental University in
Moscow in 1921, the year the CCP was founded.

"Ren Bishi never talked to me about revolution, though when he was in the
USSR he wrote me," Chen Zongying said. "I still have some of the letters."

When Zongying was 21, she left the stocking factory to study. "I didn't think it was good not to know how to read and write," she explained. She enrolled in a private vocational school in Changsha, one of the progressive schools that sprang up all over the country in the surge of new ideas during the previous five or six years, following the May Fourth Movement.

Zongying and her classmates studied in the morning and in the afternoon worked to support themselves in a clothing factory. They bunked in a one-room dormitory, made their own clothing, and earned a little extra from their work in the factory. Life did not seem particularly hard to her, she said, because she was simply happy to be supporting herself.

Ren Bishi finished his schooling in Moscow and returned to Shanghai in 1924 as a Russian language teacher at Shanghai University. He became an official in the Communist Youth League (CYL), a CCP organization, as soon as he returned from the Soviet Union, working closely with other young revolutionaries such as Zhou Enlai at the central, or highest, level. By 1926, when Chen Zongying was twenty-three and Ren Bishi a year or two younger, he was ready to marry her and bring her to Shanghai. However, just as he prepared to leave for Changsha, he received notice of a special party meeting in Beijing.

Ren Bishi asked a friend to bring Zongying back to Shanghai for him. Having their wedding plans suddenly disrupted by a summons to attend a meeting in another city foreshadowed the pattern of their lives as a revolutionary couple. Following the progressive practice, the young couple had no elaborate wedding ceremony. The year before, when Zhou Enlai and Deng Yingchao were married in Guangzhou, they had set a precedent for simple weddings among friends and comrades rather than following traditional elaborate family ceremonies and banquets. Deng Yingchao described her wedding in this way: "We had no marriage ceremony at all, only inviting our friends. We promised to love, to respect, to help, to encourage, and to console each other, to have consideration for each other, to have confidence and mutual understanding."[3]

When Chen Zongying and Ren Bishi were married, "We just raised our cups and toasted each other," Zongying said. They were able to invite some of their comrades to share a meal and have a wedding picture taken because Ren Bishi was earning a salary from his teaching post at the University.

Even though they had a revolutionary wedding, they were quite traditional in one aspect: Ren Bishi, unlike almost all the young revolutionaries who joined the Communist party in the early years, was happy to marry the wife his parents had arranged for him before he was born. The solid foundation of mutual love and concern that began in their teens continued throughout their marriage. Ren Bishi brought Chen Zongying into his revolutionary

Chen Zongying and Ren Beshi's wedding portrait, March 1926, in Shanghai. (Courtesy of Wen Wu Chubanshe [Cultural Relics Publishing House], Beijing)

work and kept her with him, instead of sending her back to live with his family, as others did.

Chen Zongying herself had no revolutionary leanings until she began studying in the vocational school, although she had supported Ren Bishi's revolutionary schooling with her earnings from the stocking factory. "The only thing I knew was to follow his lead, because I knew whatever he was doing must be good," she explained. She knew from the teachings at the vocational school that "revolution meant the fight against feudalism and feudal bureaucracy." After she began to work underground for the party, she acquired a deeper understanding. She said the person who most influenced her thinking was an educated woman with whom she worked in Shanghai, not Ren Bishi.

About a year after Chen Zongying and Ren Bishi were married, the situation changed drastically for all the young Communists when the Great Revolution, the uneasy period of cooperation between the Nationalists and the Communists, came to a bloody end.[4] The Northern Expeditionary Army, under Nationalist leadership, had been moving north to unify the country politically and militarily. When the army reached Shanghai, Communists inside the city organized workers to capture the city for the Nationalists. The Nationalist Army then moved into Shanghai and turned on their former comrades, killing and arresting Communists and workers. The end of the Great Revolution marked the beginning of the White Terror, and the Communist party, now illegal, went underground.

Chen Zongying worked as a messenger, delivering secret documents and messages to party members. Although she had not learned enough in the vocational school to be able to write, she could make out the addresses well enough to deliver the messages. She constantly varied her appearance, and thus her apparent status, trying to avoid the suspicion of Nationalists and their informers. On some occasions she wore Western clothes, at others a *qipao,* the traditional woman's high-collared long gown. When she carried a purse, she appeared to be a housewife; with a grocery basket, she might well be a servant.

* * *

Ren Bishi's work often required him to travel between Shanghai and Wuhan. It was important for Zongying to accompany her husband whenever meetings or work brought him to Wuhan, to help him avoid suspicion. The Nationalist propaganda of the time portrayed the Communists as proponents of "free love," intent on destroying the family. Landlords were afraid to rent rooms to single men, fearing they would be accused of harboring a Communist. They coined a saying, "No spouse, no house," believing a Communist would not travel with a wife and family.

During these dangerous years, Chen Zongying bore three babies in succession, all of whom died. Although she did not talk about the first two babies, she spoke of the third child, Ren Sumin.

Despite their precautions in portraying themselves as an ordinary couple, Ren Bishi, whose appearance was distinctive enough to make him easily recognized, was caught and jailed. Arrested in Anhui province, he identified himself as an apprentice at a shop in Changsha that sold paper. The owner of the shop, he said, was Chen Zongying. This was the shop where he and Chen Zongying met occasionally when she was working in the stocking factory and he was in school. "That shop was run by my cousin, so it was safe," she explained. "If the enemy went to investigate, there would be no danger." No danger, that was, if she was there.

Therefore, it was imperative that Chen Zongying take her small daughter to Changsha immediately and play the role of shop owner to establish Ren Bishi's identity as a shop apprentice. Wrapping her third baby warmly, she tried to catch a train in Shanghai. "The trainmen didn't want to let me on, but I told them it was an emergency. I said my father was ill at home, waiting for me to come. I just told them a lie. I also told them that I couldn't get a train ticket. So I got into the coal car holding on with one hand, holding the baby with the other, and carrying a small bundle of luggage on my shoulder."

She and her baby were traveling in the open coal car in January 1928. Her performance as shop owner successfully obtained her husband's release from prison. However, the baby caught pneumonia from the journey in the coal car and died soon after Ren Bishi was released.

Fifty-eight years later, Chen Zongying gave a hint of one of the ways women handled their grief over the loss of their children. "The first three died." Pointing to Yuanzhi, her oldest surviving child, she said, "I don't remember the ones who were born before her."

* * *

As the Nationalist attacks on the Communist party organization in Shanghai intensified, the Central Committee established a Political Bureau in the Chinese Soviet Base Area in southeast Jiangxi province. In 1931, Ren Bishi was assigned to go there as a member of the Political Bureau. He did not bring his wife with him on this difficult trip through blockaded areas because she was expecting her fourth child, Ren Yuanzhi, to be born within a week. In retrospect, the decision to leave Chen Zongying in Shanghai for her safety was ironic. Three months later she and her baby daughter were in a Nationalist prison.

When Chen Zongying was arrested, she shared a compound with a couple suspected of disloyalty to the party. The suspicion arose, she explained, "because he and his wife used to play mahjong, drink and stay out late." She was told by the organization to keep a watch on them. The suspect party member was soon arrested by the Nationalists and did in fact betray his comrades. Because Chen Zongying was living in the same compound, she was also implicated. She was arrested and put into Longhua prison with her baby, Ren Yuanzhi.

Under normal circumstances, the survival of a child's early months, traditionally celebrated at a "red egg and ginger" party, was a time for the parents' friends and relatives to first see the baby. Instead, Yuanzhi accompanied her mother to prison when she was 100 days old.

Chen Zongying said she knew what to expect when she was arrested and experienced no terror in anticipation of torture. She had seen the marks on her husband's body left by his prison torturers. She felt that, by already knowing what could happen, she could endure whatever might occur. "That's why the party thought it would be all right for me to face interrogation," she said.

She was interrogated but not beaten or tortured with electricity, as her husband had been. Her interrogators forced her to sit next to the bench where they usually tied their torture victims. When asked whether she were a CCP member, she feigned ignorance. She pretended to misunderstand the word for political party (*dang*), answering as if the question had been, "Do you go to the pawn shops [*dang pu*]?" After more questioning, she surreptitiously pinched her baby to make her cry. Her interrogators quickly sent her and the squalling baby back to their cell.

Surviving the appalling prison conditions was not easy for even the healthiest inmates. The Communists organized themselves in prison, choosing a leader who was responsible for the welfare of the others. Even though Chen Zongying had joined the CYL, she was not yet a party member. Her leader in jail took good care of her and tried to make sure she had enough to eat, although finding fresh food was a problem. Chen Zongying had few detailed memories of her day-to-day existence as a nursing mother in prison, perhaps a testimony to the grueling nature of her physical ordeal.[5]

She did remember that men and women were held in separate sections of Longhua prison. The Communist groups found ways to communicate with each other, exchanging names and information about other prisoners and snippets of news from outside the prison. The women used a fence in the men's section to hang out their clothes after doing their laundry. They took their time, waiting for the guards to go inside for a meal, then walked up and down under the men's windows to catch messages dropped down to them. The women sent back their own messages, tied to a thread lowered from the window.

They kept informed of outside events through their jailers. They knew Zhou Enlai had become a prime target of the Nationalists, who were trying to apprehend him. The women prison guards told Zongying and her fellow inmates that when the Nationalists found the house where Zhou was staying and burst into his room to arrest him, he wasn't there, but his quilt was still warm.

People could be arrested and held prisoner without being charged with a crime. Relatives and friends could try to arrange for their release, usually by paying large sums of money. The party organization, which provided food for the prisoners and kept abreast of their situation, was working hard to get Chen Zongying and others out of prison. Zhou Enlai, still in Shanghai at that time, worked with other party members through emissaries, bribing the jailers. They tried to persuade the Nationalists that Chen Zongying was simply an ignorant housewife. After almost a year in prison, Chen Zongying and her daughter were finally released, together with the wife of another high-ranking party member.

Two days after Zongying left prison, she reestablished communication with the Communist party organization. She learned that Zhou Enlai had arrived safely in the Jiangxi Soviet Base Area, where her husband also was. Zhou sent a telegram instructing Chen Zongying to leave immediately for the Soviet area. Instead, she decided to take her baby to Hunan and leave her with the Ren family first.

"It was impossible to bring her to the Soviet area," she said, "so we went to Hunan. I had to buy the tickets myself—there was no organization to help me" because she had made the decision on her own.

Chen Zongying's daughter, Ren Yuanzhi, did not see her mother again until after the Long March was over, nor did she meet her father for the first time until she was fifteen. She carefully explained her mother's decision to put her in the care of her paternal grandparents: "When Mother got the telegram and was ready to go to the Soviet Base Area, she decided to take me back to Hunan. It was better for her to go to the Base Area alone, so she could work for the revolution. So I was brought to my grandmother's place and then my mother left. She was only in her twenties then."

Chen Zongying returned to Shanghai to begin her journey along the "Red Line" into the Chinese Soviet Base Area. She was the only woman in a small group of Communists who traveled this underground railroad. One of the men in the group remembered her from prison when she passed along messages while hanging out laundry. She and the others left by boat from Shanghai, going directly to Hong Kong. From Hong Kong they took another boat to Shantou (Swatow), on the northeastern coast of Guangdong province, then went inland by train, by boat, and on foot through Fujian province.

Chen Zongying and her group were passed along the Red Line from one liaison station to another. At each station there was either a party member or Communist sympathizer—usually a relative of a party member—who was responsible for moving the group safely to the next liaison station. Liaison people bought tickets for them, helped find places to stay overnight, and warned them of Nationalist checkpoints where they might be stopped. Because bridges were rare in those times, rivers were crossed by boats. When they reached a river, they were met by a boatman, "one of their own," who ferried them across. As they neared the Soviet areas, they were in no-man's land, where the Nationalists had set up blockades at communication points: ferry landings, crossroads, and roads leading to market towns. These blockades were guarded by plainclothes guards, not uniformed ones, and security was tight. "We knew the plainclothesmen were Nationalists because we had our own underground people in the area," Chen Zongying explained. She and her group slipped quietly through several of these blockades.

> We walked at night only two or three times at most. We went through the area in February and March but it wasn't cold because we were in the South. We walked on dirt paths, past villages and rice fields at night when it was quiet and no one was around. We followed our guide silently. We weren't supposed to talk. And no lights. The people on the Red Line had a flashlight for me because I was a woman, but the guide held it. The men didn't have any.
>
> It's hard to say how long it took us to pass the blockades. We just went as quickly as possible. Sometimes we walked several hours. Sometimes the enemy stopped us. They looked into our bundles to see if we had guns. If they had suspected us, we would have been detained. I brought only a few things for personal use. We were not allowed to bring anything secret. I was a Communist and I had to be careful.

Chen Zongying thought the trip was not particularly arduous. She had grown up in the countryside, and she was accustomed to foraging in the mountains for brushwood. Perhaps because she did not feel it was an extraordinary experience, many details had completely slipped from her memory when she talked about it more than fifty years later.

Chen Zongying ended her journey along the Red Line in March 1932 at Dingzhou, Fujian province, where Ren Bishi was attending a meeting. With customary reticence about intimate matters, Chen Zongying did not talk about what must have been a touching reunion between husband and wife after a year's separation. Together they went to Ruijin, the capital of the Jiangxi Soviet Base Area.

The Base Areas were military and political units, usually in mountainous provincial border areas far away from the control of the provincial government. The town of Ruijin itself is in a river valley, close to the Fujian border. Wherever the Communists established a base, they confiscated land from the wealthy, redistributed it to the poor, and set up local communist governments. In Ruijin, the offices of the Communist leaders were in civilian homes, which usually doubled as living quarters. They picked up their meals from a common kitchen and carried their food back to the house, where they worked, slept, and ate.

* * *

Chen Zongying continued working in intelligence, as she did for the rest of her productive life. "I did this kind of thing because I'm reliable," she said. "I didn't give in to the enemy when they arrested me. And besides, my husband was a leader." Because she and her husband were living in a Soviet Base Area, Zongying was no longer needed as a disguised secret messenger for party leaders. Her new assignment was deciphering telegrams. Sending a telegram entailed assigning a number to the four corners of each Chinese word because written Chinese is a pictorial language. Chen Zongying worked with incoming telegrams, translating the four number sets of codes back into words. Barely literate, she could recognize some Chinese words but not necessarily understand their meaning. At that time, she said, she could write very little and not very well.

By January 1933, Shanghai had become so dangerous for the Communists that the leaders decided to move the Central Political Bureau to Ruijin. In May, Ren Bishi became the provincial secretary of the Sixth Army Group, the highest party position in that unit. He and Chen Zongying went to the Soviet Base Area on the Hunan-Jiangxi border with the Sixth Army Group.[6] "I was still wearing ordinary clothes," Zongying said. "At that time we just wore gray [homespun] clothes. I didn't wear a proper army uniform until Liberation [1949]."

Chen Zongying continued to decipher telegrams for the headquarters staff. "Every day I closed the door and couldn't let just anyone come in. I had little to do with other people," Chen Zongying explained. Only those directly concerned with or responsible for the work she was doing could go into her room. Her daughter added, "My mother said it was lonely being involved in intelligence, knowing little about the outside world. She rarely had any fun. She couldn't even take a walk outside the small compound."

The Soviet Base Areas were under siege by Nationalist troops, and fighting was constant. If the Nationalists captured a decoder, security would be breached because the Central Committee transmitted their documents by telegraph. The telegraph decoders lived under strict restrictions, and as a further security precaution they were illiterate or, like Chen Zongying, nearly illiterate.

During her sequestered time as a telegraph decoder in the Soviet Base Areas, Chen Zongying gave birth to two sons, one stillborn. As the military situation worsened, the Sixth Army Group was ordered to leave the Base Area. Chen Zongying and Ren Bishi suffered the wrenching process of placing their only living son in the care of a local family before the army began the Long March. Many of their married comrades in the beleaguered Base Areas were also finding homes for children they could not bring along with a fighting army. The parents could only trust the peasant families to take good care of their children. They hoped they would survive and be able to recover their children. At the time, they had no idea of the time and distance that would separate them from their children.

In August 1934, Chen Zongying and her group began the first troop movements of the Long March, several months before the First Front Army and the Central Government began their march from Ruijin.

> The 6th Army Group started off, without preparation, when we were told to do so. I just took the map down from the wall. I didn't have any idea how long we were going to walk. My husband didn't tell me anything. I was his subordinate and he was my superior. Wherever he went, I followed him. I'm his old companion [*lao po*].
>
> I don't know exactly how many women were with us then. Just a few. Staff members. I was the only wife, but I was working, too. We had to go on foot. There were airplanes bombing us. It was very hard. Sometimes we had to keep on going to a certain destination before we could rest. We had to push on, twenty-five to thirty miles some days. We had to stay up with everyone else.

The Sixth Army Group, under the military leadership of General Xiao Ke and the political leadership of Ren Bishi, went west, first into Hunan province, then Guangxi and Guizhou. Over the next three months of fierce fighting with Hunan, Guangxi, and Guizhou provincial troops, the 95,000 troops who left the Jiangxi-Hunan Base Area shrank to 4,000. Near the end of October, they joined General He Long of the Second Army Group and his troops at the border of Guizhou, Sichuan, and Hunan. Together, the two army groups established the Hunan-Hubei-Sichuan-Guizhou Red Base.[7]

They stayed in this Base Area for about a year, expanding the base and recruiting more soldiers. In November 1935, when Chen Zongying was two months pregnant with her seventh child, they began marching again. After they reached Sichuan near the end of the Long March, the Sixth and Second Army Groups became the Second Front Army, the army that had marched longer and farther than any other Red Army on the Long March.

When they left the Hunan-Hubei-Sichuan-Guizhou Base in 1935, Chen Zongying explained,

> There were not very many women with the 2nd Front Army. Li Zhen, [who would become] the only woman general, was with the 6th Army Group. Ma Yixiang joined us later in the march.
>
> The Jian sisters were with us. Jian Xianren was married to General He Long. She brought her sister with her. The younger Jian sister, Xianfo, married General Xiao Ke during the Long March. There was no ceremony when people got married on the March. They just reported to the Party that they were married, and then they lived together. At that time marriages were all like this.
>
> We had a propaganda team to keep up the morale, but I've never done propaganda work. I was still with intelligence. Other people carried the telegraph machines. I just held my code book. There were a lot of such books. If you lost yours, the leaders would publicly reprimand you. I would rather lose myself than the code book!

The army fought through Guizhou and Yunnan provinces during the winter and early spring of 1936.

> There were enemies behind us, but we didn't pay any attention to them because we were in the vanguard. The rear guard, the people at the back, did the fighting. We never met the enemy face to face.
>
> When the airplanes came, we either moved on or hid among the trees. When they bombed us, we stayed in one place without moving until the bombing was over. If there were no trees, we would lie on our stomachs. If the ground were uneven, we would find a little gully or ditch, drop into it and stretch out flat.
>
> I wasn't afraid, and I wasn't particularly anxious. Nobody cried, nobody shouted. We were used to it. We were even happy. Someone would say,
>
> "There's another one coming! Let's hide. What's the matter with you, you bastard? You want to die? Hurry up! Get down!" Usually four or five planes came together, but once in a while there were as many as ten.
>
> Several of us in intelligence shared one horse. We put our luggage and other things on the back of the horse. My old companion [lao tou] had a horse. I didn't ride a horse, not until my belly got big.

Before they crossed the upper Yangzi, or Jinsha River, they were already at an elevation above 6,000 feet. Across the Jinsha River, the nature of the Long

March changed dramatically for the Red Army. No longer were they fighting trained armies equipped with modern weapons. They were in a Tibetan area and saw very few Han Chinese until they left Sichuan and reached Gansu province. Although they were attacked from time to time by Tibetan tribesmen, their main enemy became the terrain itself. Their first ordeal was crossing a series of snow-covered mountains. *Xueshan,* or snow mountains, is a generic term in western Yunnan and Sichuan for several mountain ranges covered by snow year-round. The first snow mountains the Second and Sixth Army Groups climbed were in Yunnan, with peaks nearly 14,000 feet high. Chen Zongying was in her third trimester of pregnancy when they climbed *Xueshan,* the snow mountain range in northern Yunnan province.

> Even though I had a big belly when we climbed the snow mountains, I had to keep climbing. Otherwise I would be left behind. My husband and I were in the same group, but he was with the headquarters people and I was with the intelligence section. The people I was with helped me. Sometimes we grabbed onto the tail of a horse so it could pull us up. I didn't pay any attention to whether I was uncomfortable or not, but I was a little slower than the others. When we began to go down the mountain, when I could find a place that wasn't too dangerous, I'd just sit down and slide. I did this several times. I wasn't paying any attention to my condition. The only thing I thought about was keeping up with the group. One time I thought I was starting labor, but nothing happened and I felt better after a night's sleep.

By May 1936, they had reached the Tibetan area in northern Yunnan and what is now western Sichuan, then Sikang province. Chen Zongying had grown accustomed to the rigors of the March over rough terrain and through poor mountain villages where other minority peoples lived, but she spoke, with remembered fear, of the Tibetan tribes as primitive barbarians. Finding their appearance dirty and threatening, she used an old derogatory name when speaking about them despite the official policy to protect the minority people and treat them fairly. Zongying's choice of words reflects the way the soldiers she was with spoke of the Tibetans at the time. "Just before the baby was born, we went into the minority area. Those barbarians put animals on the ground under their houses, and lived on the floor above them. To get into a house, you have to climb. Once when I was climbing up, I fell into the pig food!"[8]

The next month, after the Second and Fourth Front Armies converged at Ganzi, they began marching northeast on the high plateau toward the marshy grasslands in the Aba area.

> My daughter was born in a tent in Aba. June 1936. The tent was a lean-to made of a big piece of cloth held up by two sticks. It was very damp inside. Another

woman was with me inside the tent. The Party Organization sent a doctor to help, although he was not an obstetrician. He was a Catholic, had been head of a hospital. He sympathized with the Red Army, donated the whole hospital, and followed the Army. He later became Minister of Health.

The doctor and Ren Bishi were waiting outside [the tent]. The delivery was quick. I lay on the grass with a pillow made of a bundle of clothes under my head. The woman helped me wash the baby. We found some old pieces of cloth in a minority hut to wrap her in. We got water from the river, boiled it over a fire. The doctor directed all this. I had a normal labor, an easy delivery.

A day or two after she was born, we started off again. We weren't with her father because he was with Headquarters. I had to keep up with the troops. If I hadn't, I would have been left behind with those minority people to become a barbarian. I grabbed some rest wherever the troops stopped—they couldn't stop just because of me. I didn't know much about what direction we were going in. I just followed along.

Headquarters arranged for a soldier, a man, to help me. When we were walking, he carried the baby on his back, and gave her to me to nurse when we stopped. She stayed with me at night. I didn't have enough milk for my baby, so all she had was thin gruel. I don't know how she survived. When Marshal Zhu De heard about my daughter, he caught some fish and took it to me. He said it was to help me produce milk. Nowadays people eat stewed chicken and pigs' feet for that, but the only thing that was available then was fish.

Marshal Zhu De was the commanding general of the First Front Army. When the First and Fourth met the previous year in the same area, a dispute developed between Mao Zedong and Zhang Guotao, who was military and political leader of the Fourth Front Army. Zhang Guotao kept Zhu De with the Fourth when Mao led the First to Shaanbei. That Zhu De would take time during that difficult period to catch a fish and bring it to her himself meant a great deal to Chen Zongying. She and her children mentioned it several times. She continued,

Sometimes as we walked on, we could find some cow's milk. We didn't buy it—we just took it from the local landlords. It was canned.

We got to Shaanbei when the baby, Yuanzheng, was only a few months old. Her name means "Long March."

Chen Zongying summed up her experiences on the Long March:

We walked in a long, unbroken line. We were happy, talking, telling stories, encouraging each other. When we got sleepy, someone would shout, "Lets sing a song!" All of us could sing Red Army songs. People in the back would sing with those in front. Our unit kept together, with the cook and staff members following along.

We ate whatever there was—beans, highland barley, even grass. We were with headquarters, not the fighting troops. It was usual for us to stop and eat the hot food the cooks fixed before we started off again. Sometimes in the middle of our meals we were told to start again, so we had to finish our food on the way. It was more important to avoid the enemy than to sit and eat—what would happen if we got caught!

We had a radio transmitter with us, but I wasn't involved with that. I never worked with the equipment, just did the decoding. During the Long March I was the only woman in the decoding group with four or five men. Every day we had to stay in contact with the other armies, especially the 1st Front Army. We told them where we were, how long we had marched, and they gave us instructions about where we should go. We were also in contact with our own advance troops.

When we stopped in a place, others in the group had to manage to get food, rice and kindling for a fire. I didn't do that kind of work because I was busy with the telegrams. As soon as we stopped somewhere, we set up the machines and sent telegrams, working into the night. We couldn't work while we were walking.

Chen Zongying and other women leaders in Yan'an, 1937–38: (*left to right*) Chen Zongying, Cai Chang, Xia Ming, Liu Ying. (Courtesy of Wen Wu Chubanshe [Cultural Relics Publishing House], Beijing)

At that time, I didn't think what we were doing was such an ordeal, but now, when I remember it, it was very, very difficult. But we were young, we had lots of energy, and we had a purpose.

By the time the Second Front Army reached the Shaanbei Base Area, the Long March had already become a symbol of the resilience of Chinese Communist soldiers. Chen Zongying continued her work in intelligence. When Ren Yuanzheng, the daughter born in the grasslands, was about a year old, Zongying took her back to the Ren family in Hunan where her older daughter, Yuanzhi, was living with her grandparents. "As soon as I gave the baby to her grandmother," Chen Zongying remembered, "I left to go back to Yan'an," the base of the Communist party headquarters.

During the next years of the War Against Japan, Chen Zongying gave birth to her last two babies. In 1938 she went to the Soviet Union with Ren Bishi,

Chen Zongying, Ren Bishi, and baby Ren Yuan-fang, born in Moscow. (Courtesy of Wen Wu Chubanshe [Cultural Relics Publishing House], Beijing)

where he represented the Chinese Communist party in the Communist International (Comintern). Her eighth child, Yuanfang, was born in Moscow.

In early 1940, they were suddenly ordered home to active participation in the War Against Japan. They again agonized over the decision of what to do with their baby—whether to leave her in Moscow or bring her to the front lines of a fighting army. Believing she would be safer in the Soviet Union, which was not then at war, they placed her in the International Nursery in Moscow and returned to China. Later that year, Yuanyuan, their last child, a son, was born in Yan'an.

Their surviving children, each born in a different place, share the generation name *Yuan,* meaning "distant" or "far from home." Yuanzhi's name means "distant aspiration"; Yuanzheng's means "distant or long march." Yuanfang, born in Moscow, is "distant place," and Yuanyuan is simply "far, far." "I gave them their names and their father agreed," Chen Zongying explained, "even though I didn't go to school and I'm not intellectual."

In 1946, after the end of the War Against Japan but during the civil war between the Communists and the Nationalists, Chen Zongying and Ren Bishi began to reassemble their family. Chen Zongying went to Hunan to bring her two older daughters, Yuanzhi and Yuanzheng, back to Yan'an. Fifteen years had passed since Chen Zongying took Yuanzhi, fresh from prison, to the Ren family home in Hunan. When Yuanzhi came to Yan'an in 1946, the teenager met her father for the first time.

The People's Republic of China was established in 1949 in Beijing. With the end of the civil war, the family moved to Beijing. In 1950, in Moscow for medical treatment, Ren Bishi went to the orphanage for foreign children to try to discover what had happened to Yuanfang, the daughter born in the Soviet Union. He was taken to a room where several Chinese children were playing and recognized Yuanfang immediately, for she greatly resembled him and his other children. His feelings for this twelve-year-old child, whom he had held as a baby in Moscow and reluctantly left behind, were especially strong.

Ren Bishi, at age 46, died of a stroke in October 1950. Trying to assuage her grief, Chen Zongying searched for the last child still unaccounted for, the son she had left with peasants in the Jiangxi-Hunan Base Area. After a long search in Jiangxi, she found the family who had taken him in. They told her he had died in childhood.

"They cried," she said. "They gave me the sweater he had worn when he was a little boy. But I still don't know if what they said was true. They may have given him to another family."

Chen Zongying's reluctance to believe that her son had died has founda

The reunited family in Beijing in 1950: (*left to right*) Ren Yuanzhi, Chen Zongying, Ren Yuanfang, Ren Bishi, Ren Yuanyuan, Ren Yuanzheng. (Courtesy of Wen Wu Chubanshe [Cultural Relics Publishing House], Beijing)

tion in reality. In the 1930s, when they left the child behind in the Base Area, it was very dangerous for a family to keep a child known to belong to a top Communist leader. If the Nationalists came into a Base Area after the Red Army moved out, the family would be in danger of being executed as Communists. Under these circumstances, it seems equally likely that the family gave the child away or that he died during the long years of war with the Japanese.

Chen Zongying, Ren Yuanzhi, and Ren Yuanyuan spoke in the present tense of the five children lost or dead. Yuanzhi called them "my sisters and brothers," just as she did Yuanzheng, Yuanfang, and Yuanyuan, the ones still living.

After Ren Bishi's death, Chen Zongying continued to work and later became a member of the Chinese Peoples' Political Consultative Conference and the All-China Women's Federation. In 2001, Chen Zongying and her daughters were still living in Beijing. Her son, Ren Yuanyuan, whose physical appearance was so remarkably close to his father's, died when he was about fifty years old.

3. Little Devil

THE PICTURE Ma Yixiang paints of her childhood is extremely grim, without any folksongs, stories, or legends to lighten the image of ceaseless drudgery and anguish that poverty and hunger can bring. Her father was continually disappearing to avoid his debts and family responsibility, her mother disliked her and blamed her for the deaths of her siblings, and her foster family seemed to take great pleasure in tormenting and abusing her. Yet she reflects little hopelessness and was resourceful in finding solutions to her problems, sometimes following her father's pattern of running away, sometimes persuading others to change their minds or attitudes through her dogged persistence.

Ma Yixiang was born in May 1923 in the rolling mountains of northwestern Hunan province, about 100 miles west of Jian Xianren's hometown. Although she didn't realize it at the time, her family was not Han Chinese but Tujia, one of the fifty-five minority peoples in China, the majority being Han Chinese. Her memories of her grandparents are positive, though minimal; she described them only as "honest and kind." Her grandfather, a long-term contract laborer, worked raw, previously uncultivated land that he rented from the landlord—the least lucrative, most arduous kind of farming. They lived beside a river bank at the foot of a mountain. "There was so little land around our place that we might fall into the water if we weren't careful," Ma Yixiang related.

When his sons married, the grandfather added a single room for each couple, following the usual practice of keeping the grown sons within the family. Ma Yixiang's father, the fourth of five sons, lived with his wife and children in one room furnished with one bed. They cooked and ate in the room, and all slept together on the bed. When their fourth child, Ma Yixiang, was born, the family had two living children. The infant mortality rate at the time was extremely high, especially for baby girls. Their first child, a daughter, died perhaps from natural causes, or perhaps not, for the family was poor. Ma Yixiang's father, a self-taught carpenter, was at the lowest social and economic levels. Her mother sold firewood and pig fodder she gathered in the mountains to add to the family income. Ma Yixiang explained,

> My father could only earn three to four copper coins a day and with that he could buy just one *jin* of rice. It was so hard for him to support a family of five.
> When my mother sold firewood and pig food, she had to beg people to buy it. We ate rice gruel and cornmeal mush. If we had it for breakfast, we wouldn't have any for supper and we would go hungry.

One *jin* of raw rice makes about eight cups of cooked rice. Because this family could not afford to buy meat, they received all their protein from grain. One pound a day of rice or cornmeal would not sustain a family of five people for very long.

Every family needed a constant supply of brushwood for cooking, which the women and children usually gathered in the surrounding hills and mountains or bought from destitute people like Ma Yixiang's mother. The pig fodder she sold probably was a cooked mush of rice husks, vines, and grasses she had gathered and boiled. This mixture was consumed in huge amounts by pigs owned by families fortunate enough to afford them. In addition to the rent they paid and the rice or corn they bought, Ma Yixiang's family needed cash for salt, oil, clothes, needles, and thread.

In 1923, when Ma Yixiang was born, China's economy was rapidly restructuring in a move toward commercial agriculture.[1] Civil unrest, fed by warlord armies and bandits, was plaguing the countryside. Depredations by soldiers and bandits and the unsettled nature of the economy caused great hardship for many mountain families in western Hunan. When Ma Yixiang's father could not scrape together enough money to pay the rent, he left home for a year or two, hiding from the landlord. In recompense, the landlord insisted that Ma Yixiang's mother send her older children to work for him to help offset the family's debt. The children took care of the landlord's dogs and chickens, swept his floors, and collected firewood from the mountains.

When her brother, who was then about eight, fell ill, the family had no money for medical care, but the landlord insisted that he continue working. "He fell down the mountain and died," Ma Yixiang remembered her mother saying later. She was about two years old when her brother died. Shortly after, her sister drowned in the river, leaving Ma Yixiang the only child left.

Her mother was superstitious, Ma Yixiang said, and believed that the two older children died because Yixiang was born with "something evil" in her. "She didn't like me very much," was Ma Yixiang's understatement. This was a marked departure from the rosy picture she had painted of the close, loving relationship between her mother and herself in her fictionalized autobiography, *Sunflower*.[2] In the opening passage she describes the famine conditions that were an integral part of her childhood.

> Western Hunan had not had one drop of rain for two months. The air was scorching dry, stifling; the road was burning hot, each footstep sending up a cloud of dust. The grain was just ready to head, with dried, shriveled, curled, burnt yellow leaves, seemed to be roasted when you pulled off a head. The rich soil had become like a turtle's shell with cracks two fingers wide.
>
> Night fell. The bright moon hung high in the deep blue night sky; the starry heavens winked in my eyes.
>
> In our narrow hut a tong oil lamp was lit. The lamp light, resembling a bean, flashed in the gloom.
>
> The little insects outside chirped, the frogs croaked annoyingly.
>
> I climbed on my mother's knee, raised my head and weakly asked,
>
> "Mama, the insects and frogs are calling. Are they hungry?"
>
> Mama bowed her head and asked me,
>
> "Xiaolan, are you hungry?"
>
> "Uh huh." I dropped my head and said, "Mama, listen. My stomach is calling, too."
>
> Mama stroked my head, and lovingly said,
>
> "Little one, we'll have something to eat when your father comes back."

A few years after her brother and sister died, her father lost the house and small bit of land he owned through gambling. "He was cheated at cards," Ma Yixiang believed. "The landlord took everything and then we had no house or land of our own."

For a time they lived with other people in the village, then left during one of the frequent famines of that time and area, roaming from place to place in the mountains of western Hunan. Knowing they could rely on support from relatives, they asked for help from a great-aunt whose son had been like a brother to her father when they were children. The great-aunt arranged for them to stay with a distant relative who shared the same surname as her mother, possibly somehow related to both her parents. His house had one larger central room and a smaller room, hardly adequate to absorb another family. After a while, Ma Yixiang's father built a lean-to with walls of stalks and tree branches covered with straw mats near her great-aunt's home. By that time, they were a family of four, for another daughter had been born.

Following the common strategy for economic survival, Ma Yixiang's destitute family decided to sell her to another family. Not only would her family receive money from the sale, but, perhaps of greater importance, her great-aunt felt it imperative to place her in a more economically stable family so that she could at least get enough to eat. It is unclear whether there was not enough food for anyone in Ma Yixiang's family at that point or whether, in light of her mother's feelings about her, she was given a lesser share.

Thus, when Yixiang was seven or eight, she went as *tongyangxi* to her "mother-in-law's" home, about two miles from the shed her family occupied. She described her "in-laws" as

> very cruel people. They didn't have much money, but they had enough food. I guess they just wanted to get richer, because they only fed me leftovers. I served the family at each meal and after they finished, if they had left anything they would give it to me. If there weren't any leftovers, I went hungry. They beat me and cursed me all the time. When I ate the leftovers, they all watched me eat, saying things like,
> "You don't do anything but eat, you wretched devil!"

The "in-law" family included the paternal grandparents, parents, a son, and a daughter. Both the son and daughter were younger than Yixiang. In addition to waiting on all of them, she had to feed the son. She also helped with the cooking, cleaning, and other household tasks. The physical drudgery was made worse by the family's behavior toward her. After half a year of constant mistreatment, Ma Yixiang ran away from her "in-laws" to her mother's place. Her mother beat her and sent her back to her foster family.

> Sometimes I could hardly stand it, but I didn't dare fight back. The only thing I could do was run away. I ran home all the time, but my mother always sent me back. There was no food at home. My father came and went. My little sister died of hunger. Later my mother had another son about ten years younger than I am. He's still alive now. My father kept going further and further away so the landlord couldn't find him.
> My "mother-in-law's" house was about ten *li* from my own mother's. At first, when I went back home, I walked on the road, but that made it easy for them to catch me. Then I started going up the mountain and taking a footpath. There was a marshy area with a lot of reeds as tall as a man where I could hide until dark and then make my way home. Sometimes they caught me on the way, but if I got back home, my mother would take me back [to them] again. After my mother left, they would give me a beating and curse me:
> "You miserable wretch! You ran away but you had to come back. Your family can't take care of you."
> I wasn't allowed to cry.

Finally, during the autumn harvest—July or August in Hunan—they beat me black and blue and I ran away again. This time, I knelt down in front of my mother and begged her to let me stay. This time my mother was very sad and didn't send me back. I worked very hard at home, collecting firewood and pig food. I wanted to please my mother so she would let me stay.

"Then, in September 1934, when it was time to harvest the rapeseed," Ma Yixiang said, "the Red Army came." General He Long led the Second Army Group fighting Nationalist and warlord soldiers. In the mountains they said He Long was a human being during the day and a dragon at night, Ma Yixiang explained. They said that even if there were no light in a room, the room became bright when he entered it because his army fought for the poor people, raiding the rich to help them. "When we first heard about the Red Army, they hadn't been to our village because we were in a remote area. We had seen the White Army. What they said was that they had come to find the bandits, but what they did was plunder."

Bands of soldiers were notorious for conscripting able-bodied men and confiscating any food and clothing they could find. When the Red Army came, the men in her family, her father and uncles, hid inside, not knowing whether the soldiers would prey on them or help them. The whole family watched through the door and windows as the soldiers came past.

> We had never seen troops like that. My parents said they were strange because they didn't have uniforms. The Nationalist troops all had gray uniforms. These soldiers wore clothes of blue, black or brown. Some had jackets buttoned on the right, some wore jackets that buttoned down the front and some were in student uniforms. The bills of their hats were long, and every hat had a red star. The soldiers also had red stripes on their collars.
>
> I was too small to see over the window, so I stood on a stool and watched the soldiers marching with torches in their hands. They had broken up the bamboo poles we used for drying the clothes and lit them for torches. It was drizzling. The road was wet and muddy and some soldiers slipped and fell into the fields [from the raised paths]. The soldiers went to the threshing ground and sat around their campfires to get warm. They didn't come into our houses. We weren't sure whether these soldiers were really the Red Army or not, because we hadn't seen the Red Army before; we'd only heard that they came but didn't plunder. That's why we thought they were good troops.

Drawn by the singing around the campfires, Ma Yixiang's father and uncle slipped out to the threshing ground. When they learned the soldiers were truly in the Red Army, they invited some of them home. The soldiers asked to use the family stove and insisted on paying for the firewood they used, Ma Yixiang said.

They said if they didn't pay they would be criticized. They followed the "Three Main Rules of Discipline and Eight Points for Attention."[3] When the soldiers needed vegetables, they didn't help themselves from the fields. Instead, they asked the town people to pick and weigh the vegetables before the soldiers paid for them.

The soldiers needed seven or eight *jin* of rice. The mess officer in charge of provisions came to ask my mother if he could buy some from us. He politely called my mother, "old village woman." My mother gave him all we had. The mess officer didn't have any money with him, but he had brought a piece of cloth. He told my mother if he didn't come back to pay us in ten days, she could use the piece of cloth to make clothes. Two weeks passed. He didn't come, but my mother didn't use the cloth. A month passed. He still hadn't come, so my mother made clothes from that cloth. I can still remember the color—dark blue. We never saw the mess officer again.

The soldiers advised Ma Yixiang's parents to send the children away because the Nationalist troops were coming close. Yixiang and her baby brother were sent up to the mountains to stay with an uncle who was in an isolated area working uncultivated land. She reported, "The two sides began to fight near our home. They built some defensework in our kitchen." This was probably a trench in the dirt floor and some pieces of wood piled up for the soldiers to take cover while shooting. From her uncle's house where she and her brother were hiding, she could hear shots and explosions.

The next morning the Red Army had disappeared and "the old folks said the troops must be supernatural." Ma Yixiang climbed up a tree to watch the Nationalist troops and listen to the fighting. She could hear the Red Army soldiers calling to the Nationalists to surrender.

I didn't know what it meant. I was eleven years old, then. My aunt kept me hidden under the bed with my younger brother and a cousin. We didn't dare move. Some soldiers came and asked my uncle to lead them into the mountains. We were afraid they wouldn't let him come back again, but he returned after an hour or two and told us the soldiers were from the Red Army. As soon as they found the right path, they told my uncle to go back home because his family would be worried about him.

Then my brother, my cousin and I all came out and watched the Red Army searching in the mountains. The enemy was wiped out and very few escaped.

A few days later, Yixiang's father came for the children. She explained what she learned about the fighting:

Our town was between two mountains. The soldiers took cover in the marshy area where there were a lot of reeds. Since it was just after the autumn harvest, there were rice stalks in stacks that could provide cover for one or two soldiers.

Others took cover up in the mountain. When the enemy came, the fighting began. The Red Army won a brilliant victory. The enemy tried to escape, but many local people came out of their houses and blocked the way with tables, chairs, rice stalks. The local people hated the Nationalist troops, because they had often left the town in a terrible state—they didn't even leave the dogs and ducks and chickens in peace!

After the enemy was wiped out, the Red Army set up camp in our town. It was September 1934 on the lunar calendar—October, on the modern calendar. They told us not to be afraid because they were conquering the country for the poor people. They spread propaganda and recruited new members. The Red Army asked the local people to go up into the mountains to collect guns and bullets for the Red Army.[4] My uncle and my father took part in this activity.

With the Red Army stationed in our town, a local government was soon set up. My Aunt Peng was the head of the Women's Union.[5] She asked me to attend their meetings. Since I was a *tongyangxi,* they all sympathized with me, and they all liked me because I wasn't naughty. The women soldiers in the Red Army spread propaganda together with the men soldiers. Many young people joined the Red Army because they fought to help the poor people. It was the winter of 1934.

I also wanted to join the Red Army, and told my mother,

"If I go back to my 'mother-in-law's' family, they'll beat me to death. Do you want that?"

She said she didn't want me beaten to death, but she was afraid I was too young for the Army. My aunt spoke up for me. I had attended two meetings, since the local government was only two or three *li* from my home. I didn't quite understand their propaganda, but I had seen women soldiers. They wore the same kind of clothes as men and they took part in the same activities that men did. In the Nationalist Army, the women were all officers' wives and they looked like demons or monsters.[6] The women soldiers in the Red Army wore leather belts around their waists. I envied them.

If Ma Yixiang had run away to the army from her own home, her "in-laws'" family would have demanded that the Ma family return the money they received when Ma Yixiang was sold. In addition, running away to the army would bring shame to her family. With the approach of Lunar New Year, the time to settle moral and financial accounts, they were very afraid of the trouble the "in-law family" might cause them. "Our family was poor. The poor people were always bullied by others, and we couldn't speak up for ourselves," Ma Yixiang explained.

Therefore, Yixiang's mother persuaded her to return to her "mother-in-law's" family. This time she didn't cry, for her mother explained, "If you want to join the Red Army, you must run away from their home. It is time for you to find a way out, so you won't be beaten to death."

As soon as Ma Yixiang returned, her "mother-in-law" took her to the local government office to file a complaint against her. Many of the people who
became officials in the new government were sympathetic to the Communists but not necessarily qualified to conduct civil business. The man who
heard Ma Yixiang's case had been a singer with traveling puppet shows before the Red Army came. He either did not know about or chose not to follow the Communist policy that protected *tongyangxi* from mistreatment. He
scolded Yixiang and promised that he personally would catch her every time
she ran away. She decided he was like a dog trying to catch mice, putting his
nose into something that was not his affair.

Then her "in-laws" accused her of stealing a quilt when she ran away the
previous time—ironically, the quilt her own mother had made for her use.

The whole family started beating me. I wasn't afraid of them now the Red
Army had come. I shouted for help and some neighbors came and tried to stop
them. The family falsely accused me of stealing the quilt. How could I have stolen it? They'd beaten me and I just ran away empty-handed.

Then they brought a Buddhist idol home—they were superstitious people.
They wanted me to swear before the idol that I had not stolen the quilt. They
said they would kill a cat and make me drink a bowl of cat blood to see if I had
stolen the quilt. If I didn't throw up, it would show I hadn't taken it. If I did
throw up, then I must have stolen it. Who could stand to drink cat blood? Who
wouldn't throw up? Even though I had nothing on my conscience, I knew I
would throw up if I drank cat blood.

Before they went to bed that night, they ordered me to chop and cook food
for the pigs. I often worked until midnight after they had all gone to bed. If I
didn't finish the work before they got up, they'd beat me the next morning. I
was too short to reach the stove, so I stood on a stool to cook. I chopped and
cooked the pig food and put it in a barrel. That night I left the gate open so I
wouldn't make any noise when I left. Before I had left my own home to come
back to that family, an uncle of mine—my mother's uncle's son—had told our
local government he would come and fetch me. We were supposed to meet at
a place where some people had just been killed [the execution ground]. My
uncle promised to come and get me at midnight.

I crept out of the house. I was really frightened, but there was nothing else I
could do. I had to escape. I held a knife for cutting kindling in my hand. A dog
I had raised from a pup came with me. My "mother-in-law" and her son slept
upstairs and she used to make me carry the dog upstairs to eat the boy's shit.
When the dog got too big for me to hold in my arms, I carried it on my back.
The dog was very friendly to me and ran along in front of me.

When I got to the meeting place, I couldn't see anybody. I coughed softly,
but no answer. I knocked a piece of stone against a huge rock, but still nothing. I was in a cold sweat. By this time all the dogs in the nearby villages had

started barking. I was so frightened my hair stood on end. My uncle didn't come. I turned back, the dog following behind me. It seemed my heart would jump out of my body until I quietly got back home. I got on my bed and stayed awake until daybreak.

Nobody in that family knew I had been away because I left quietly and came back quietly. It was fortunate they didn't find out, or they would think I really was guilty.

The next day they continued to curse me and said they would kill the cat the following day and force me to drink the cat's blood. They said every kind of thing to torture me. I had a lot to do that night, but I didn't have to cook the pig food. I put some water on the door hinge to keep it from squeaking. I tried it once. It didn't make any noise. Then I lay down on my bed and waited until daybreak [the false dawn]. I knew after daybreak it would get dark for a while before it would be light again.

I left when it was dark. I climbed over a fence, then I was on the mountain-side. I went to my aunt's home about ten *li* away, because they wouldn't expect me to take this road and wouldn't look for me there. I walked across a marshy area, and finally reached my aunt's home.

My aunt had just gotten up and my uncle was still in bed. I started crying. She led me inside her house. I told her there was nothing else I could have done and asked her to take me to join the Army. She told me she would hide me in her house. After breakfast she went to make arrangements.

Ma Yixiang's aunt first spoke to people in the local Communist govern-ment. She told them Yixiang might not be old enough to be in the army but that she was quite capable. They told her to bring Yixiang in to see them, but when they found out what an undernourished, skinny little child Yixiang was, they told her to come back in a couple of years.

They were afraid I couldn't keep up with the troops and they would have to carry me when they marched. I told them I could do a lot of things: I could collect firewood and wash clothes for them. The Red Army soldiers were on the march a lot. I said I knew I could walk a long way because I often went up into the mountains to collect pig food, but they said Red Army soldiers marched tens and hundreds of *li*. It was against the rules to recruit such young children. They wanted young people who could fight, young people at least seventeen or eighteen. They didn't want me. My aunt took me back home. But how could I afford to wait?

Ma Yixiang's aunt took her to a field hospital next, hoping to place her with the laundry team. They left before daybreak, afraid they might be seen by someone who would alert Yixiang's "in-laws." As they walked along, her aunt instructed her to work hard, to call her elders "aunt" and "uncle," and to try to please the people in the Red Army so they would let her stay.

Finding only women in laundry teams when they reached the hospital, Yixiang's aunt stressed how Yixiang had been severely mistreated as *tong-yangxi.* The head nurse refused her plea for help, saying that Yixiang was too young and too weak to be in the Army. Ma Yixiang and her aunt refused to leave.

> I told the head nurse, "Auntie, you can't let them beat me to death!"
> I kept begging, and my own aunt kept speaking up for me. A lot of people gathered around and took pity on me.
> "We are fighting to liberate the poor people. She is a poor *tongyangxi.* Let's liberate her."
> Finally, the head nurse told me, "All right, we'll see what we can do. But we'll have to send you home when there is a battle."

In the meantime, the "mother-in-law" went to Ma Yixiang's mother's home to find her, demanding that she be brought out of the house immediately. Her mother truly did not know where Yixiang was because her aunt did not want to let anyone know her whereabouts until she was safely with the army. Because the social and economic climate had changed with the coming of the Red Army, Ma Yixiang's mother was no longer afraid of the "mother-in-law" and told her, "My child was jumping with life when she left home. Now she's disappeared. I want my child. If she can stand up, I want her to be able to jump. If she can sit down, I want her to be able to smile. If she's dead, I want her body." The "mother-in-law" went away, vowing she would find Yixiang.

Ma Yixiang was assigned to the General Hospital of the Second Army Group, a rear hospital with nine companies attached to it. The nurses gave Yixiang a form to fill in, asking her name, age, and family members. They helped her with it, of course, for she had never been to school and could not read or even write her name. She began to cry when the nurses cut off her braid, a required and visible commitment for young revolutionaries. She quickly stopped crying, however, when they told her they would send her home if she did not have short hair. Then they issued her a hat and new clothes.

> I was very pleased when the head nurse sewed the red star on the hat and when I put on the flower-print cotton clothes I stood in front of a well and looked down. I was overjoyed to see the eight-sided hat on my head. I was a grown-up now!
> The communications squad leader was passing by and saw me.
> "What are you doing there, Little Devil?"
> I didn't know how to answer. I told him I was measuring how deep the well was, but my face turned red. I was ashamed, because I had really gone there to look at myself.

Always afraid of being sent home, Yixiang worked so hard the soldiers laughed at her, advising her to take it easy. She built fires, washed vegetables and rice, and helped the walking wounded wash their clothes.

The severely wounded were another matter. The first one she saw, head swathed in bandages, had been shot in the mouth. She was terrified of the man, who looked like a ghost with only eyes and mouth showing, and ran away. The second time she saw him, she started to run away again, but he caught her and asked, "How can you be a revolutionary if you are afraid of a wounded soldier? You shouldn't be afraid of the wounded." But Ma Yixiang was still terrified.

One day when Ma Yixiang was washing clothes, she caught sight of her father and began to cry. When one of the wounded soldiers brought her father to her, her father told her he had known where she was but had not come to see her sooner for fear her "mother-in-law" would hear about it and accuse him of keeping Ma Yixiang—her "property"—away. He urged her to be obedient, learn from the nurses, and be respectful. He instructed her to work hard and try to get along with her elders. He thanked the hospital staff for bothering with Yixiang, and asked them to treat her like a little sister.

Then Ma Yixiang's mother came to warn her that the "mother-in-law" would be coming to look for her. Her mother told her not to be afraid, to defend herself against the "mother-in-law's" accusations, for otherwise she would be sent back. She encouraged Yixiang to pour out all her sufferings, for the hospital staff was prepared to help her if she defended herself. If she were sent back to the "mother-in-law's," she would die. Even if she were sent back to her own home, she would not be welcome because it was shameful to run away from home. Distancing herself again from her daughter, Yixiang's mother said she would not be there when the "mother-in-law" came because then they could be charged with conspiring against the "in-laws."

Ma Yixiang's "in-laws" came to the hospital that same day.

> I was frightened, and hid under the bed of the director of the professional work section. He told me to come out and defend myself, but I didn't dare. Then he swept a spear [under the bed] to drive me out.
>
> "Don't be afraid," he said. "There are so many people here, they won't dare beat you. If you don't come out, I'll send you back." I was afraid of being sent home, so I quickly crawled out.
>
> I asked four people to listen to us: the political instructor, the head of the hospital, the head nurse and the director of the professional work section. I let my mother-in-law speak first. I wanted her to tell them if I had done anything against the rules of the house. She told them I was not obedient and talked back, but she really couldn't justify herself. Then I began to talk. I said

I hadn't talked back at first, but then I couldn't bear it any longer. I poured out all my sufferings. The soldiers in the hospital told me not to be afraid of her and tell them everything. I told them how they tortured me. How they had given me leftovers to eat and while I was eating they stared at me and cursed me, calling me a "miserable devil." How they said the only thing I could do was eat. How all of them had beaten me. I said they disliked me because my family was poor. If they disliked me why didn't they find a wealthy devil to be their child bride? My mother-in-law was unable to convince the people in the hospital that I was not obedient. They all thought I was the one who had been wronged, so they all defended me. Even though my mother-in-law was unable to justify herself, she kept insisting on getting me back. I told her I would rather die than go back with her, because they would beat me to death anyway. She was reprimanded by the people in the hospital and then she left. She never came again.

In April 1935, Ma Yixiang had been with the Red Army for two months when they began an offensive in Sangzhi county, the home of He Long, general of the Second Army Group. Ma Yixiang had not been told directly that the army was going into battle, but she knew the wounded were being transferred to homes in the villages. Secure in the knowledge that the people she worked with were fond of her, she didn't believe they would keep their promise to send her home when the Army marched to battle. However, when the wounded had been placed with peasant families, Ma Yixiang was ordered to go home until the battle was over because, she was told, they could not take a child with them. They did not listen to Yixiang's pleas that she was not a child but a Red Army soldier who would die if she were sent home.

She was ordered to report to the same man in the local government who had promised to catch her himself if she ever ran away again. Determined not to be sent back to her "in-law" family, Ma Yixiang waited until the soldier assigned to escort her part of the way left to return to his unit. Then she ran to the village where the Provincial Revolutionary Committee was headquartered, for she knew the committee would move with the troops.

There she met Jian Xianren, He Long's wife, and other women soldiers. When asked for a letter of introduction from the hospital, a document verifying her identity and clarifying her status, she told them she had been sent there from the hospital, insisting a letter wasn't necessary.[7]

I told them I could do anything and I walked around trying to find things to do. I couldn't take care of the wounded because they had all gone to stay with local families. I helped make fires, found clothes to wash. I made people take their clothes off and let me wash them.

Later, when we started marching, I saw one woman soldier carrying her baby on her back. I thought, "If she can march with a baby on her back, I can march, too."

Ma Yixiang was returned to her hospital unit when the Provincial Revolutionary Committee caught up with them. The nurses were surprised to see her but far too busy to deal with her. To show she wasn't afraid, Yixiang went to the front to help with the wounded, but was later criticized for going. She did not know how to handle the wounded: "I pulled on them to make them walk." The soldiers, understandably, cursed her, calling her "dead child." Later, however, during a lull in the fighting, they praised her courage and determination and let her stay and continue to work.

> I delivered medicine to the wounded, helped them drink, washed their faces. I didn't sleep at night, but I didn't know how fatigued I was. I was too busy attending the wounded. There were many soldiers who were slightly wounded in the battle. I did all I could for them. I washed their clothes. I washed their ankle socks for them, because they all wore straw sandals. After a day or two of walking, we would stop to rest. There were troops behind us to defend us. Our surgical team was in between because it had no fighting capability.

When the army moved to capture Long Shan county, Ma Yixiang and several of the women soldiers were ordered home. Again the Red Army soldiers sent to escort the women went only a short distance before sending them on alone. None went home. Ma Yixiang found a company of wounded soldiers to stay with, playing games with them and sharing their food. "But I couldn't go on like this, eating their food." She went to work at the local government headquarters, washing clothes, making fires, chopping vegetables, and making herself generally useful.

Ma Yixiang tried to avoid being seen by any of the troops or hospital people. She hoped they believed she had returned home, although her hometown was in the hands of the Nationalists. But the people in the hospital knew where she was, and when they became shorthanded, they brought her back. "I was very pleased. I thought once they took me in they would never send me away again."

* * *

Ma Yixiang's hopes to stay with the army were short-lived. While the Second Army was fighting to take territory and establish a firm Soviet Base Area, the party was mobilizing political campaigns to "comb out" potential counterrevolutionaries. Landlords and those who owned property or hired others to work for them were targeted for expulsion. Those with the worst reputations for exploiting the poor were killed or ostracized. Some of the landlords and rich peasants who had joined the Communists were dismissed from the army and from the local governments. And Ma Yixiang, the luckless child, was caught up in this political campaign:

> The local people in my hometown had taken in some wounded soldiers because it was an out-of-the-way place in the mountains. Although some of the severely wounded died there, the surviving soldiers rejoined their troops. One of them came to the hospital to see me.
>
> "Little Devil," he said, "there were a lot of landlords' bandits in your hometown. When we were hiding there, they all came to search for us."
>
> He joked with me: "You don't look like a child from a poor family. Children from poor families have dark, coarse skin, but your skin is like a child from a landlord's family."
>
> When I was a little girl, I had fair skin. After I joined the Army, I worked indoors, so my skin was even fairer.
>
> I said, "My family was so poor we didn't even have a house. How could I be from a landlord's family?"
>
> He teased, "Your parents were landlords. They were afraid of us and they wanted people to think they are different so they sent their child to join the Red Army."
>
> It was just a joke. I didn't take it seriously. Later he left to catch up with his own troops and I forgot all about it.

In the fall of 1935, when the autumn harvest began, Ma Yixiang fell ill. She never knew what caused her illness. She only knew that she was running a high fever and was too weak to walk. Falling behind when the hospital moved with the troops, she was picked up by the "collecting team," a group given the job of rounding up the stragglers and bringing them in when the troops stopped for the night. The team put her on a mule and took her to a section of the hospital that had halted in a village. She became a patient along with a company of wounded soldiers. Her memories of her illness are understandably confused, but she remembers spending a night in bed with a woman who had already died.

While she was still very ill, the rumors, which had spread after the wounded soldier had joked with her, caught up with her. She became a target of the revolution and was expelled from the Red Army for being a member of a landlord's family. "They went to leftist extremes. They thought I was an alien class element [landlord class] so they drove me out of the Soviet Area."

Too weak to walk, she pulled herself along the village street by holding onto the walls of the houses. She hid in the home of a woman who had just had a baby, sleeping on the woman's bed during the day and at night sharing a straw pallet on the floor with the mosquitoes and mice.

Ma Yixiang recovered in a week or so. She began to make friends in the village and, following her usual pattern, made herself useful. People who sympathized with her gave her rice, which she shared with the family who hid her.

Not long after she was expelled from the army, a cousin who was a messenger for the Red Army found her. He told her to move in with some relatives named Ma, where he thought she would be safer.

The Ma family, barely subsisting, sent Ma Yixiang to get some rice from people in the administrative section of a branch hospital who had just overthrown a landlord and confiscated his storehouse. Yixiang had to make many trips back and forth through the village because she couldn't carry much rice at a time. She was spotted by a wounded soldier whose husband was head of the administrative section. They allowed the Ma family to keep the rice she had collected, enough to sustain the family for a few days, but the political commissar ordered her to leave the village, telling her she would be shot if she stayed. The Ma family promised to send her away. She hid nearby and crept back to the house after dark to sleep.

> I wouldn't talk about this in the past. Now I want to tell all I have experienced. The class struggle at that time was very complicated. I was unable to find people who could prove who I was. One soldier from my hometown could, but one wasn't enough. I had to find a few more people to prove who I was, people who had been to my home.
>
> Even though they knew I was a mistreated child bride, I couldn't explain myself clearly. At that time there was a movement to eliminate the counterrevolutionaries when many people were wronged and killed. It was impossible that nine investigations out of ten would reach correct conclusions. Since my hometown had been occupied by the enemy, they couldn't go there to investigate. They believed the rumor that I was from a landlord's family. I was lucky it ended when it did or I wouldn't be alive today.

When Ma Yixiang was expelled from the army, a woman soldier named Wang tried to verify who she was. She stated that she had known Yixiang as a suffering child bride before she joined the Red Army. The officials, not believing what she said, accused her of trying to protect a landlord's child and expelled her from the Red Army. After that, no one else dared speak up for Yixiang.

Ma Yixiang left the Ma family to go with a supply depot company charged with guarding the rice on the boats en route to Sangzhi. Because the boats were too full for passengers, Yixiang walked with the soldiers, who did not know she had been labeled a landlord's child and expelled from the Red Army. When their meals were ready, they invited her to eat with them.

Ma Yixiang found the woman who had defended her, Lao Wang, in Sang-zhi, hiding with a local family. Wang, having made arrangements to eat at a Red Army school before Yixiang came, shared her food with Yixiang. Wang also made her a padded jacket in anticipation of the cold weather and found work for her, washing clothes for the school personnel so that she could buy some rice for herself.

Officials in the Sangzhi provincial government knew Yixiang was staying with Lao Wang. When Lao Wang left to go to her mother's home in a nearby town, they brought Yixiang to their office, together with about ten women soldiers. Some had children with them, some were not in good health and some had crippled feet because their feet had been bound and later unbound. The women put straw on the office floor and slept there.

In November 1935, the Red Army in Sangzhi started their part of the Long March.[8] The First Front Army, with the Central Soviet Government, had already arrived in the Soviet Base Area in north central China, just over a year after leaving the Central Soviet Base area in Jiangxi province. General He Long of the Second Army and General Xiao Ke of the Sixth Army decided to leave Sangzhi, the center of their base area, and move west.

Ma Yixiang and the motley group of disabled women and children were given travel money and ordered to go home. However, they were quietly informed that the provincial office was moving out with the Second Army the next morning before daybreak. Ma Yixiang and the others were told to follow, but not too closely, and cautioned not to fall too far behind, for the enemy was nearby. The group was given a bag of newly harvested rice to carry with them.

> We left Sangzhi and started the Long March in November, 1935. I was thirteen years old.[9]
> The villagers watched us leave from the windows. At first, we all walked together. We were starting the Long March, though we didn't know it. The people below the leadership didn't even know about it. We just followed along half a *li* behind them and didn't get lost.

The Second and Sixth Armies, numbering 18,000–20,000 men and 20–40 women, at first moved slowly under enemy fire. "The Nationalist planes flew after us, dropping bombs. The planes flew so low even machine guns could hit them." By the time they reached Dayong, thirty to thirty-five miles south of Sangzhi, the bag of rice they had been given in Sangzhi was already empty and the November cold had set in. Ma Yixiang plodded along, grateful for the traditional black cotton padded jacket Lao Wang had made for her.

The first night in Dayong, she and another "Little Devil" found a place to sleep in an orange grove where they were supposed to be keeping watch, protecting the ripe oranges from thieving hands. Instead, the little girls crawled into a barrel used for husking rice and slept soundly side by side, oblivious to the battle preparations going on around them. When they woke the next morning, it was to find soldiers dismantling the bridge that separated them from the main body of troops. They raced across the bridge, just seconds before it blew up.

To present a smaller target for Nationalist bombs, the troops began to fan out, and the two girls followed. "They didn't know I had been labeled a landlord's child. If they had known, I would have followed them anyway!" Yixiang asserted.

Soon after they crossed the river near Dayong, Ma Yixiang's presence was discovered by people in headquarters. Li Zhen, a woman who later became the highest ranking female general in the People's Liberation Army, was consulted about what to do with the group of women and children who had followed the army this far. She was director of the political section in the field hospital and knew Ma Yixiang. Li Zhen thought kindly of the curious little girl who often came to play games and ask questions of her.

Ma Yixiang reports that, when asked about the group, Li Zhen replied,

> "We have already crossed the river at Dayong. Where can we send them? They each come from a different place. If you send a company of soldiers to escort them, they can't escort each one home, and the soldiers may not get back. No use losing a company of soldiers. Since they are here, just tell them to follow some distance behind the main troops."
>
> Many years later she told me if she had not spoken up for us, we would have been sent back, but at the time we didn't know that Li Zhen had protected us.

Ma Yixiang's group walked behind the troops until they reached Xupu county, about eighty miles south of Dayong, across the Wuling Mountains. As the women and children trekked through the river valleys, local people tried to persuade the young girls to come away and stay with them, offering to adopt them, "but I refused to leave the Red Army," Yixiang reported.

The army stayed in Xupu county for five or six days to rest, reorganize, and gather supplies. Yixiang and four others from her group hid in the house of a landlord who had fled, leaving only an old man to guard the house. When workers from the Red Army school came to distribute rice, Yixiang hid while the other four were given several bushels of unhusked rice. The girls husked the rice, planning to trade some of it for vegetables, salt, and oil.

Three days later, people in the Political Department who had discovered where she was hiding disposed of Ma Yixiang's case. They decided to readmit her into the army, though not without conditions. Yixiang remembers the head of the General Affairs Section saying, "This child may be from a landlord's family, but she's not afraid of hardship. Since she herself hadn't exploited anyone, we'll let her stay." However, because she had been labeled a landlord's daughter under conditions that made it impossible for the leaders to go to her hometown to investigate her case, she was required to do hard labor. Her "hard labor" task was to wash clothes for the cooks of the Revolutionary Committee.[10] "If I washed their clothes, they would weave straw sandals for me. Straw sandals rotted quickly when we walked during rainy days. They wore out in less than two days. At that time, I didn't know how to express my gratitude. I didn't even know how to say 'Thanks.' The cooks were older than me, so they watched out for me. Of course, I felt very grateful to them. If they hadn't woven straw sandals for me, I would have had to walk barefoot. Anyway, the soles of my feet became so thick!" Ma Yixiang was soon transferred from the Revolutionary Committee back to the Health Department.

Shortly after being readmitted to the army, Ma Yixiang was washing clothes in the river when the fighting resumed. To her surprise, she found everyone packing up, ready to leave. She had not yet realized they had begun the continuous movement that would keep the Second and Sixth Armies on the Long March for almost a year.

> During daytime, we marched and fought. After we took up quarters somewhere, we were busy changing dressings for the wounded, washing bandages and strips of gauze. At that time we were so short of supplies we couldn't throw away the gauze strips. After we had washed them, we dried them by a fire made with bundles of twigs.
>
> Every night we changed the dressings for the wounded. As for the severely wounded, once was not enough. We also changed their dressings early the next morning, using a torch for light. We didn't have many kinds of medicines. We had mercurochrome, and another kind of western medicine which was green. Sometimes we had to collect medicinal herbs for the severely wounded.

It is hard to remember when reading Ma Yixiang's description of her duties during this stage of the Long March that she and her companions were performing their tasks after marching under fire, sometimes on forced marches of up to fifty miles. With the hospital unit were ambulatory patients and more seriously wounded soldiers who were carried on pack animals or on stretchers. Those whom it would be dangerous to move, "the ones with pulverized-bone fractures," she said, were placed along the way with poor families who were given a little money for their care.

Ma Yixiang's unit was secure in the middle of the marching troops. When they were ready to rest, they tried to find the places where advance troops had laid down straw for sleeping a night or two previously. With her own piece of sheeting under them and another child's blanket to cover them, Ma Yixiang and several other little girls pressed closely together in exhausted sleep after a fifty-mile march.

In a fog of weariness, Ma Yixiang often was on the verge of tears as they marched. Even a stumble made her cry. Sometimes she walked along holding the tail of a horse or mule which carried a wounded soldier, but she often dropped behind. If night fell when she lagged behind the others, the team whose job it was to collect the stragglers gave her a hand and an encouraging word as they brought her to the hospital unit.

> Sometimes, when I was too tired to move, the other soldiers gave me a pull. The men were usually the ones who pulled me along, because they were stronger. They carried guns and rice bags with them, while we children walked empty-handed. When the soldiers pulled me along, they would say, "Little Devil, stay close. We're going to take up quarters soon."
>
> I felt very warm in this big family. Nobody beat me and nobody cursed me. I was equal to everyone else. Even though the Army tried to send me home several times, and expelled me, I didn't feel wronged. I didn't have the feeling that nobody cared about me. It was a hard time for everybody. I didn't expect them to watch out for me all the time and I worked very hard myself. As long as they didn't drive me away when I caught up with them, as long as they didn't kill me.

Ma Yixiang saw Chen Zongying almost every day because they were both in units attached to Sixth Army Group Headquarters. Yixiang's hospital unit in the Health Department was directly under the Army Headquarters and Chen was with the Headquarters telegraph unit. Chen Zongying advised her, "Stick close or you'll be caught and killed by the bandits who are running after us," and added the usual words of encouragement: "We are going to take up quarters soon." Yixiang found her to be gentle and quiet. Chen, twenty years older, was about the same size as Ma Yixiang, who went on to say,

> I'm short now, but I was even shorter then. I had gone through many hardships in my childhood, so I didn't grow up normally. I went hungry quite often. I don't know whether I was born to be short or not, but I know that I wasn't able to grow normally.
>
> I didn't know how to address my elders, people like Chen Zongying. I don't remember what I called her. I couldn't call her "sister", and we didn't use "aunt" very often, then. She called me "Little Devil."
>
> I called Li Zhen, Li *Bu Zhang* [Department Head]. She knew my name and

called me, "Xiao Ma." Li Zhen was quite impatient and often encouraged me by saying,

"Hurry up! Stick close! We are going to take up quarters soon."

Sometimes people said, "We are going to reach a prosperous town. They'll expropriate the landlord's property and get a lot of pork. Probably there is a meal already prepared. Let's go and eat!" Then I would walk faster. But I always tried to walk as fast as I could.

The women leaders were not the only ones to mother the little girls. One of her surrogate mothers was Wen Xingmei, to whom Ma Yixiang felt especially close.

We all often helped each other. Sometimes we just fell down on the straw and went to sleep with our bags still on our backs, and with muddy feet. If we had a good rest and washed our feet, we would feel better the next day. Sometimes I didn't even know who had washed my feet for me, but it was usually Wen Xingmei. And sometimes I couldn't even think of eating anything and she would pull me up and feed me while dozing off herself. We were very, very tired. One of the children had her mother with her. She and her mother joined the Red Army together. Many people looked after me on the way, especially Wen Xingmei who was wounded later.

Sometimes when they had got our food ready, we would fill our enamel cups with rice and eat while we marched. At that time we would eat whatever we could find. Before we reached Guizhou, we still had plenty of rice. After that, we would have corn grits. Sometimes they fried it.

Under daily bombardment from enemy planes, the army moved into eastern Guizhou, into an area where the Sixth Army Corps and the Second Army had converged a year or so earlier. Prevented by the enemy from establishing a base there again, the army moved to western Guizhou. "We got to Guizhou after Spring Festival. Then we had more times when we ate nothing but grits, and there were more rainy days."

It was snowing when the Army reached Bijie in mountainous northwest Guizhou near the Yunnan and Sichuan borders. They stayed there for about two weeks to rest and regroup. During this time, Ma Yixiang and the other children went into town with the head nurse to recruit soldiers and porters.[11]

We couldn't keep the porters for more than three days, or they wouldn't be able to get back home. We spread propaganda among the masses and tried to mobilize people into the Army. I was young but I knew the name "Nationalists." I told the local people that they suffered from poverty because they had been oppressed by the Nationalists and exploited by the landlords, that they should join the Red Army to conquer the country for the poor people and distribute the land.

They asked me, "Do you miss your mother?"

I said, "No, or I couldn't be a revolutionary." I had been away from home for a year, so I had some idea of what revolution meant.

I knew the Red Army was going [north] to resist the Japanese. Japan was an imperialist country which was invading China. But what was Japan like? What was the situation like at that time? I didn't know. I didn't know what imperialism was. When we were in Guizhou and caught some British missionaries, I thought that they were imperialism. I thought people who had high-bridged noses and green eyes were imperialism and that to fight imperialism was to fight them. Actually, I still had no idea what *imperialism* meant. I was [so] simple and naive, I thought "imperialism" was a person.

As Ma Yixiang's experience grew to include working with propaganda teams, she asked the party secretary to teach her how to read and write while they were resting and regrouping. The first words she learned to write were "study hard" (*nuli xuexi*), which she practiced by writing on the ground with a stick. The pace of the march was such that she learned very little, although she did learn a few more words by asking people who were literate to read slogans written on walls of villages they passed through. One slogan she said she remembered learning was "Resist the Japanese and Oppose Chiang Kai-shek! [*Kang Ri, Fan Jiang!*]"

In 1931 the Japanese had invaded Manchuria in the Northeast and by 1936 were posing a real threat to eastern and southern China. The Nationalists were conciliatory, hoping to avoid full-scale war with the Japanese, but the appeasement policy became increasingly unpopular with the ordinary people. In December 1935, after the First Front Army ended their Long March, the Communist party adopted the policy advocating the formation of a United Front with the Nationalists to fight the Japanese. Fighting the Japanese invasion was a common rallying cry among many diverse groups in China and was one of the most effective propaganda slogans the Communists used as they moved through the villages on the Long March.

The Second Army and the Sixth Army Group moved to the Pan River valley on the border between Guizhou and Yunnan provinces, setting up headquarters in Xuanwei on the Yunnan side of the border. The leaders were considering establishing a Soviet Base Area in this remote, fertile river valley, far from large cities or strong warlord armies, when they received orders to march north to join the Fourth Front Army. To do this, they had to cross Yunnan province before crossing the upper Yangzi River into Sikang.

Yunnan, China's most southwest province, derives its name, "South of the Clouds," from the persistent cloud cover over Sichuan province to the north. Yunnan is well known for many things. The weather in the area around Kunming, the capital, is similar to the weather in northern California and described as "eternal spring." It is also especially well known for Yunnan ham.

Once in Xuanwei, before we started the night marches, we had been hiding in a capitalist ham company where hams were hanging in rows along the walls. The capitalists had run away.

Then we were surrounded by the enemy and we retreated. I saw Wen Xingmei take a ham, so I took one, too, for the wounded. It was the upper part of the pig's leg. Fresh, not smoked. I had to run because the enemy was chasing us and their planes were bombing us. The ham weighed six or seven *jin*. I tried to carry it on my shoulder, but it was too heavy and I had to throw it away.

It was very hot and the rape flowers were in full bloom.

It was getting dark when we retreated. After we left Xuanwei, we covered about seventy *li* and reached a village. The enemy planes dropped a lot of bombs. We happened to be on a mountain slope where there was a pine forest. The other side was a cliff with overhanging rocks. The Health Department and the Supply Department were all on the mountain slope, so we made a very big target. Our medical kits were covered with metal and reflected the light. The Supply Department had a lot of these metal cases. The enemy planes flew over and bombed us without having to circle around and look for the target. I was lying on the ground watching the airplanes. I wasn't afraid. I wanted to see where the bomb would hit. I had experienced this before and I knew that the plane would dive at a slant instead of dropping straight down. The bombs were coming down. I was lying between a wounded soldier and Wen Xingmei. I clung to the wounded soldier and we rolled down together into a ditch. A bomb exploded near us. We were buried under the mud splattered by the bomb. The wounded soldier was killed, but I was lucky. I wasn't hurt. Wen Xingmei was hurt. She was lying somewhere higher up. Her arm was broken and there was a gash in her leg and it was broken, too. There was a piece of shrapnel in it. I cried and cried.

When it was getting dark, those who were in charge of the wounded began to check the casualties. I cried while we buried the dead. There was a mute who had been hurt in the head. They had the mute bandaged and dressed. He was still able to breathe. It was already quite dark when the mute came down from the mountain. He tried to talk, "Yi ya ya. . . ." He had been hit in the head somewhere near his ear. The bullet was probably still in his head. He had to be sent away.

One of the mules had been hit in the legs so it couldn't carry the medical kits. They got the kits off its back and put them on the side of the road. The mule tried to stand up, but it fell down because both of its front legs were broken. I really felt sorry for it. The mule was our major means of transportation at that time. It carried the medical kits and the wounded soldiers. We would be very happy if we could have a mule to ride.

Wen Xingmei was to be sent away because her leg was broken and she couldn't walk. I sobbed and sobbed because she had been with me all along the way. Wen Xingmei had been very good to me. Who would take care of me if she left? She counseled me saying,

"Stop crying. It doesn't do any good. Be a good girl and stay up with our troops. I don't want to leave you, but I have to. If I stayed, they would have to find someone to carry me, and then I would be a burden to the troops."

She said, "I want to cry, but I have no tears. My leg hurts a lot." But she was very strong. She was three or four years older than me.

I wanted to follow her to the provincial committee, but our commissar said to me, "You can't go with her. Each person is one part of our total strength. If you leave it will mean a loss for us. You can't go with her. She has to leave us now. When we come back, we'll find her."

"Who knows when we will come back?" I retorted.

Wen Xingmei said, "When I get better, I'll catch up with you." Then they carried her away on a stretcher. I cried for several days. The others pulled me along because I was in such low spirits.

Of course, she did not know then that Wen Xingmei would survive her wounds and be living in her hometown at the time of our interview.

* * *

To cross the upper section of the Yangzi River before the Nationalists blocked them, the Second and Sixth Armies left the Pan River valley on April 1 for three weeks of forced night marches across the mountains of north central Yunnan.[12] The strenuous marching, bombardment, and fighting left Ma Yixiang little time to grieve deeply for her companion and surrogate mother, Wen Xingmei.

By this time, Ma Yixiang had been in and out of the army for more than a year, yet in her descriptions and reminiscences she demonstrates no longing for the familiarity of home and the ease of communication with family members. The constant hunger, fatigue, and danger kept her focused on the present.

We didn't have enough time for rest. Sometimes we were so sleepy that we would fall into a dry ditch beside the road and sleep. When the collecting team came, they poked sticks into the ditch to see if anyone was sleeping there, because it was too dark for them to see clearly. Then they would pull us up. Sometimes when we were marching, we would stop now and then because the going was rough. Then we would stand there, dozing off because we were so sleepy. When there was fighting, we had to run as fast as we could. The bullets were flying. If you were hit, that's it. If you weren't hit, you could break out. Sometimes the bullets went through the bottoms of my trouser legs, but I didn't have time to think about it. If you were killed . . . you had to trust to luck.

I saw people being killed every day, so I wasn't afraid of death. I was afraid of getting injured and being sent away. If I were injured in the leg, then I couldn't walk and I'd have to stay in the home of one of the local people. What would I do if I were sent away?

In Yunnan, at first we marched about 140 *li* during daylight, but the enemy planes followed us like flies. They wanted to bomb us. We lay down on the ground, not daring to move for fear of exposing ourselves to the enemy. Since the road was very wide, the Army marched in several columns. Just after we had moved into the line of defense, the sun came up and the enemy planes approached.

I was taking care of a regiment commander who was sick, and a chief of staff who had a broken leg. We were staying in a landlord's house. They were lying on stretchers. I told them to stay where they were because I wasn't strong enough to help them get up and the stretcher carriers were still asleep. Just as I started out to find something for the wounded to eat, the enemy planes came and pinned us down. I quickly woke up the carriers. They picked up the stretchers and we broke out of the house. We climbed the mountain behind the house, holding onto the trees, two carriers carrying each stretcher.

All the people in the Health Department were breaking out [of the area under bombardment] together, but only the soldiers in the communication squad had guns. The rest of us didn't have any. The fighting started. The cooking squad also went up to resist the enemy in order to cover us. It wasn't easy for me. My sleeves and the legs of my pants were shredded by the bullets, but I wasn't hurt.

After we broke out, Commissar Yan's 16th Army came to help us. He said, "There will be fighting every day when we have night marches." That was my husband, but I didn't know him then. I was still very young.

Another night we covered over 140 *li* and we were still marching after the sun came up. The enemy planes were still following us. [Where we were in] Yunnan was not far away from their airport, so when they ran out of bombs, they would fly back to the airport to get another load. We were up in the mountains, very tired, nothing to eat. Two of us fell fast asleep—our legs were so tired. The sun was shining on us. Our faces were red from the heat and our clothes were wet with sweat. Then the collecting team came. They pulled us up and said, "The enemy is coming. You'll be taken prisoner." We were so scared that we jumped right up.

We hadn't had anything to eat for hours. When we finally took up quarters, the others all went to sleep, but we got something to eat first and then had some sleep. When the sun went down we started out again.

Among Ma Yixiang's strongest memories of the exhausting march across Yunnan were those of relationships among the people she traveled with.

The happiest days I had were when we won a battle and got a lot of booty and took a lot of prisoners. Many Nationalist soldiers in Yunnan and Guizhou were opium addicts. We called them "the troops with two guns." The other gun was an opium pipe. When they needed a smoke, their eyes watered and their noses ran. We thought it was strange. How could such soldiers fight? They could only become our prisoners. We were contemptuous of them, but since they had given up their arms and weren't our enemies any more, we didn't beat them and curse them.

We were most happy when we captured medicines and medical instruments like stethoscopes and tweezers, because we were short of these things. Usually, after a day's march of seventy *li,* I couldn't think of anything to make me happy except to take up quarters and sleep. Or having pork to eat. When I heard that the town we were going to reach was prosperous, and that there would be pork for us to eat, I would laugh and sing and skip with joy while we walked.

Actually, when we were marching at night, we were often encouraged to sing so that we wouldn't doze off. Sometimes the head nurse would say, "Let's sing." Sometimes the wounded soldiers would say to us, "Little Devils, sing a song." Then we would sing folk songs and songs like, "Send Our Husbands and Fiancés to the Red Army" and "Three Rules of Discipline and Eight Points for Attention." When we sang while we walked, we wouldn't be very sleepy, so the adults always encouraged us to sing and they would lead our songs. I used to have a good voice. After I joined the Red Army, I was so happy to be liberated and no longer beaten and cursed that I often sang for the wounded when we stopped somewhere.

When I saw that soldier with the bandage covering his head not long after I joined the Army, I was so frightened that I ran away from him. Now, sometimes, my own comrades were killed right beside me. I had to deal with the wounded and the dead every day, so I stopped being afraid.

Every day we marched. The enemy was behind us. They were intercepting us in the front, surrounding us from two sides and their planes were flying over us. You were lucky if you escaped because otherwise you'd be killed. I knew the reason we marched every day was because we were heading for a good place, but where that good place was, I didn't know. I just walked with the Red Army, simple-mindedly. We were revolutionaries. To be a revolutionary is to go and look for a good place.

Our most difficult times were when we crossed the grasslands and the snow mountains. But I never had the feeling that we wouldn't make it and I wasn't scared. I knew the Red Army was going north to resist the Japanese.

Many of the survivors recounted their most compelling experiences as those occurring during the last half of the March after crossing the upper Yangzi River, also known as the Jinsha (Golden Sands) River. When the Sixth and Second armies reached the Jinsha, they found no boats on the river banks, a result of the Nationalist attempt to keep the Red Army from crossing the river. The soldiers, having encountered many rivers and streams during the past six months, quickly organized their own transportation to get their units safely across the river at many places along the thirty-mile stretch of river bank between Shigu and Judian. They were under pressure to move quickly, for the enemy troops were not far behind. They made wooden and bamboo rafts and repaired abandoned boats of questionable seaworthiness.

Ma Yixiang's health unit crossed at Judian, where the river was about half a mile wide. They found a decrepit boat they thought would do. Because the horses could swim, she explained, they were tied to the side of the boat. Passengers kept themselves afloat by bailing out the water while others rowed. There were too many people in her unit for all to cross in one trip. "It took my unit one whole night to cross the river," Ma Yixiang stated. "After we crossed the river, the enemy stopped chasing us."

The enemy Ma Yixiang referred to were the Nationalist and their provincial troop allies who had been bombing and attacking them since they had left their base in Hunan.

> The day before we crossed the Jinsha River, we could see the snow mountains. They were very high and white all over. We thought it must be very cool up there, so we all wanted to get up there and cool off a little. Yunnan is very hot in October.
>
> After we crossed the river, we talked and laughed while we walked. Some said the snow mountain was a sugar mountain. Someone said it was a salt mountain and somebody else said that it was a cotton mountain.
>
> The night before we crossed the river, I took off my muddy clothes and went to sleep with two Dajie. Someone washed my clothes and gave me a sweater she got when the property of a landlord was expropriated. In the morning she told me to throw away the padded coat Wang Dajie made for me.
>
> I said, "I won't. It's still new."
>
> She said, "Throw that away and take this sweater." The wool sweater had been knit with several colors—red, green—and it had buttons and two pockets. It was a man's sweater, so big I had to cut the sleeves.
>
> She said, "This one is better."
>
> I thought, "I don't like it. I like my coat. Wang Dajie made it for me. It has been with me for a long time." But after a while, I gave it up and took the sweater.
>
> When we had covered twenty or thirty *li* after crossing the river, we stopped at the foot of the snow mountain and took up quarters there. That was when I lost my sweater. I went to change the dressings for the wounded and when I came back, my sweater had disappeared. A porter took it. I recognized it, but I didn't dare ask him for it.
>
> Since I had thrown away my padded jacket and then lost my sweater, I crossed the snow mountains in just an unlined jacket. I put on all the old clothes I had. If you had two sets of clothes, that was not bad. We often traded clothes. When

mine got dry after washing, [someone else] would have a change. Then when mine got dirty, I would wear hers. I had a small bag which didn't have much in it. We climbed the mountain empty-handed. All I needed to do was not fall behind, just stick close to the others.

The troops traveled as lightly as possible. The soldiers put their rice bags and bedrolls on the pack animals, which also carried medical kits. The porters carried some of the medical supplies and helped transport the wounded soldiers who were on stretchers. Some of the slightly wounded rode horses, which did double duty—the children hung onto the horses' tails and let themselves be pulled up the mountain.

"We climbed the mountain from the very bottom," Ma Yixiang said, although they were already about 6,500 feet above sea level. The army had been in the mountains fairly constantly since Guizhou. Ma Yixiang continued,

> The first snow mountain was very high. Lower down on the mountain, there were green branches and leaves and virgin forests. Higher up there was a lot of snow. We could hear water running, but couldn't see it because it was flowing under the snow. The water in the gullies up high in the mountains was yellow. We didn't dare drink that water because if you drank it your belly would swell up. Higher up, everything was frozen and arid. No grass or trees could grow. There was nothing but snow. The higher we climbed, the more tired we got. We felt sick and dizzy. Everything got dark and we felt like we might fall down.
>
> We climbed and climbed because we couldn't sit down. They told us, "Little Devils, you can't sit down or you'll go to heaven. Then you won't be able to go with us. You can't find us then." As soon as I sat down, they would pull me up. They didn't let me sit down for even half a minute.
>
> The most difficult time came after we had climbed two or three *li*. There was a cook from Yunnan who carried a big pot on his back. He fell down and lay there and foamed at the mouth with his eyes open. They couldn't get him up, so he died there. There was no place to bury the dead because there was snow all around. Some people never got up, but none of the children died there because the adults scared us and coaxed us while they pulled us along.
>
> When I was tired, I often walked holding on to a horse's tail and that made it much easier. I was on very good terms with the horses. I still have a special feeling for them. When I see films I like to see the horses in them. Horses gave me a lot of help. I have been thinking of writing something about horses, but I haven't written anything yet.

Ma Yixiang's affinity for horses could be considered quite natural: Her surname, *Ma,* means "horse."

> I was still with the Health Department when we crossed the snow mountains. One of the big-bellied women who were with us had been pregnant for seven

or eight months. Her feet had been bound and later let out. She had to hold onto the horse's tail. Those who were strong would give her a pull. When she fell down into a hole in the snow, it took a lot of people to get her out of it. She was quite fat.

We felt easier and easier after we had gone down the mountain two or three *li*. When we got to a smooth spot, we would roll down. After we had gone half-way down, we didn't feel dizzy as if we'd been drinking any more.

Quite a lot of people died when we crossed the first snow mountain because it was so high.[13]

On the other side of the mountain was Zhongdian county. We saw Tibetan people, their hair in braids, wearing robes which were both skirts and pants at the same time.

While the army groups rested in Zhongdian, a county on a high limestone plateau, they regrouped and prepared for the coming march across the next group of snow mountains. They set in supplies of grain and hot peppers, having been told by the locals that they should eat pepper to ward off the cold of the high mountains. The staple in Zhongdian was highland barley (*qingke*), which they husked, roasted, and ground for field rations to sustain them before they crossed the next mountains. The soldiers packed the grain into "rice bags."

Barley must have been difficult for Ma Yixiang to digest: "I didn't take much barley with me, just took three or four ricebags of it. When I had it before, I got the runs." This was no small matter; diarrhea could be extremely debilitating for the exhausted troops, fatal if unchecked.

Before leaving Zhongdian, the two army groups divided, taking different routes north. The Second Army Group took the westernmost route, in the Tibetan areas. During the regrouping, Ma Yixiang was transferred from the Health Department to Headquarters and assigned to do propaganda work in the Political Department.

Ma Yixiang insisted there was no highlight, nothing to report about crossing several snow mountains other than extreme hunger and losing comrades to ill health during the ordeal. "The more mountains we crossed, the fewer people we had," she explained. "Our health went from bad to worse. We didn't have much to eat. When we had no barley left, we began to eat wild herbs. At first we picked the ones we knew. Later we had to eat the ones we didn't know. We ate fennel and wild rape. We just crossed the mountains like that. There was nothing special to talk about. We just struggled against nature."

They seldom encountered the Tibetan (*Zang*) villagers. Whenever they came to a village, they found it empty of people. Often the villagers buried their grain or took it with them into the mountains and cut off the water supply.

When we were crossing the snow mountains, we were in the region inhabited by the Zang people. Usually the Zang people had run away. The grain in the fields was getting ripe, so we got something to eat. We roasted the grain over the fire, rubbed it between our hands to make it puff up, and then we would eat it. We would pick the leaves from pea vines before they bore fruit and leave some money in the field. Or we would leave a note and some silver in the empty houses. Those people might not be able to read, but it [paying for food] was part of our discipline.

The other problem was being attacked by the local bandits and landlords. We had left the enemy behind on the other side of the Jinsha River. They didn't dare follow us [into Zang territory.] After we had crossed the river, we mainly fought the bandits in the Zang area. They were crack shots and they fought on horseback. We were marching on the road and they were hiding in the forest, so we couldn't see them but they could see us.

The Second Army Group continued their climb north over snow mountains into an arid area Ma Yixiang described as "hot as the Flaming Mountain," referring to a mountain in Xinjiang province that a favorite folklore figure, the Monkey King [*Sunwugong*], had made familiar to children everywhere in China.[14] The few villages in this area in Sichuan were supplied by water brought through a viaduct made by hollow pieces of bamboo.

High up in the mountains where no trees grew, we got dehydrated because we were sweating and had nothing to drink. It was so dry we could hardly stand it, and when we got to a village the savages had destroyed the waterpipes. They had cut parts of the pipe so we couldn't get water. The bandits were hiding in the mountains. They could see what we were doing. Quite a few of our soldiers were killed when they tried to reconnect the pipes.

In the snow mountains, our everyday life had been a struggle against hunger and against the bandits who had tried to stop us. After we crossed the snow mountains, we joined forces with the 4th Front Army in Ganzi. The 6th Army Group also met us in Ganzi.

The Second and Sixth Army Groups merged to become the Second Front Army and traveled north and east together toward Shaanxi province.

When we left Ganzi, we would have to cross the grasslands. In preparation, the 4th Front Army made leather shoes for us. They made a few holes in a piece of ox skin and threaded a string through the holes. That made it a shoe. When the shoes got wet, the soles would slip up to the tops of our feet. When I had nothing left to eat in the grasslands, I ate my leather shoes.

A few of us in the Political Department of the 2nd Army Group were sent with a squad of soldiers to join a Company of 4th Front Army soldiers. We crossed the first grassland with them. We couldn't get along with them very well because they had the warlord style of Zhang Guotao—they beat and cursed people. We couldn't always understand what they said when they cursed us. When they saw us wearing long pants, they cursed us, calling us "Little Miss" soldiers, student soldiers [*xiaojie bing.*] They wore short pants and carried a lot of things on their back, while we just carried small bags with us. They were jealous of us because we had been given a horse to carry things.

The Company got some barley flour. They distributed some of it to us, but we could only use it to make very thin gruel. They themselves made roasted barley [*zanba,* the Tibetan staple.]

While we crossed the first grassland, Qing Jinmei had her baby. Or maybe we hadn't started across yet, but we were about to cross—there were mountains and virgin forests around us.

Qing Jinmei's first baby had been given to some local people after her first husband, a specialist in repairing guns, was killed by the enemy. Her second husband was killed just a couple of weeks before this baby was born.

The Supply Department gave her a horse and sent her to us when she was about to have the baby. One of the women with us was over thirty and more experienced than we children were. We only knew that she was pregnant because she had a big belly. Qing Jinmei had the pains for quite a long time before she got off the horse. She had kept going in spite of the pain, gritting her teeth. When her pains got too strong for her to bear, several of us who were taking care of her helped her to the side of the road. The troops were still marching on. She screamed while the baby was being born. She left her baby in a thick clump of grass by the side of the road because it was impossible to take her along. It was hard enough for adults to survive, let alone children.

In my novel Chen Zhenmei [actually Qing Jinmei] takes the baby with her. Otherwise, she would seem to be too cruel. Her first husband has died, her first baby has been given to a local family, and now her second husband has also died. If she leaves her second baby, the readers wouldn't feel good about it.

Actually, there was nothing else Qing Jinmei could do. She insisted on not taking the baby with her, so the baby was left in the bushes while it was still alive. She lost her baby because we were about to cross the grassland and there were no local families to leave it with. The Zang people had all run away. After the baby was born, we helped her to quarters. We got a lot of dry straw to put on the ground and let her lie down. Comrade Bishi's wife [Chen Zongying] and Jian Xianren came to see her with what little yak butter and [barley] flour they could spare, because we had no grain left. After the baby was born, we rested there a few days. Then we crossed the first grassland.

It took us more than twenty days to go across the first one and reach Aba. The troops stopped in a small village to try to collect grain. Every day we went out to look for grain. We would even try to get grain from the husked wheat straws and picked up the heads of wheat left in the fields, one by one. We ate wild herbs. Wild rape in the fields.

When we were in Aba, Xiao Ke came to see the man who was head of the Grain Bureau [in the Fourth Front Army]. He was from Hunan—we were landsmen, from the same province. When we heard that Xiao Ke had come, we several Little Devils went to complain to him. We had been hoping that we could go back with him because they bullied us here. We told him that the soldiers often beat us and cursed us. Once, when one girl was suffering from malaria, they kicked her while we clung to each other and cried.

We complained to Xiao Ke, not taking into consideration the fact that the head of the grain bureau from the 4th Front Army was right there. We didn't understand. But he said, "The women soldiers in the 4th Front Army may be a little rough. I'm sorry you Little Devils have to go through all this." We were still crying when Xiao Ke said, "All right. Stop crying. I'll take you back." Then we all stopped crying and burst into laughter.

When Xiao Ke took us back, we had to borrow grain, making preparation for the second grassland, which was a marshland. Several people were assigned to carry Qing Jinmei on a stretcher. Everybody was weak at that time, but she couldn't ride yet. Later she went to help Jian Xianren take care of her baby, He Jiesheng, who was less than a year old.

When we were in Aba, we went back to the propaganda team because the people in the Headquarters of the 2nd Front Army hadn't arrived yet. When they arrived, we went back to the Political Department. During our rest days after we got back to the Political Department, we went to look for grain but we couldn't find much. The Zang compatriots had either taken it up to the mountains, or buried it in the storage pits. We got little bits of grain here and there. We hollowed out some tea and rice from the stomachs of Buddha idols. Whenever I saw men soldiers who had a lot of grain with them, I would ask them to give me some. One day I saw that they had a heap of wheat. I sat down on it, putting my hands into it and wouldn't get up.

I said, "I've been looking for grain and this is the only grain I've found. You've got to give me some."

"Go and ask our senior officer for permission. Then we'll give you some."

"You've got some grain," I told [the senior officer]. "They told us to get your permission."

"Go help yourselves. Little children don't need my permission. Don't be afraid. Act like little brats and they'll give you some."

We went back and said, "We don't need permission. Give us some."

"OK, we don't have any choice. We don't have much, but we'll give you some."

It was as if we took one mouthful of grain from each of them. Altogether we got four bowls of grain apiece. But that was quite a lot, because we couldn't have found that much in several days. With what I'd gotten before, I had five or six *jin*. I roasted it and ground it after the others had ground theirs. Actually, there were just two flat stones slabs we could use for grinding grain. After I put my grain into the rice bag, I put it under my pillow so it wouldn't be stolen.

At that time, some dependents of the soldiers in the 4th Front Army were crossing the grasslands with us. They carried large baskets. They were sleeping beside me but when I woke up the next morning, they were gone. So was my grain. I couldn't talk or cry. I just sat there stunned, miserable.

In my novel my grain is not stolen, but is washed away in the river. I was very cautious when I was writing. I couldn't spoil the image of the Red Army.

Ma Yixiang reported her grain missing, only to learn that the meager grain supplies had already been distributed among those in her group. There was less than ten pounds of grain left. "People were so hungry that they could eat up that much in two meals, but the grain had to last ten or twenty days." She continued:

I had no tears. I thought I was destined to die in the grassland. I had followed the Red Army for such a long time. I hadn't died from the cold or from hunger in the snow mountains, but now I wouldn't survive the second grassland. I would die from hunger. I didn't want to die. I hadn't had enough of life yet.

That night, when the others were having their meal, I boiled the wild rape which I had collected during the daytime and then dried it over the fire. I worked all night, but there was only a little left after I dried it. While I was sitting there drying the wild herbs over the fire, the head of the propaganda team came over with his rice bag. It was this long and that wide. He gave me two bowls of parched flour and told me not to let anyone see it. With these two bowls of flour, I could survive three or four days if I ate just a little at each meal. The next morning, I also put the wild rape I had dried into my bag.

We had taken turns carrying a small pot. Now I didn't have to carry it because I had nothing to cook in it.

As she started across the wet grasslands, Ma Yixiang was so dispirited that she began to fall behind. Qing Jinmei, carrying Jian Xianren's baby on a horse, found her. She gave Ma Yixiang enough grain to fill two or three bowls. "After I ate a little, I figured with my fingers how long it could last."

Still certain that she would never survive the grasslands, she walked more and more slowly. Some of the soldiers noticed her empty grain satchel and gave her a little grain. One group leader asked everyone in his charge to give her a mouthful until she had accumulated enough to fill her cap.

Ma Yixiang survived this way until she had eaten all the grain she had been given. Then, with no way of knowing which grasses were edible, she began to eat some of the wild grasses that grew in the area. She was soon screaming with stomach pains. Too weak to carry her, the others pulled her along. To keep her moving, they scared her with tales of what would happen to her if she fell down. Fortunately, a doctor came along with some medicine which had proved effective for others who had been poisoned from eating wild grass. Later she wondered if the medicine was opium.

For three weeks Ma Yixiang had trudged along through the marshy grasslands with the rest of the bedraggled army. When they finally reached the edge of the grasslands, they were at a place where they could find some fresh grain, meat, and vegetables. Her leaders fed her a little mutton, and Ma Yixiang began to revive. Understandably, her memories of the next few days were solely about food:

> The wheat was ripe, the peas were ripe enough to eat, and the broad beans were getting ripe. When we saw the peas, we went deep into the fields and wouldn't get out. We picked the old ones and put them in our bags and we ate the new peas. That night none of us got back. We were all in the pea fields picking peas. When it was getting dark, we made a big fire. There was a mess officer from the Army Headquarters who didn't go back, either. He had a ladle with a long handle for serving soup. We sat around the fire and cooked the peas. We ate all night long and still felt hungry, but we were very happy and our faces were black.
>
> At daybreak, we began to look for our troops who had stopped not far ahead. When we found our troops, we rested for a few days. Meanwhile, we prepared the wheat, husking it, rolling it between our hands, then roasting it. That's how we got our rations. The grain we got was still not enough because it would take us a few more days to get out of the grassland and we had so many troops. Everyone just got a small share of it, three or four *jin*. I ate up all mine quite quickly.
>
> Before we reached the Han area, we crossed another mountain. There we saw local people in straw hats, husking wheat. Unlike Zang people, they wore trousers and their clothes had buttons. When we were in the Zang area, we couldn't see anybody and we couldn't find any grain, because the Zang people had all run away and had hidden the grain in the mountains. If we went into the mountain to look for grain, they would shoot us.
>
> It was still early when we took up quarters in the Han area. I was ravenous, so I went to a local home. I put some wheat straw under the eaves and lay down on it. There was a pig in that house but I didn't have any money with me. Two of the others had silver coins with them. They said, "You don't have to pay much. If you can find firewood, we'll help you butcher the pig, help you kill it, clean it."
>
> It was very difficult for the local people to find firewood and we couldn't collect any, either. I wanted to eat pork so much! When I heard the pig grunt, I would go and look at it. How I wanted to eat it! That night, when it was time to eat, we ate wheat gruel without any wild herbs in it. The herbs were good enough, but I still wanted to eat pork. I was so hungry for something to eat besides gruel, and the pig wasn't behaving. It kept grunting again and again. I kept getting up, looking at it, and lying down again.

Early the next morning we started out again. It was September, 1936. The frost season had started. I walked barefoot because I didn't have any shoes. I cut my foot and it was bleeding. Our squad leader bought half of a pig's head and four pigs feet for one yuan. They had been cooked. We women soldiers were really excited. After one had taken a bite, she would pass it on to another. We were still gnawing on the bones when we reached Hadapu. Seven or eight of us were still chewing on the four pigs feet after we'd walked forty *li!*

When we marched into the streets of Hadapu, we could see [good things to eat] and peddlers selling steamed bread. The delicious smell kept coming into our noses. When we took up quarters, my squad leader bought a *jin* or two of pork and cooked it in a local home. We ate that and half a pig's head. That night we ate dumplings. It had been a long time since we really had food to eat, so we should have eaten our meal more slowly and we should have eaten something lighter. That night, I felt so full that I couldn't sit up but my mouth still wanted to eat.

Hadapu is in Gansu. After we entered Gansu, we had noodles and steamed bread to eat. But for most of the time, we had dumplings because we didn't know how to make leavened bread. Sometimes we would have millet and I could eat two bowls of it without any other food except a little bit of salt. Before we crossed the grasslands, Li Zhen had given us some salt which she had brought from Yunnan. Each one of us was given only a little of it, but even with that little bit, we felt stronger afterwards.

We rested a few days in Hadapu and while we were there, we went out to recruit new soldiers. They took me along with them. Li Jingxiang and Ho Ye-ying also went along. At that time, the main thing we did was recruit new soldiers. Later I went back to the Political Department. We also had some performances, such as "Send My Love to the Red Army." When we took the new soldiers away with us, the women cried loudly. Then we would counsel them, saying, "Don't cry, Sister-in-law. It's not a bad thing to join the Army. Look at us. We left our parents when we were very young." We had to convince them, but I didn't know how. I could only say those meaningless words.

That they were recruiting new soldiers strikingly suggests that those in the armies were not thinking in terms of a Long March now over but simply about the next task they faced. The Second Front Army joined forces with the First Front in Huining, Gansu. When the armies reached Qingyang, eastern Gansu province, in December 1936, they learned about the events taking place in Xi'an, Shaanxi province, where a warlord had captured Chiang Kai-shek, holding him until he agreed to commit his Nationalist Army to form a United Front with the Communists to fight the Japanese invaders.

Even then, Ma Yixiang had no realization of the magnitude of what the armies—and she herself—had accomplished on their year-long trek from Hunan province. Not until she reached Yan'an, the seat of the government of the Soviet Base Area, did she hear the term, "25,000 *li* Long March."

While many of the soldiers moved on to fight the Japanese, Ma Yixiang and the other little girls were sent to the rear. She remembers being told before they left Gansu province, "We are sending you to Yan'an to learn to read. We are going to the front because we have finished the Long March and our new job is to fight the Japanese." She knew she had been through some trying times, but she had no sense of making a new beginning until she was with Han Chinese again and had reached the safety of the Chinese Soviet Base Area in Shaanxi province.

Ma Yixiang was taken into the Communist party the following year, probably at the Youth League level because she was only fourteen, and was considered a Model Party Member. She attended the party school, where she became literate, and worked in the local government. Following the pattern she set for herself when she was a child, she worked so hard during a push for increased production during the war that she was named a Model Worker.

In January 1989, when we interviewed Ma Yixiang at our hotel in Guangzhou, she mentioned seeing a TV program about the Second Front Army on the Long March a year before. "It brought me back to the 1930s," she said. She continued to reminisce about some of the people she had been close to during the Long March:

> Li Zhen and Chen Zongying are in Beijing now. Chen Zongying is eighty-five or eighty-six now. She is twenty-two years older than me. She was over thirty at that time and Li Zhen was twenty-seven or twenty-eight then. Many people looked after me on the way. . . . [Several] have died, some are in rest homes for senior cadres in Hunan and Jiangxi provinces. Jian Xianren is in Beijing. Her

Ma Yixiang in Guangzhou, 1988. (Author's photo)

younger sister, Jian Xianfo, is also in Beijing. She is Xiao Ke's wife. There are others still in Beijing. The one who recommended me for Party membership has died. There was a mother and daughter, Zhang Jinglian and Fan Qingfang, who were on the Long March. The daughter was a year younger than me. She has died, and her mother is in the county rest home for senior cadres. She's ninety years old. I lost contact with Qing Jinmei [who left her newborn in the grassland] after she joined the New 4th Army.

Now I'm in Guangzhou. There are no former 2nd Front Army soldiers in Guangzhou except me. I know two who were in the 4th Front Army. One can't express herself clearly and the other's memory isn't good. The last time we talked about the Long March, she said she wasn't able to remember anything.

Ma Yixiang continued, "When I was writing the book, I was still young and I could stop to think while I was writing. When I'm talking, I don't have time to think, so it is impossible for me to cover everything." She added, "Now

The cover of Ma Yixiang's book, *Chaoyanghua*. (Courtesy of Qingnian Chubanshe [China Youth Press], Beijing, and the artist, Wang Shenglie)

I'm getting old. I was under attack during the Cultural Revolution and it affected my memory."

Ma Yixiang's novel, *Chaoyang Hua*, first published in 1962, was acclaimed for her vivid portrayal of the lives of medical personnel during the Long March. During the Cultural Revolution, however, she was criticized for her heroic portrayal of General He Long, who was under attack. She is a leading member of the provincial branch of the Chinese Writers' Association. When we interviewed her in our hotel room in Guangzhou, she was living on a military post as a retired Red Army soldier.

4. From Soldier to Doctor

THE CHINESE Communist armies on the March were small mobile cities. One women's regiment was actually a clothing factory; there was a print shop, and of course there were hospitals. Probably the most unusual service was a medical school that conducted classes and graduated students during the March. He Manqiu was one of two women who graduated from this medical school and was among the first of the women army doctors in China.

Like many of the women who had run away to join the Red Army in their midteens, He Manqiu was already something of a rebel, someone who did not fit the mold. But although many of the women in the Fourth Front Army were from the most destitute peasant families, she explained,

> My family was an intellectual family in the old society. In the area where we lived, my family was considered comparatively rich. This meant that we didn't lack food and clothing. My father, grandfather and great-grandfather were literate, and my own generation was the same. Such a family in China was called a literary family, "a family with a taste for books [*shuxiang zhijia*]," but our family fortune declined to the point that we could be considered a bankrupt landlord family. My grandfather had passed the imperial examination at the county level during the Qing dynasty, but he didn't realize his ambition and just stayed at home. My father and my uncles also went to school, but my father didn't finish. He thought it was useless to go to school, because having an education no longer assured anyone of having a good position. In the Qing dynasty, before the 1911 revolution, you had to pass the Imperial examinations in order to receive an appointment as a civil servant at any level. My father became a businessman.

He Manqiu in the 1950s,
after she became a doctor.
(Courtesy of Shanghai
Wenyi Chubanshe
[Shanghai Literature and
Arts Publishing House],
Nubing Liezhuan)

She and her brother were the only children in her family. She was closer to her grandmother and her father than she was to her mother "because she didn't like me. She thought I was ugly. As soon as I was born, she wanted to throw me away." Although her grandmother had very traditional ideas, her father was liberal for the times.

Even though he was against women finding their own husbands, he was for women cutting their pigtails and not binding their feet. At that time women still had the golden lily, but in my family we had been "big feet" all the way back to my great-grandmother. However, my grandmother had wanted me to have bound feet. She told me that big feet were not beautiful. I thought that was fine, so I had my feet bound, but it was very painful. When you bind your feet, you have to wear at least two pairs of cloth shoes, plus several layers of cloth strips binding your feet tightly inside the shoes. Young people today have never seen that kind of thing. I screamed and cried, but when they wanted to unbind them, I wouldn't let them. I thought it was great, walking on tiny feet, swaying from side to side.

The traditional standard of beauty was not set by a woman's face, but by a woman's feet, shoulders and waist. A beautiful woman should have round, sloping shoulders, but mine were big and square. That's why people thought I was ugly. To be considered beautiful, a woman's waist should be very small and supple, and her feet should be about three inches long.

My father objected to these ideas and thought the binding of women's feet was cruel, so he joined a Nationalist propaganda campaign called the "New Life Movement," which followed Sun Yatsen's Three Principles. I went with my father when he participated in the New Life activities, and I became liberated and unbound my own feet.[1]

Her father was enough of a liberal to let her leave her hometown to attend a missionary school in the city of Chengdu, even hiring a tutor who helped her pass the entrance examinations.

The high school I had attended in Chengdu, *Hua-Ying* [China-England] High School, was a Catholic school run by British nuns. The dean of my school was an unmarried Chinese woman, an old maid. I was in the high school less than two years before I had to leave because of the unstable situation in that area. The classes I took were mostly traditional Chinese subjects, but we were also given religious instruction and had to attend Mass. I hated that sort of thing, but my family was religious. They were Catholic.

At school, we lived in an old-style house with a moon-gate, several students sharing one room. Actually, the conditions at that time were better for students than they are now. Several students pooled their money and ate together, or got food from the stands on the streets. The snacks that you can buy on the streets in Sichuan are very popular: glutinous rice cakes of all kinds, noodles with hot sauce.

In 1932, He Manqiu had to leave before she finished high school because of the fighting among the local warlords and the threatened advance of the Communist Army. Back home in the small town of Zhongba,[2] her grandmother wanted her to uphold the traditional Confucian values of obedience and virtue: obedience to her father before marriage, to her husband after marriage, and to her son after the death of her husband, and the virtues of

morality, proper speech, modest manner, and diligent work. However, because she was a tomboy and she didn't fit the ideal of beauty, traditionalists
such as her grandmother did not consider her behavior proper. Her grandmother wanted her to become the Confucian model of a chaste and obedient woman.

I had wanted to participate in the revolution and help liberate women for
a long time. A lot of students in Chengdu were organized to cut off pigtails
and unbind feet, to propagate the spirit of the May 4th movement against
feudal ideas. Although I was young, I accepted the idea of women being liberated. When the Red Army came to our area, I was staying at home with
nothing to do really, but to read novels. I was bored and very unhappy. My old-
fashioned, very feudalistic grandparents thought they had better find a mother-in-law for me. I knew that if that happened, I would follow in my grandmother's and mother's footsteps and become a "virtuous woman and good
mother"—something totally incompatible with my personality.

Then the bell of the time struck and I started on the road to revolution. In
1932 the Fourth Front Red Army, led by the Chinese Communist Party, came
to northern Sichuan from a Soviet Base Area in Hubei, Henan and Anhui. They
had expanded their base area, which threatened the local warlords who had been
fighting among themselves. The warlords then united to fight the Communist
Party. So the Chinese Communist Party began to withdraw from the expanded areas in 1933 and 1934. In late 1934 the Nationalists started operations against
the red bases and the Red Armies began to prepare for the Long March.

In March 1935 the Red Army passed through the area where our town was. I
can't remember the exact time of year, but I do remember that it was when the
opium poppies were in bloom. When we heard that the Red Army was coming, although the rich families had fled, we didn't. My father was popular because he offered help to those who needed it, writing documents for people who
were illiterate, helping with lawsuits. A lot of people came to our house to advise my father to leave. They told him that since he was well-known in the area,
he would be ill-treated when the Chinese Communist Party came. They also
said that his daughter was vulnerable and he had better run away.

My father told the neighbors that he didn't see any reason to leave. He said
that the people in the Chinese Communist Party were human, too. They couldn't
plow the fields and make clothes while they were fighting, so they would have
to rely on the local people for these things in the same way the Nationalists did.
He didn't believe that the Chinese Communist Party shared wives and property, and anyway, he told them, his daughter would be the last one anyone would
want. So my family stayed. I must admit that my father did have some worries,
but what could he do? We couldn't afford to run away.

Before the Red Army came, the Nationalist Army, the White Army, arrived.
They had been driven back by the Red Army and they came, one group after

another. They were awful—their caps were on backwards, their clothes were unkempt and shabby, they held their guns upside down and used them for walking sticks. They all had two guns—a rifle and a "smoking gun" [opium pipe]. My father said we'd better stay out of their way because these Nationalist soldiers tried to take everything they could from the local people. So we went away and hid for several days.

When we returned to town, as soon as we got close to the village we heard firecrackers, drums and gongs. It was more exciting than the Spring Festival celebrations—I had never experienced such an exciting scene in all my 15 years! I grabbed my father's arm and ran toward the village. We could see a wall of people standing and listening attentively. My father was cautious and didn't dare go any further, but I wasn't at all afraid. I went on and squeezed into the crowd next to a neighbor who was a good friend of my father's. I asked him what the matter was. He said, "What do you mean, what's the matter? And where have you been hiding? Look! This is the Red Army."

Our neighbor, who was himself a poor man, told me that this was the poor people's army, and that they were being welcomed because the Red Army came here to liberate the poor. I went back to where my father was waiting and said, "Father, hurry up, come and look. The Red Army is here. Everybody is welcoming them."

So my father and I went on into town. We looked and looked and looked, walked and walked and walked, and saw line after line after line of soldiers. The soldiers were in high spirits, most of them in their 20s, very strong, carrying tommy guns, wearing eight-cornered [Mao] hats and belted gray uniforms, and marching along in good order. To us they seemed both powerful and mighty. The local people were offering them food and all kinds of other things.

As my father and I watched all this, we spotted my uncle who was with the army, and embraced him. I was so excited because I had heard that there were women soldiers in the army and I had been bored at home for so long. Although I couldn't ask my uncle about these things in the middle of the street, from that time on I began thinking about joining the army, joining the revolution.

The army was resting and reorganizing in the villages, so my uncle had time to come to our home to see my grandmother and the rest of the family. I remember that it was already dark when he came and that the opium flowers were blooming, huge fields of flowers called *ying hua*. In Sichuan every family used opium—my family, too. Our village was on a small plain where each family planted their own opium. They sold most of it, but kept some for their own use. I broke my father's opium equipment several times to try to get him to stop smoking. I was really strong-willed about things in the family.

My uncle and Comrade Li, who was head of propaganda for the 31st army group in the 4th Front Army, came to our house together. My grandmother was overjoyed to see my uncle because he had been gone for so many years and she hadn't heard from him for a long time. My father knew that my uncle was a revolutionary but he told my grandmother that my uncle was a student. I couldn't wait to see him and talk to him.

My uncle introduced me to Comrade Li as his rebellious niece. I asked him straight out if it were true that they had women soldiers, and told him I wanted to join the Red Army. My uncle shushed me so that my grandmother wouldn't hear what I was saying.

My father said, "Before you've even greeted them, you ask if you can join the army! That's impolite."

But Comrade Li answered, "No, that's all right. The Red Army believes in equality between men and women, between people of different levels. We don't bother with manners."

That really impressed me. When he told me that it was true the army had women soldiers, I relaxed. Before this, I had felt that my future was black and hopeless, but now it looked brighter.

I asked them immediately, "Can I join the army? Can I join the army?"

Comrade Li replied, "It's up to your uncle. I will accept you."

My uncle said, "It will be impossible for you to go if your grandmother finds out about this. She wouldn't agree to let a man in our family join the army, much less a young girl. You know the Chinese saying: 'Never use good iron for a nail; never use a good man for a soldier.'"

Then they left.

A few days later, my uncle came again. Actually, his purpose was to take me away with him.

My uncle told my father, "Since Hui Xiang (my family pet name), can't continue in school, and no one in the family can teach her, it's better for her to join the army."

My father agreed that I could go with him, but we couldn't let my grandmother know. I packed my things quietly, waited until dark when my grandmother had gone to bed, and then I left my home to join the Red Army. My family found out what I had done soon after I left and I heard later that my mother and my grandmother both died of anger shortly after I had joined the army.[3] I was the only woman from our area who joined the army.

Whether or not her mother and grandmother actually died because she joined the army, there is no question that they must have been terribly upset. Most people had poor opinions of the soldiers and even poorer opinions of the women who went with the soldiers. A woman from a literary family, however impoverished, running off to join the army would bring unbearable shame to the family. On the other hand, from the point of view of those in the Red Army, her class background could prove to be a serious problem because she was joining the army during the political campaign to "comb out" people of questionable background. Her uncle advised her,

"First, never tell anyone that you are literate." Actually, my uncle himself was literate.

"Second, don't talk about your family owning land or having a small business; say as little about it as possible.

"Third, don't write anything or draw any pictures." He knew that I tended to be open, not secretive.

The reason for this was that the far left party line dominated the Red Army at that time and there was a movement to eliminate the counter-revolutionaries or unpure elements from the army. The head of the army led the elimination movement, which was at its highest peak in 1932 and 1933. When the Long March began, there was no time for it any more and by 1935 the movement had almost come to an end.

He Manqiu, assigned to the propaganda team, had her first experience of being under fire during a battle. Soon after that, she contracted malaria and was sent to the hospital.

I saw so many things in the hospital. We were so short of medicine, so short of doctors. Most of the best doctors had been in the Nationalist army. After they were captured, they became liberated officers and served in the Red Army. Some of them didn't have a good attitude toward the patients, but the leaders didn't care about that. There were a lot of women patients because there were so many women soldiers in the 4th Front Army. They had all kinds of female problems, but most of the doctors hadn't been trained in gynecology. If a patient completely recovered, she really had a strong constitution!

After I saw what the true situation was, the idea of studying medicine began to germinate in my mind. I thought some of these women patients had either been victims of a wrong diagnosis, or had not been treated as soon as they should have been. For example, whatever the problem might be, the doctors would just say they had a form of a tubercular disease found in women which was characterized by abnormal menstrual patterns, low fever and general debility. In addition, the women themselves held feudal ideas. They were ashamed to explain their problems and were reluctant to be treated by men. As a result, a lot of women died unnecessarily. I saw many such cases and decided they could have been helped if they had had a woman doctor. It would be great if I could be a doctor!

She was torn between going back to her original unit to participate in battle, and by her desire to enter the medical field. However, when she found her closest friend in a traditional hospital, dying of tuberculosis—unnecessarily, she thought—she decided to stay with the hospital unit and study to be a nurse.

The nursing schools at that time didn't really teach nursing, but we had a textbook called, *Questions and Answers about Physical Treatment,* which included dissection procedures, physiology, pharmacology. We had just a couple of classes each day and spent the rest of the time caring for the injured soldiers. We cleaned the wounds, helped the doctors treat the patients, took care of the sterilizing. Most of what we learned wasn't from textbooks—we learned from practice. We listened to the doctors and memorized or wrote down what they taught us, but most of the other students were illiterate. Since I could read, I always got good marks on the exams, though people wondered how I could be so good because they thought I was illiterate, too.

Her hospital group traveled with the army. When the Red Armies met in the Tibetan area of western Sichuan, they settled down to rest and regroup. The top leadership was locked in a struggle for control of army and party policies, but the soldiers were busy training and preparing food and clothing for the next phase of the March. A medical school, which had been established in the Jiangxi Soviet Base Area in southeast China, had already graduated five classes and the sixth had just enrolled when the students and faculty were ordered to rejoin their original units and leave on the Long March. The leaders of the school decided to start the sixth class again when they were resting in western Sichuan. "One morning when we were doing our morning exercises, the head of our battalion told us, 'I have some good news for you. The Central [1st Front] Army's medical school came to ask about enrolling new students. Whoever wants to apply for it, can sign up to take the exam tomorrow.'"

He Manqiu had a difficult decision to make. If she passed the exam, she would have to give up her pretense of being illiterate, and although the campaign to "comb out" people with bad class background was almost over, she was still afraid of the consequences of letting people know that she had been to school before she joined the army. On the other hand, she knew that she could learn much more than she was being taught in nursing school and that as a doctor she would be able to give medical treatment.

> So I gathered my courage and asked a close friend, "What do you think? Do you want to apply?"
>
> She answered immediately, "Okay, let's do it!"
>
> We were almost the same age, and our personalities were also similar. So we raised our hands, along with quite few others, and the next day we went to take the exam. It was held in an old, empty, ramshackle lama temple. The monks had all run away, leaving only a few statues of Buddha in the cold, gloomy temple. There were no lights, but we had torches which burned resin from the pine trees. Our desks were made of rough planks supported by tree limbs, as were our stools. This "examination hall" later became our classroom.
>
> The exam was quite simple. It tested our knowledge of language and litera-

ture; we were asked to explain some words and sentences, and then we signed our names. We were asked to give some pharmaceutical terms, to name the organs of the human body. As for politics, we were asked to explain why we had joined the Red Army, and to name the three tasks of the Communist Party.[4] The exam was completely oral. Why was it oral? We didn't have anything to write with! It was all oral, except for the math test for which we had to do some simple arithmetic using the abacus. None of these things were obstacles for me.

So the sixth class was organized and school began in August. Life in the school was very hard, not at all what we had expected. We had imagined quiet classrooms, all kinds of equipment, qualified teachers, but the reality was that there were only six teachers for 60 to 70 students. Each teacher taught several subjects. I had imagined it would be like my high school, but it wasn't the same. There were no bright classrooms with beautiful desks and chairs and a variety of equipment and teaching materials. We didn't have even the most basic thing: a skeleton. They told us that they had had one skeleton and one microscope when they set out from Jiangxi, but they had to discard them along the way to lighten their loads. At first I was a bit disappointed and thought I would have been better off in the nursing school, where at least there were enough teachers for us, and we had the opportunity to work with the patients. Life there wasn't as hard, either. I struggled with my doubts, but then I realized that this was a formal medical school, and that after I had finished school I would be able to make a greater contribution.

Our focus was on western medicine. Many of the teachers who were liberated prisoners of war had been trained in the Nationalist army, in the White areas. Most were college graduates, had good, solid professional training and had had a lot of experience. They were experts, but it was hard for us to tell how good these doctors really were because we lacked the necessary facilities. There were no patients at the school, no hospital, no facilities for research, not even the most basic equipment. They could teach us theory, but they couldn't teach us to use a microscope since we didn't have one. If we hadn't found a cadaver, we wouldn't have been able to learn how to dissect. Their attitudes were good. They supported the Communist Party policy of killing the rich and supporting the poor, even though they themselves came from all kinds of backgrounds. They were Red Army soldiers, too, and were given preferential treatment. Their monthly salary was high, and each of them had a horse and an orderly.

I said our life at the school was hard. We could never use our time off to rest, because we had to go up into the mountains to look for things we needed. We collected resin from pine trees—the older the tree, the more resin. We peeled the resin off the tree and put it on the end of a stick, to use for light at night when we studied. We also collected grass and kindling, and dug wild roots for food.

Some of us lived in the lama temple; others lived in the homes of local people. Since there were no beds in the temple, we slept on the dried grass we gathered in the mountains. There were only three women, so we took a corner in the temple for sleeping. We had nothing: no quilts, none of the most basic things for living. We spun our own yarn from sheep wool, then sent it to the weavers in the army for them to use to make clothes for us. Our main food was highland barley. Every day we had two to four *liang*,[5] but it was far from enough, so we had to find food for ourselves. That's why we spent our holidays in the mountains, collecting roots. We had almost no salt. Each of our three meals every day consisted of very thin barley porridge mixed with wild roots, three bowls at each meal. Our political commissar volunteered to take care of apportioning the food to be sure that everybody got the same amount in an orderly way. I thought a political commissar who volunteered to be responsible for the food distribution was really something! Every day she took a stool to the food stand and sat there putting the porridge in each bowl, and then supervised the food lines. After the last one took his or her bowl, she blew a whistle so that everyone could start eating at the same time. Then people could line up again for their second, and later, third bowls.

What were our classes like? We just memorized everything mechanically. We had almost no texts, but the teachers sometimes had materials which they wrote out by hand on the paper the monks had left in the temple for their sutras. The students weren't able to get any paper, nor were there any pens. We asked our dean what we could do.

"You don't have any paper? It's easy to take care of that. We can use the ground for our paper. That's one resource which is never used up. We can use sticks for pens."

Each of us found a square of flat ground to write on. We'd wipe it out and write again. Usually we'd use a good stick until it was completely worn down. In addition to the sticks and the ground, we also used charred pine branches to write on our palms, the backs of our hands, our arms. That way, wherever we went we could memorize the words we had written. And that's how we overcame our difficulties and learned all the Latin words that we needed to know.

We usually attended classes during the daytime and reviewed the lessons or taught ourselves at night. We were always memorizing mechanically. At night we lit torches of resin so that we could study. There was a big fireplace in the middle of the temple. We usually sat on the ground around the big fire and helped each other study. One would ask the other, "How many bones in the skull?" and the other would answer. The teacher would sit nearby and listen to us.

Everything we needed to learn in medical school was based on being able to dissect a human body, but we had no preserving solution, no human bones, no cadaver. What could we do about it? Some of our teachers sent us out to find a cadaver. We went to every mountain and valley around Songgang, starting out at daybreak. I volunteered to go because I really liked to go out and try to find things we needed. We walked and walked looking for a corpse, but we couldn't even find a dead bird. How frustrating to have to return empty-handed!

But on our way back we just happened to find an intact, fresh corpse in a cave. We felt sure that this person had had no family to prepare him for death and that no one would try to find the body because this corpse had had no funeral or burial. We had seen several funerals in this Tibetan area. The family always claimed the dead body and disposed of it in one of several ways. One funeral practice was to flay the skin and expose the body to the vultures. Another was cremation, and the third was to put the body in a river or stream. Sometimes when a person died, the body was tied to a tree and stones were piled up around until it was completely covered. That's why it wasn't easy to find a cadaver in such a place. Of course, we couldn't use our own soldiers or prisoners of war. Usually when our soldiers died we claimed the bodies and then buried them, because the Communist Party was humane. If we hadn't found that person's body in the cave, we would have had to wait for the body of a criminal who had been sentenced to death.

That was why, when we found our cadaver, we were as overjoyed as if we had discovered a treasure. We were so happy that we hugged each other and shouted to each other. It was a miracle! We collected some grass and tree branches to bind up the corpse and carried it back to the school. We sent someone ahead so that one of the teachers who was skilled at dissection would be ready for us as soon as we got back with the body. We stayed up all night watching the process, because the cadaver wouldn't stay fresh very long. It was late summer and we knew the flesh would putrefy because we didn't have any antiseptic preservatives.

We washed the body quickly, opened it, looked at the veins, the muscles and all the organs. After the body had been dissected, we put the pieces into a big pot and boiled it because we needed the bones for a skeleton. Two people watched the pot—I was one of the two. I wasn't afraid of anything. I hadn't believed in ghosts or spirits since my childhood. Even now, I don't mind killing and drawing any kind of poultry. I'm fearless, but some of the women were scared and refused to have anything to do with a dead body. We put the pieces into a huge pot which had been used to feed the hundreds or thousands of people in the lama temple who "ate from the big pot." We put that big pot in the middle of the temple and started the fire. When one of the women saw the steam from the pot she screamed and ran away, thinking it was a ghost! We put ashes into the water because they had soda in them which would make the meat come off the bones more easily and would bleach the bones. What did it smell like? It smelled just like any other meat cooking.

That was how we made our skeleton. First we looked at the different organs—the liver, the heart and everything. We saw how the muscles functioned, looked at the arteries, veins and the nerves, then stripped off the flesh, and, when the bones were boiled clean, put together the skeleton. We could identify the number of bones in the skull and other parts of the body. There are lots of different kinds of bones in the human body and every day we identified the bones. This is the very foundation of medical study. And that was how we overcame our difficulties when we started our school.

Of the seventy people enrolled in the class, only forty-odd graduated. Two of the three women completed the course. The one who thought she saw a ghost in the steam rising from the boiling cadaver withdrew because "she was afraid of the things we were learning."

* * *

He Manqiu stayed with the Army and received further training after the Fourth Front Army reached the Soviet Base Area in northern Shaanxi. The medical school she attended in Sichuan became a medical university, and the year she turned eighteen she returned to school for further study and was transferred from the Communist Youth League to become a member of the Communist party. She rose to responsible positions in the Health Department of her army unit during the War Against Japan. In the 1950s she became chief of the women's and children's health care section in the Health Department of the People's Liberation Army (PLA), where she and her colleagues compiled several standard reference books on women and children's health care. She left the army in 1958 to head the biophysics department of the newly established University of Science and Technology. In 1960, when all women soldiers were directed to return to their original force, she returned to the army and became the deputy director and the secretary general of the Communist Party Committee of the Information Department of the Medical Science Academy.

Because of her surname "He," General He Long spoke of her jokingly as his adopted daughter. During the Cultural Revolution, she was interrogated, mistreated, and forced to do hard labor because of her alleged relationship to him, but in the 1970s she was reinstated in her department at the Medical Science Academy when He Long was exonerated. She retired in 1984, and at the time of her interview she was working on her memoirs.

5. Why We Joined

THE WOMEN soldiers on the Long March whom I interviewed told stories of leaving children behind with peasant families, crossing glacier mountains in the third trimester of pregnancy, leaving babies where they were born, or carrying them along a day or two after birth. They described the work they did as soldiers, carrying stretchers, doing propaganda work, recruiting laborers and soldiers, and carrying gold for the army. Rich as these stories are, the greatest wealth of material came in response to the question, "Why did you join the party and the army?" Their answers, framed by their understanding of Marxist ideology at the time of the interview, contain details from their childhood, their family situations, how they perceived their future, how and when they were politicized, and how they understood their own decision to join the revolution. From the responses of these women, it is possible to find ways to understand what motivates women anywhere to become revolutionaries and go to war.

All the women, those who joined Communist organizations before entering the army as well as those who enlisted in the Red Army directly, spoke not of joining the army but of "participating in the revolution." What "becoming revolutionary" meant was as varied as the women themselves. To some it meant freedom from exploitation and abuse at home, the hope of escape from the chaos of poverty into the safety of a secure, regimented environment with enough food to eat; for those whose future was unsettled it was a way to avoid marrying into a strange family or remaining an unmarried, unpaid worker on the lowest rung of the family ladder; for the educated and educable, it was an exciting way to fight for social justice and work for national sovereignty. For almost all, participating in the revolution meant

The women featured in this chapter: (*row 1, left to right*) Chen Zongying, Deng Liujin, He Manqiu, Jian Xianfo, Jian Xianren; (*row 2*) Kang Keqing, Li Guiying, Li Jianzhen, Liao Siguang; (*row 3*) Lin Yueqin, Liu Jian, Liu Ying, Ma Yixiang, Qian Xijun; (*row 4*) Wei Xiuying, Xie Xiaomei, Zhang Wen, Zhong Yuelin. (He Manqiu and Zhang Wen photos by the author; remaining photos courtesy of *Liaowang Zhoukang She* [Outlook Weekly Press])

finding a place to belong. One, echoed by several others, said, "The Party was my family." However, the revolution, unlike their families, offered them opportunity to allow their unsubmissive, independent traits to surface.

When asked, "Why did you join?" the women spoke about the social and economic situations in their families, their family relationships, and the level of education they received. They described the geographic setting of their home cities or villages, including proximity of home to the Chinese Soviet Base Areas or the path of the Red Armies. They emphasized the opportunities they had to learn about the revolution from Communist underground workers in the village, by joining revolutionary organizations in the village, in listening to progressive teachers in school, and from family members, usually men, already in the revolution.

From the founding of the Chinese Communist Party (CCP) in 1921, the male party members had been serious about equality of the sexes, although they interpreted equality within the boundaries of their own cultural consciousness.[1] They organized schools for their sisters, wives, and mothers, established literacy classes for women workers and peasants, and wrote sexual equality into their documents, advocating emancipation of women and an end to child marriages of all kinds. They guaranteed protection for women and offered them access to the economic and cultural life of the society.[2] The CCP has continued this top-down policy of liberation of women within the patriarchal society.[3]

During the first three decades of the twentieth century, there was little institutional support for girls and women in China. In the poorest families, baby girls were unaffordable luxuries, to be disposed of as quickly as possible by death, sale, or marriage. Unlike sons, daughters were part of the birth family only until they married and joined their husband's family, giving rise to the common Chinese saying, "When a girl is married, it is like throwing water on the ground" (*jia chuqude nu, po chuqude shui*); once water is poured away, it can never be returned to the jar. In the same way, a daughter was lost to her birth family once she married. In those harsh economic times, surviving girls from poor families were sold into marriage as *tongyangxi*. Four of the twelve *tongyangxi* among the women interviewed were infants under one year old when they were given to other families. Li Jianzhen, born to poor peasants in Guangdong, was sold to another poor family for eight copper coins when she was eight months old. She spoke of the plight of some girls in rhyme:

> Eighteen year old wife, three year old husband.
> At night the wife puts the little husband to bed,

Works hard to take care of him until he grows up;
When the husband is grown up, the wife is old;
The dream has been hidden away.[4]

She continued,

There were two different situations. There were younger baby brides as well as
younger husbands. In the old society, families with money would buy a girl, but
actually she would be a servant or daughter rather than a wife.

My own mother had twelve children: four dead, eight living. The three of us
girls were sold, leaving five. Four of my brothers were sold abroad in Southeast Asia. Finally, there was only one younger brother left.

In the old society, we called it "selling baby pigs." There was no alternative.
You bore one child, gave it away, and bore another.

In Sichuan, Liu Jian's destitute family gave their first child, a daughter, to
another family when she was three days old. Then two more daughters were
born and, Liu explained, "People didn't have any choice but to put them in
the urine bucket and cover it."[5] She was more fortunate than her sisters. When
she was born in a paddy field and left to die, her grandmother picked her up.
A year later, when her mother gave birth to a son, "They said I was good luck,
because I brought my mother a boy." A son was old age insurance for his
parents. His wife came into his family to work and to continue the male family
line. Together, husband and wife took care of his parents when they were too
old to be productive.

The girls who became *tongyangxi* when they were older had a much more
difficult time. Four of the five women who were sold into another family
between ages six and eight spoke of maltreatment. Their experience was typical.[6] The abuse of *tongyangxi* was widespread, and for all four, their mistreatment was a crucial factor in the decision to run away and join the revolution. Two believed they would be beaten to death by their "in-law" families
and chose the uncertainty of life and death in the military over the certainty
of death in their adoptive families. The other three *tongyangxi* were sent to
their families "in-law" just before puberty, in one case to prevent her from
joining the army.

None of the twelve *tongyangxi* was educated as a child. However, several
spoke of standing outside the schoolroom, listening to the teacher after they
had taken the boys in the family to school. Two, whose designated "husbands"
were revolutionaries, received some schooling as teenagers, one in a CCP
school, the other in a progressive work/study school.

* * *

The three who were from poor peasant families but not sold as *tongyangxi* had no education. The other seven, who grew up in more comfortable families, received some schooling. Even in wealthier families, however, girls were seldom educated with their brothers because girls were not highly valued. Money spent on education for girls was thought to be a waste. Lin Yueqin, from a mountainous area in Anhui province, explained,

> At that time, China was governed by feudalism and there was no equality between men and women. Chinese women had no freedom, no right to education. Boys from rich families could go to school, but girls from rich families could not. They had no right to freely choose whom they would marry. When you were in your mother's belly [laugh], your parents arranged your marriage. Women had no status. They were at the lowest level of society, doing household chores, home labor.
>
> My father was a businessman in our small town and was comparatively accepting of the idea of equality between men and women advocated by Sun Yat-sen after the May 4th movement. So, although men and women were not equal, I did get some schooling. I studied at home, first, and later went to a primary school for three years.

Liu Ying, an educated woman from Hunan province, came from a family ruled by a traditional father. She had to fight for her education, with some support from her mother, who was literate. In her "rather feudalistic" family, Liu Ying explained,

> The sons were more important than the daughters [*zhongnan qingnu*]. My father wanted the sons to go to school, not the daughters. But I also wanted to go to school. I struggled and struggled, studying by myself until I could pass the entrance exam for the Women's Normal School in Changsha. (At that time, boys and girls didn't go to school together.) An early communist revolutionary, who had just come back from studying in France, established this progressive girls' school where we didn't have to pay tuition. Many of our men teachers had been classmates of Mao Zedong when they were students in the Number One Normal School in Changsha. Under the influence of these teachers, we joined the revolution.

Later, Liu Ying continued her schooling at the college level in Moscow, the only one of the women interviewed to receive tertiary education before the Long March.

Four of the others also attended progressive schools and became political activists as a direct result of what they learned from their teachers. They did not follow the usual pattern in society of the time, for they came from families that were more enlightened than Liu Ying's. Jian Xianren, also from

Hunan, was educated in the village, along with her brother. However, when it was time for her to go to middle school, her grandmother became ill and she was kept at home to help while her brother went to school in the provincial capital. He became a revolutionary and brought her material to read. After her grandmother died, she joined her brother, entered a branch of the same school in Changsha that Liu Ying attended, and also became a political activist.

He Manqiu alone was educated in a missionary school after some grounding in Chinese classics. She was perhaps the most direct in expressing her desire to avoid marriage as one of the factors in her choice to join the Fourth Front Army when it came to her hometown.[7]

He Manqiu, like the other women interviewed, remembered the coming of the Red Army positively. When the Red Army stopped moving, even for a brief time, they established local Communist government and mass organizations. They redistributed the land and shared the landlords' grain with the local peasants. The Chinese Soviet Base Areas they established were in poor, remote mountainous regions, often straddling provincial borders. The advantage to the Communists included proximity to a supportive population, terrain favorable for guerrilla warfare, and distance from the scrutiny of national and provincial authorities. Of the twenty-two women interviewed, sixteen lived in or near Soviet Base Areas, in places where the Red Armies were fighting, or in the path of a moving Red Army. These areas, poor in normal times, were even more devastated by the depredations of the warlord and Nationalist armies on the civilian populations. Not only did these armies feed and clothe themselves by living off the land, but they also took the young men to be soldiers and laborers.

As early as 1928, the Party Congress passed a resolution emphasizing the need to bring women into the revolution and linking women's interests with revolutionary activities.[8] Three of the seven women from Sichuan and Anhui who lived near the path of the Fourth Front Army cited the CCP propaganda advocating women's liberation as one of the reasons they joined the revolution.[9]

Many of those who lived in proximity to the Red Armies reported that nothing in their village had ever been as exciting as the coming of the Red Army. Certainly the attraction of adventure existed for all of the women, although it was never directly cited as the reason they joined. And no one else was quite as straightforward as Li Yanfa, who said, "Why did I join the army? To go find food to eat. There was no food at home." Several others mentioned hunger as a factor, but they also spoke of the effects of propaganda that promised equality between men and women and a chance to change the social and economic structure in China. The powerful attraction of a different way of life, an alternative to being a wife in a poor family, clearly was important for many. Even Li Yanfa, like the others, expressed several reasons for joining, although her basic reason for joining the army was simply hunger.[10] She found life in Sichuan with her opium-smoking father intolerable and her life after he sent her to her in-laws even worse. She explained,

> The first time I saw the Red Army, I went to the meeting in a big village. My father was lazy—you know, he smoked. I went by myself. Children weren't afraid any more. The meeting was led by a woman. At the first meeting, I didn't dare say anything. At the third meeting, I asked if I could join the army. They said yes, but asked,
>
> "What about your family?"
>
> "My mama died. My two brothers don't live at home and my father smokes opium." I told them everything. And they said, "Yes."

When her father found out that Li Yanfa wanted to join the army, he told her, "If you join the army, I'll pull the tendon out of your leg!" Then he insisted that she get married immediately into the family to which she had been betrothed before she was born.

> "Whatever you say, it's okay with me." I knew that I was going to join the army anyway, so I went to my in-laws.
>
> The bed that family gave me was only a frame with a shabby rain cape made of palm-leaves on it, not even any straw or stalks on the bed. When I got up in the morning, I had to take the ox out to graze. Five families owned one ox. I carried pails of water on a shoulder pole for the five families. After I fetched water for each family, I gathered kindling and cut grass while the ox was grazing. You know what I ate when I got back? They fed the dog sweet potato leaves mixed with the rice that had stuck to the pot and some water. After the dog ate, I would eat what was left.

Li Yanfa bided her time until she could safely run away to army headquarters one morning while the ox was grazing.

> I ran ten miles without stopping, but they wouldn't let me in. There were two guards at the gate.
>
> "What do you want? What's a little girl doing here?" I was thirteen.
>
> I said, "The team leader says I can be a soldier."
>
> "Let *you* be a soldier?"
>
> My clothes were shabby, just hanging in threads.
>
> "*You* join the army?" He went inside to see if the team leader knew anything about it. Then he said,
>
> "Come in." I saw the team leader and ran to her, crying in her arms.

After we filled in some papers, I had a bath in a basin of water. Then they took me to eat. I ate one bowl of meat and vegetables, one bowl of rice.

"Is it enough?"

"Give me one more serving." I finished, and they asked again,

"Enough?"

Still not enough, so I got another, until I had three bowls of meat and vegetables, three bowls of rice. The salty vegetables were so tasty, sweet potato, pumpkin, tofu, pork, all mixed up together. They wouldn't let me have any more. They said I'd burst!

"We eat this every day. Don't eat any more now."

The shabby clothes I came with were burned and they gave me a set of clothes which had been taken from the local tyrants—two sets of underclothes and one set of padded clothes. We used red cloth for the epaulets and the star on the hat.

That was how I joined the army. No one in our village joined with me. There was no food at home. When you join the army, you have food to eat and clothes to wear.

The only *tongyangxi* sold in her mid-childhood years who did not talk about maltreatment, Zhong Yuelin emphasized the accident of life that put her in proximity to the Red Army. She had been sold to a family living in a larger village in Jiangxi province when she was eight years old, a happy circumstance, she said:

If I had stayed in my mother's village, I probably wouldn't have taken the revolutionary road. My mother's village was in a mountain valley. It was rather backward and isolated from outside ideas. When I went to the family as *tongyangxi*, I had more opportunity because the village was larger, much more open and receptive to Communist Party propaganda.

There were quite a few people who could read and write because a lot of young people were concentrated there. They officially organized the local government and some mass organizations like the Children's Corps, the Young Pioneers, the Women's Unit. I joined the Young Pioneers by myself, just because I thought it was good.

At that time, we believed that women had been oppressed for thousands of years. One time I was told to go to a women's meeting. At the meeting they asked what my name was. I said,

"I don't have a name."

I never had a name before that!

The Communist organizations not only gave individual women the most basic recognition but also provided social legitimacy for women, who occupied the lowest position in the family as well as in the society.[11]

Among the women who lived near the Soviet Base Area in Jiangxi province, where the central Communist government was based, only Wei Xiuying joined the army directly, before joining a local Communist organization. After carrying messages for the soldiers, she joined the army with several men from her village. They encouraged her to enlist with them, she said, because of the daily abuse she suffered from her "in-law" family.

Deng Liujin followed the usual pattern for the women in this area and joined Communist organizations before joining the army. She described a woman who came to her village, befriended her, and persuaded her to make a revolutionary commitment:

> I was still waiting for the son who hadn't been born yet. My foster parents half-adopted a son, borrowing him from another family. I was supposed to be his fiancé, but I didn't like him at all. Later he got sick and died.
>
> I lived this way until 1929 when Mao Zedong, Zhu De and Chen Yi brought the army to western Fujian where I lived. Because of the Nationalist reactionary propaganda, most of us ran away to the mountains to hide when the Red Army arrived. We were naive at that time, so we believed what the Nationalists said and didn't trust the Red Army. Gradually we began to understand and we moved back to the village.
>
> I know now that even before the Red Army came there was an underground organization in the township. A woman who often came to visit us asked me if I wanted to become active in helping the poor people. I knew my family wouldn't interfere if I tried to do this kind of work, so I said,
>
> "Of course, but what can I do? Nothing can be done."
>
> "Why not? You are so poor, you've suffered a lot—you have to liberate yourself."
>
> "How can I liberate myself?"
>
> She suggested that we two be the first to cut our hair, to set an example. At that time, I wore a pigtail. As a married woman, she wore her hair in a bun. In the old society, nobody had short hair, so cutting hair was abnormal. If you cut your hair, everybody laughed at you. She had to persuade me several times until I finally gave in. We cut our hair. People stood around and looked at us but we thought, "Think what you please, we're cutting our hair."
>
> After we cut our hair, and after I accepted the things she told me, she said, "Now that the Red Army is here, we want to overturn the landlords. You are a poor person. Would you like to join the Party to help in the work to liberate the poor people?" So in 1931, three years after the Red Army came, I joined the Party and she was my sponsor. Before I joined the Party, I didn't participate in any revolutionary activities. I just had advanced ideas.

Cutting away the symbol of marital status in cutting hair, joining Communist organizations, running errands for the army were all paths to involvement for the women living near the Central Soviet Base Area on the Jiangxi-Fujian border. In some cases the families supported the girls, especially *tongyangxi* such as Deng Liujin, who had no one in the family to marry. In Li Guiying's case, she was compromised by the revolutionary act of joining a literacy class and had to make the break with her "family," not unwillingly. "I was sold when I was seven years old. My foster family was also poor. I was just sold to this family—there was no husband for me. The son was much older than me and had left, so it was only the old woman and me. That old woman was very fierce, terrible. She wasn't good to me. I had to do almost everything—men's work, women's work. I shouldered everything in the house. At that time we led a bitter, hopeless life. Then, Chairman Mao and General Zhu came to our county. I was about eighteen or nineteen."

When the mass organizations were established, Li Guiying secretly joined a literacy class organized by the Communists.

> I'd go to the class when that old woman wasn't home. When she was at home, I didn't dare go. When she found out, she threatened to kill me with the kitchen knife and tried to beat me to death. She gave me a black eye. The comrades in the literacy class told me to go back to class, but I said,
> "I don't dare go. It's all right as long as you're here, but when you leave, that old woman will beat me to death!"
> They made that old woman wear a tall hat and paraded her through the village, shouting, "Don't abuse child brides!"

After Li Guiying joined the army and began the Long March, her husband was wounded in battle. She and her husband were sent to join a guerrilla team near her husband's hometown. She was wounded during a skirmish, and her husband died. Pregnant at the time, she endured terrible physical suffering, especially when she was captured and jailed. When Li Guiying talked about the difficulties she experienced, both before and after she joined the army, she spoke in a matter-of-fact voice, neither dramatizing nor minimizing the violence she suffered. She gave no indication that she was aware of the irony of escaping domestic violence only to experience military violence but seemed, in retrospect, to understand violence as simply a part of life. Neither she nor the others interviewed expressed any regrets over their initial decision to join the revolution.

Jian Xianfo gave more complex reasons for joining the Red Army. Her sister, Jian Xianren, already politicized by her brother before she entered the Women's Normal School in Changsha, was a student activist wanted by the Nationalist police. To avoid putting her family in jeopardy, Xianren left and joined the Red Army. Xianfo, seven years younger, explained that her thinking was influenced by the political ideas of her older brother and sister, the patriotism of progressive teachers, and the Nationalist threat to her family.

My older sister and brother went to school in Changsha, but in 1927, after Jiang Jieshi[12] betrayed the revolution, there was an official order to arrest them. They escaped to our hometown, but the official order was sent to all the counties, so they were on the run and joined the Red Army. Afterwards, our family life wasn't peaceful any more. I was always haunted by that.

Of course, I was influenced by my sister and brother. They told me about the October Revolution and described how the Soviet Union was building socialism there. I listened very eagerly, and although I was young I understood.

After the older children found refuge in the Red Army, the family was harassed by the Nationalists, who arrested Jian Xianfo's father. When the family bought his release, he worried about his vulnerable sixteen-year-old daughter and sent her away to the Women's Normal School in Changsha.

When the September 18th incident occurred, I was in school.[13] During our lessons, our teachers told us how our country was humiliated. We felt so sad when we listened—sometimes we were in tears. After the September 18 incident, Jiang Jieshi refused to put up any resistance against the Japanese. The Nationalist policy was to establish internal peace before resisting foreign aggression [*rang wai bi shu an li*]. They wanted to fight the Red Army in a civil war.

Under such circumstances, I couldn't go on with my education. I had gone home during vacation and hadn't wanted to go back to school. My father comforted me and said, "When there is an opportunity, go join the Red Army and fight the Japanese." I already had such a thought. In December 1934, the 2nd Army Group guerrilla troops came to our town. Some of the guerrillas knew about my family, and they welcomed me to join the army.

"What can I do in the army?"

"You are a student, you are educated, there are a lot of things you can do. You can be a teacher, you can do propaganda." I was very happy and I followed them. At that time, my younger brother went with me. He was fifteen and I was eighteen. But, of course, when I left I knew the Nationalists would not leave my family in peace.

Although the Jian sisters' stories about the entire family suffering because of the political activism of the children were the most poignant, all those who belonged to revolutionary families told stories of ostracism, execution, and incarceration of members of their families. In several accounts by women from revolutionary families, there is a hint of inevitability, a suggestion that they never considered any choice other than participating in the revolution. This was probably because of both the propensity of Chinese family members to engage in the same work and to make the same commitments as others in the family and the fact that, in the eyes of the authorities, the whole family was guilty of the crimes of one family member. Because they were already compromised by the activities of a revolutionary family member, they may well have felt they had no choice but to become revolutionaries themselves. When they talked about their earlier life, they either detailed their growing intellectual commitment, as the Jian sisters did, or simply recounted the experiences with no evaluation of the nature of their commitment.

Xie Xiaomei, whose life was marred by bad luck, had one brother who was a Communist. When her non-Communist brother was executed, Xie Xiaomei was briefly jailed, then exiled from her hometown along with her mother. She continued working for the party, married a fellow worker, fought in skirmishes and battles with the Communist guerrillas, and in 1934 left on the Long March—after finding a family who would provide a home to her newborn child. Although she and her husband eventually were turned out of the party and were not readmitted until the 1980s, she spoke only about the circumstances that had made her life so difficult, expressing no regret about having joined her brother in revolutionary work.

Jian Xianfo and Ma Yixiang were the only interviewees to credit a female family member with contributing to her involvement in the revolution. Ma Yixiang joined the army to save her life when her "in-law" family threatened to kill her. She ran away to her aunt, who was already working with the Red Army. Her aunt took her to a Red Army field hospital, where the doctors and nurses took pity on her and let her work in the laundry, although she was only eleven or twelve.

Usually the revolutionary relatives who brought women into their work were men: uncles, brothers, fathers, male cousins. In three cases, it was the "husband" of a *tongyangxi* who played a role in the process.

Chen Zongying, who went to her husband's family as *tongyangxi* at twelve, was the only one who stayed married to the husband her father had arranged for her. The two families were related by marriage and the youngsters had developed a strong relationship before they knew the details of the betrothal. Her husband was one of the early Communist leaders, and, she said, "I just followed him. I knew what he was doing must be good." But she also explained that she had been politicized through the influence of a woman with whom she worked and at a work/study school she attended briefly.

Qian Xijun's "husband" also was an early Communist. He told her that he considered her his sister, not a wife, and arranged for her to attend schools organized by the Communists for their female relatives. She joined the party, did underground work in Shanghai, married Mao Zedong's brother, then moved to the Chinese Soviet Base Area with her husband.

The third *tongyangxi* whose "husband" helped her was Zhong Yuelin, the woman who did not have a name of her own before she joined the Communists. Her "husband," also a revolutionary, helped her run away from his family. In most cases, the women had to run away from their "in-law" families to join the army; not only would the family of a girl who joined the army be looked down on in the village, but the *tongyangxi* were economic assets to the "in-law" family.

Of the sixteen women who mentioned having revolutionary relatives, only six indicated that the relatives' involvement was crucial to their decision to join the revolution. Most of the ten who mentioned revolutionary relatives only in passing spoke of their own political participation in local organizations.

Kang Keqing said she didn't know of her father's involvement in the revolution until the guerrillas came to her village a second time. At fourteen, she had joined the underground Communist organizations and had already made up her mind to join the army. When the army returned to her village three years later, she ran away to become one of the most fearless fighters in the Red Army.

Of those who had not mentioned having revolutionary relatives, Zhang Wen's story is unique. She was the only one who used the plural when she told of joining the army. She was working in a clothing factory when the Red Army came to her town and set up headquarters near the factory. "That year, 1933, hundreds of men and women joined the Red Army, not as soldiers but as laborers, because they had to make clothes for the army." Her entire factory, men supervisors and women workers, were recruited. After she became politicized and adept at propaganda, she was transferred to more interesting work during the Long March.

Although the women themselves did not suggest that age was a factor in joining the revolution, twenty-one of the twenty-two women interviewed joined the army or other Communist organizations when they were under twenty-one, fourteen of them before they were eighteen years old. They had not yet borne children and had the time and opportunity to work for the revolution that older women, bound to their husband's family by marriage and children and ground down by poverty, did not have. Chen Zongying, who joined the Communist Youth League (CYL) at twenty-four, had transferred her loyalty to her husband even before they were married. However, she did not sever ties with his family: Two of her daughters were brought up in his family.

The reasons the women joined the revolution were primarily gendered, for the men who joined did not have the same impetus as the women. For example, the men with whom Wei Xiuying joined also may have been looking for safety and for the thrill of adventure, as she was, but they, as males, had not been sold into abusive families; the revolutionary "husbands" of Chen Zongying and Qian Xijun joined from political conviction that came from the schools their "wives" were prohibited from attending. On the other hand, men as well as women were brought into the revolution by their fathers, brothers, sisters, and cousins. Men also joined the local Communist organizations in their villages and became active in the CYL and the party, finding security in a strong organization and a cause to believe in. And they also were predominantly in their teens and early twenties, ready to leave home on their own terms.

Although the attraction of participating in the revolution as a path to a new life certainly was a factor for both sexes, the urgency that impelled the women to join the revolution rose directly from their being women. They expected even greater changes in the way they would live their lives than the men did. As the nameless Zhong Yuelin so clearly demonstrated, Chinese girls had no place, no status, apart from their relations to a male in the male families. They had little legitimacy or social identity, or, to borrow Linda Kerber's concept in the context of the American Revolution, no citizenship.[14] As part of the Communist Revolution, they were no longer just the property of the men in their families; they demonstrated their independence by cutting their hair and thus cutting the symbol of marital status. The army paid off the families they ran away from, sheltered them from abusive families, gave them jobs that took them outside the prescribed confines of their homes, and taught them to read and write. The appeal of belonging to the revolution was powerful to a woman who had been sold into child servitude, prevented from going to school, or physically abused and offered her a way to avoid being married into a strange family or living the half-life of an unmarried servant in her "in-law" family. In offering an end to *tongyangxi* and to unequal treatment of girls and women, the revolution held a gendered attraction for women who were strong and independent, an essential element for their participation.[15]

The men were joining by the thousands, but the women interviewed often were the only ones in their village to join the revolution. Why did these particular women join when most other women did not? Some followed their revolutionary "husbands" or male relatives into the revolution, not really making a clear-cut choice for themselves. For more assertive women, the CCP propaganda advocating equality for men and women persuaded them that the revolution would allow them to be strong and aggressive.[16] Even the women whose subsequent experiences had included disgrace, physical suffering, and death of those close to them expressed no regret over their decision to become revolutionary activists. While helping them escape from hunger, physical abuse, low status, boredom, and marriage, the revolution drew them into an exciting new life, a safer and more interesting place in society, and granted them a sense of belonging and a patriotic purpose.

6. Women at Work

THE FOLLOWING stories about the work done by women during the Long March are drawn from translations of a series of interviews by the author between 1986 and 1989. The twenty-three women who were interviewed represent a fair selection of Long March veterans. When they began the Long March, their ages ranged from twelve to thirty-two; fourteen were seventeen years old or younger when they joined Chinese Communist Party (CCP) organizations and the Red Army. They came from seven different provinces and quite varied backgrounds. Eleven were sold or given to other families as infants or small children; twelve were illiterate when the Long March began, and the others had some kind of schooling, although only one had gone beyond junior middle school. Three of the interviewees were married to generals, others to political commissars, some to lesser leaders; the rest were unmarried or had left their husbands to join the revolution. Three gave birth to babies on the March, and one carried her infant daughter with her.

The interviewed group, although representative of the women who made the Long March, were not representative of Chinese women generally. Because there was so much regional variation in the way women were treated in China and wide variation in both class and individual family attitudes, it is difficult to generalize about the status of women, except to say that women were in an inferior position. The families that followed the hierarchical Confucian ethic of emperor above subject, father above son, husband above wife, and upon husband's death, eldest son above mother also believed in *zhongnan qingnu,* putting emphasis on boys and treating girls lightly. There was also an economic basis for this saying: Girls married into other families, which then claimed their labor and allegiance, while the sons stayed with their parents, supporting them in old age. In the early twentieth century, foot binding was still prevalent in some areas and some levels of society, although there was governmental effort to change this practice. None of the women interviewed had bound feet, although several had their feet slightly crippled before they rebelled against the practice when they were young girls. Even though one woman with bound feet accompanied her husband on the Long March with the First Front Army, she was an army dependent rather than a soldier and did no work.

What work women soldiers did on the Long March reflected the nature of the political and military leaders with whom they traveled. There were about 30 women with the strictly disciplined First Front Army, which included the top political leadership of the CCP. The First Front Army left the Central Soviet Base in Jiangxi province in October 1934. The Fourth Front Army, which had approximately 2,000 women and was constantly moving and fighting, included support services similar to those in a small city. The Fourth left the Base Area in north central Sichuan in March 1935. The Second and Sixth Army Groups, which were reorganized as the Second Front Army during the Long March, included about 25 women. They left the Chinese Soviet Base Area they had established in the mountains, where the borders of Hunan, Hubei, Sichuan, and Guizhou provinces converge, in November 1935, almost one year after the First Front Army ended their March.

When the First Front Army left the Jiangxi Soviet Base Area, many of the women who had been students at the party school were grouped together as a work team. They were given a physical exam to ensure that they did not have tuberculosis or other ailments that would prevent their making an arduous journey. They were also tested for color blindness, night blindness, and sharpness of vision and hearing. The women who had the exam were not wives of high leaders, although many later married men of importance. They had previously demonstrated their leadership qualities as political workers, cadres, usually in the Women's Department of the Communist Youth League or the Communist Party in their home villages. The Base Areas had both a civilian government structure and a military one. Communist government organizations in the Base Areas operated at the village, county, district, provincial, and central, or "national," levels. Most women who participated in the Long March worked at the provincial or central level.

In addition to the work team, there were women who were attached to a special unit within the Health Department in the First Front Army. Some were high-level leaders' wives who were brought along not only because of their husbands but also because they themselves held high-ranking jobs. Several were ill. Deng Yingchao, Zhou Enlai's wife, had an active case of tuberculosis and traveled much of the time on a stretcher. Some of the women were pregnant when they began the March; others became pregnant during the year they were on the move.

Before the army left the Jiangxi Soviet, the decision was made to leave all children behind. Those who were mothers had to find local families willing to adopt their children. Those who suspected they were pregnant knew they would not be able to keep their babies once they were born.

The women in the First Front Army traveled with the top leadership, well protected by the fighting solders. The tasks they fulfilled on the March varied from situation to situation and from person to person. The illiterate peasant women in the work team, accustomed to heavy work in the fields, carried boxes of medicines and sometimes stretchers while also performing the ongoing job of recruitment and replenishing supplies. Educated women had responsibility for changing the minds and attitudes of the peasants toward Communists, soldiers in general, the national government, and landlords. They created propaganda material in the form of posters and drama and taught women and men soldiers to shout slogans, sing songs, put on plays, and make speeches to the people in the towns and villages they traveled through. They went into village homes to talk with the peasant women, to persuade them to sell or contribute grain to the Red Army. They also recruited soldiers and transport workers by obtaining the consent of the women to let their husbands and sons go.

Zhong Yuelin, the youngest of the First Front Army women, was an illiterate teenager when the Long March began not far from her home in Jiangxi province. When she was eight years old, her father became ill with jaundice and was not expected to recover. Farm families in China who did not own land were barely able to subsist. Losing adult labor through the illness or death of a parent was so devastating that most families could not survive intact. Zhong Yuelin's mother, fearing she could not raise all her children alone, sold her daughters into other families, keeping her son with her. Zhong was in her teens when the Red Army came to the village into which she had been sold. Touched by the rhetoric promising land to the poor and equality between men and women, she joined a young women's organization. At the first meeting, she was asked to introduce herself, but could not: She had never been given a name. Heretofore known only as her father's daughter or her brother's sister, she chose her name and began her work with local Communist organizations, becoming one of the youngest leaders in the Women's Department. Just before the First Front Army left on the Long March, she and other cadres were sent out to recruit soldiers from the surrounding towns and villages.

Recruitment continued after the Long March began and was complicated by the negative ideas the peasants held about the Red Army. They had heard about "Zhumao," a contraction of the surnames of the Red Army leaders, Zhu De and Mao Zedong. *Zhu* has the same pronunciation as the word for "pig" and the word for "red." *Mao* can be understood as both "sword" and "hairy." Thus the Nationalists used visual images of hairy red pigs wielding swords in their anti-Communist propaganda.

Zhong Yuelin described the work she did on the Long March:

> Our main job was still to recruit for the Red Army. Another job was to find transport workers to help us, and to do propaganda work with the civilians. The route we were taking had been occupied by the Nationalists. The civilians had been deeply influenced by the Nationalist reactionary propaganda which said that the Communist Party shared property and wives, telling how bad Zhumao was. The Red Army had never been along this road and these civilians didn't have any idea what [kind of army] we were. In many places, when we arrived the civilians had run away. The road we took was in the mountains, where the houses were isolated and there weren't any large villages.
>
> We marched everyday. When we arrived at a place, we immediately went out to find transport workers. Do you know what I mean? They were the people who carried things. When we first started out we had stretchers and documents in iron boxes. [Our group] didn't carry the boxes, just the stretchers.

The young women in the work team with Zhong Yuelin marched at night across Jiangxi province with the Red Army, breaking through the Nationalist blockade of the Base Area. When they reached Hunan province, night marches continued, for they had been spotted by the Nationalists, and daylight bombing raids began. As they fought their way across Hunan and into Guizhou, they worked at four principal tasks. First, they constantly sought out civilians willing to be hired as short-term transport workers who traveled with the army several days before returning home. Because the Red Army had no motor vehicles and was short of pack animals, transport workers played a crucial role in the early part of the Long March. The second task of the women's work team was to counteract the Nationalist propaganda with their own, to persuade local peasants to support the Red Army, often using what we would now call street drama to help the peasants understand the nature of their own oppression by the landlords. Third, they investigated the areas they marched through to locate homes of landlords and confiscate grain, which was shared with the peasants and used to feed the troops. Their fourth task, to care for the ill and wounded, became increasingly important as casualties mounted. They not only found transport workers to carry wounded soldiers but also shouldered the stretchers themselves if carriers could not be found. When they stopped to rest, the women fed their charges and dressed their wounds before they themselves ate and rested. They also had the difficult job of locating village families with whom they could leave the severely wounded whom they could not carry along.

Healthy women who were not part of the work team did similar work. Xie Fei, allowed to attend school by an indulgent father, became a revolutionary when she was a thirteen-year-old student on Hainan Island. After her entire family became involved in revolutionary activities, they were exiled. She became a Communist underground worker in Hong Kong and Singapore before returning to China and going into the Jiangxi Base Area. Although attached to the Security Bureau, she traveled with the other women in the Health Department and participated in recruitment and propaganda.

Kang Keqing, wife of commander-in-chief Zhu De, marched with the Military Headquarters as a political instructor. She not only did the same tasks the other women did but also carried a weapon (sometimes two) and may have fought in battle on one occasion.

Liu Ying, who defied her father by going to a tuition-free school established by young socialists and communists, was the most educated of the women interviewed, having studied at the college level in Moscow before returning to China and joining the Red Army in Jiangxi. She worked directly under the political commissar of the First Front Army in the Logistics Department. Explaining the nature of her work, she said,

> The Logistics Department was in charge of things like money, guns and ammunition, uniforms, machines, printing presses—all the things that we moved [from the Base Area]. A great many of the soldiers we recruited had to carry those things. As a leader in the Political Department, I managed things in the transport team. When we didn't have any transport workers, I had to go out to recruit them. When they were unwilling, we had to do some political work. When there wasn't any food, I had to scrounge some. There were many other cadres in the Political Department besides me who also did this kind of thing, but I was the leader.
>
> When we stopped at a campsite where ordinary people and local tyrants were nearby, we separated the rich and the poor very clearly. We divided what we gathered [from the wealthy] among everyone because we couldn't carry a lot of things. If we took some things from a poor family when they were not at home, we wrote a note and left some money. When the ordinary people came back home and found it, they believed we were truly the army of the poor people. Later on when we came to a place to stop, the people didn't run away. They helped us and gave us food. We gave them money, silver. I kept doing this on the Long March until we got to Zunyi.

The First Front Army was fluid not only in troop movements but also in organization and in leadership. The deep schisms within the party over military tactics also reflected political disagreements. Leaders who had been educated in Moscow and adhered to the instructions of the Communist International (Comintern) were in opposition to Mao Zedong and Zhu De, who advocated guerrilla warfare. Mao and Zhu believed their tactics, which earlier had been successful in establishing and maintaining the Chinese Soviet Base Areas, should not have been abandoned, as the Comintern agent had directed.

In addition, the Red Army efforts to move north in Hunan province and join Communist troops in the Hunan-Guizhou-Sichuan Base Area were thwarted by the local Hunan and Nationalist troops. The route north blocked, they were forced to continue west into Guizhou province. By the time the First Front Army had been traveling three months, they had lost more than one-third of their forces. They stopped in the area around Zunyi, second largest city in Guizhou province, to regroup, reorganize, and replenish supplies. During this time, the Political Bureau (Politburo) leaders met in what has become known as the Zunyi Conference, where Mao Zedong regained power.

Most of the women had little understanding of what the leaders were doing unless they were married to high-level people. Even then, they had their own work to do. Kang Keqing said she knew something was going on because the place where she and Zhu De stayed was being used for meetings, but she was busy collecting grain in another part of the city and knew none of the details. Qian Xijun, on the other hand, reported that she was aware of the divisions in the leadership. As the wife of Mao Zedong's brother, she had been traveling with wives whose husbands held high positions and heard their discussions about the conflicting policies. Although they were cadres, most of the women knew only what the ordinary soldiers knew: that the army was taking time to rest and to gather supplies while the leaders were holding meetings. Only later, as the information about the decisions at the Zunyi Conference was reported to lower levels in the military and political hierarchy, did they learn that Mao Zedong's policies had been adopted and that there had been a shift in power away from the group supporting the Comintern.

Liu Ying continued,

> After the Zunyi meeting, we jettisoned many things, because it had been a mistake to try to carry so many things. When the enemy attacked, we couldn't fight. We weren't "moving house," we had to travel lightly. The people who could walk were sent to the front. I was sent to the Center. Three people were in charge of the Central unit: Chairman Mao, Zhang Wentian, Wang Jiaxiang.

This team was equal to the Central Government. Because of the reorganization, many soldiers were freed to fight at the front, making the army more effective. Chairman Mao thought the women could do the work: manage the everyday living, raise the morale of the bodyguards, take notes during meetings. I was General Party Secretary for a while.

For the next two months, the First Front Army moved and fought in Guizhou and Yunnan in a futile effort to reach the Fourth Front Army in Sichuan. It was during these months that the first two babies were born on the Long March, and another dimension was added to the work the women performed. In this case alone, their work was gender-specific: Men did not assist at childbirth. The first baby was born to Liao Siguang and the second to He Zizhen, Mao Zedong's wife.

Liao Siguang's story is translated from a written account of her recollections of the Long March because she became ill immediately before our scheduled interview.

> I had a premature birth when we entered the minority nationality area of Guizhou. I remember on that day we plunged through two or three lines of the enemy blockade and continually ran more than thirty miles. Just before reaching the camp area, I began to have stomach pains. My back was aching, and perspiration was rolling off me like peas. The Company Commander and the doctor recognized the symptoms and gave me their horse to ride. [The pains] still didn't ease up. Deng Dajie[1] understood the situation. She quickly got off her stretcher and gave it to me. During that time, relations between women comrades were closer than hands and feet. When we reached camp, my seventh-month baby was born. It was a male baby, and cried loudly as if he wanted to announce his arrival. Deng Dajie happily said, "He is a future Red Army soldier who should be carried on a stretcher to the people's area to be raised."

Liao Siguang did not actually have the option of carrying the baby with her because the First Front Army had decided to leave the children behind. She wrapped the baby in a towel and wrote a note in which she included his birth date, the fact that he had been born when the Red Army was traveling through the area, and her hopes that the baby would be well cared for. When she left her baby in an empty farmhouse and continued marching, she did not know that she would never be able to find her child again.

* * *

After the First Front Army traversed Yunnan province and crossed the upper reaches of the Yangzi River, they were in the foothills of the Himalayas, in areas where many Tibetans lived. As they moved from northwestern Yunnan into western Sichuan province, they finally joined troops from the Fourth Front Army. They crossed several snow-capped mountain ranges at altitudes around 3,000 meters, and at this time the nature of their work again changed. Although the local Tibetans often were hostile to the Han Chinese Red Army, the greatest enemy was the terrain itself. The principal task for the women became finding food for themselves and others in their unit. While part of the work team was foraging for food in the mountains, Zeng Yu began labor. The inexperienced young women with her delivered her baby before leaving the child in an abandoned Tibetan house.

Again there were political conflicts at the top, this time between the First and Fourth Front Army leaders. Some of the women were detached from the First Front Army and transferred to the Fourth. In Kang Keqing's case, it was because her husband was kept with the Fourth Front Army. She was relieved of her position as political instructor at Headquarters and was sent to the party school to be party secretary. Wang Quanyuan and Wu Fulian worked with women in the Fourth Front Army to buy grain from the Tibetans and were unable to rejoin the First Front Army before it moved north and east, toward Shaanxi province.

Because of the conflict between the leaders of the two armies, the First Front Army slipped away after they crossed the grasslands. The grasslands in northern Sichuan are high-altitude prairies, some dry and some marshy, taking at least a week to traverse. The First Front women had a single purpose: to survive the grasslands crossing. They prepared grain for the crossing, shared ground cover and blankets, and took turns carrying cooking pots and basins as they trudged across the vast expanses. Exhausted, their clothing in tatters, barefoot or wearing makeshift shoes made of pieces of leather, they did little other work until they reached their comrades in Shaanxi province in October 1935.

When the Long March had ended for them, they had little perception of the heroic aspect of their ordeal. They resumed working at many of the same tasks they had been doing before and during the Long March.

* * *

The women in the Fourth Front Army also perceived little difference in the kinds of work they did before, during, and after the Long March. In fact, Lin Yueqin believed that the Long March actually began for her in 1931 or 1932, when the Fourth Front Army left the Soviet Base Area on the borders of Hubei, Anhui, and Henan provinces to move and fight their way to the border of central Sichuan and Shaanxi, where another Base Area was established.

Lin Yueqin was fifteen in 1929 when the Red Army guerrillas came to her hometown in Anhui province. Daughter of a shop owner, she had been to school for a year or two and was facing a future that included being married into another family. "Every girl in our small town was wandering around the town talking all day long about joining the Red Army," she said. Her relatives gathered to talk her out of it, but she cut off her pigtails, joined the Communist Youth League, and left home. She became a bureau leader in the Children's Corps, a Communist party organization. Then, she said, "Spring 1932, the blow came." The Communist party was waging a campaign to drive out members whose class status was "bad." It was assumed that those who had some schooling could not have come from poor families and therefore must belong to the landlord class. Lin Yueqin, who was literate, was among those dismissed from her job. "That was called being 'combed out.' I couldn't work in the Children's Corps. Where could I go?"

Before a decision could be made about the disposition of those being "combed out," the Nationalist encirclement forced the army to abandon the Soviet Base Area and move on. Lin and the others followed the army, refusing to return home for several reasons. Most important, was the fact that the Nationalists had retaken their hometowns and, as Communists, they would be subject to imprisonment and execution. Even if they were kept safe from the Nationalists, their reputations would be ruined because they had run away and joined the Red Army. Also important was their commitment to the Communist party: Even though they were under suspicion in the Red Army, they did not want to leave. Therefore, they helped with whatever needed doing in the army, although not in a leadership capacity. They mimeographed notices, parched rice for field rations, and changed bandages for wounded soldiers. Finally, by the end of 1932 they were accepted into the propaganda team. "To be a member of the propaganda team meant that you had joined the Red Army," Lin Yueqin explained.

> Each of us was given a lime pail and with a brush we wrote slogans on boulders: "Overthrow the local tyrants and divide the fields. Workers and poor people, don't run away, don't be afraid. We are the Red Army. [We] overthrow the rich and help the poor." Wherever we went we had the lime pail with us.
>
> When we came to a campsite where there was a big village, we would investigate the landlords. We would look at their homes to see whether the family had many places for grain storage, whether they collected rent. Then we would ask the masses if this family was rich or not. When the masses would nod their head, saying they were [wealthy], we would open the grain storage places and confiscate the grain.

The Fourth Front Army set up a base area in north central Sichuan on the border with Shaanxi province in an area where opium was flourishing. Lin

Yueqin said almost all the heavy labor was done by the women because many of the men were opium addicts. The men stayed home, cooking and caring for children. "There were fewer males [available] to be recruited, so we had to recruit women." Men and women in the Fourth Front Army then helped the husbands give up opium. They broke opium pipes, prohibited the peasants from growing opium, and promoted raising larger crops of food.[2]

* * *

Lin Yueqin was transferred out of the propaganda team and assigned to logistics in charge of a women's clothing factory which, after induction into the army, became a Women's Engineering Battalion. When she was made battalion commander, her class status was resolved positively on the basis of her continued devotion to the army even after she had been combed out. The battalion was composed entirely of women, (with the exception of one man "who kept the accounts and was in charge of the mess"). She continued,

> When there was cloth we made clothes. When there was no cloth and there were battles at the front, we went to the front to help with the transport. When we had nothing else to do, we usually had some training, including military training and literacy lessons. At that time, Women's Engineering Battalion didn't mean engineers at the front who built bridges, paved roads, set up ambushes. We didn't do this kind of work. The women mainly remained in the rear, helping with logistics. We were soldiers from the clothing factory, so we were [also] called the Women's Factory Battalion. In the 4th Front Army there were many others [women's units] besides the Women's Factory Battalion: Women's Independent Battalion, [later the] Independent Regiment. Different counties had Women's Independent Battalions. There were an especially large number of women working in the rear doing logistics, including those working in the local soviet governments, those working in the post offices, hospitals—especially hospitals. Nurses and doctors in hospitals, [were] all women.

Zhang Wen was one of the young women who worked in a clothing factory. When she was a child, her parents were tenant farmers in debt to the landlord. To ensure that she had food to eat, they sent her to work for the landlord. Badly beaten after being falsely accused of stealing flour, she returned home and began working in the factory when she was thirteen. Her story continues:

> The factory was very simple. We worked with our hands and needles—there were no machines. The clothes we produced were [the kind of] clothes worn by ordinary people, sleeves and body all in one piece. The work was hard. We were each supposed to produce one set of clothes a day. If a person was quick,

it was possible, but a slower person couldn't do it. What I described was the situation in the ordinary times.

I was fourteen when I joined the Logistics Department of the 4th Army Group of the 4th Front Army, with the quilt and clothing factory. The woman who was head of the Group went to my home to ask my mother if she would be willing to let her daughter join the Red Army. My mother said she couldn't oppose it because men and women were equal now, and because I wanted to. My mother let me go.

Zhang Wen's mother probably did not object to her daughter's joining the Red Army for a variety of reasons. The fact that almost everybody who worked in the factory was joining must have been important in that collective society. Also, the knowledge that Zhang Wen would soon be of marriageable age and would leave the family anyway would have made it easier for her mother to let her go. Additionally, if she were still in the army when she became old enough to marry, it would be the army's responsibility to find a husband for her, relieving her parents of the task.

Zhong Wen described her early work in the army: "When the army moved, the factory moved. When there was a battle at the front, and quilts were needed at the battlefield, we sometimes worked until midnight. The work was hard, but when we worked, everyone was in high spirits. We sang revolutionary songs while we worked. We felt happy in this way. Our entertainment was what we made for ourselves because there was no other entertainment at that time."

* * *

Li Yanfa, also from the same county, was in a far more desperate situation than Zhang Wen because both her parents were addicted to opium. Her mother died and her brothers left home, leaving her alone with her addicted father. When she was twelve, she decided to join the Red Army, explaining, "I said I would go join the revolution to get food to eat. I had no other purpose. [I was] just a starving teenager." Her father, who threatened to pull the tendons from her legs if she joined, sent her to the family to whom she had been affianced before she was born. She ran away when she was thirteen. Underage, she talked her way into a nearby army unit and was assigned to do propaganda work until she became ill with typhoid and was sent to the hospital. "They didn't let me leave and I started working in the hospital" as a nurse, she said. Her tasks included medicating wounds, dressing wounds, and giving injections. "The doctor told us what injections [to give]. I never went to school. The doctor taught us." She rolled bandages of gauze or any other available cloth and sterilized cotton for dressings. "The cotton came from quilts we got from the local tyrants. [We] put the cotton in a basin, boiled it and sterilized it. We used that to dress the wounds."

When Li Yanfa was asked whether she knew when the Long March began from the Sichuan-Shaanxi Soviet Base Area, she explained that they were simply told they would be going a long distance. In preparation, they returned the slightly wounded soldiers to their units and carried the severely wounded soldiers on stretchers.

About her work on the Long March, she said, "The thing I remember most was burying the dead. There were a lot of dead people, because we were in the general hospital. Every day we carried the dead out. At first, we could find some soil to cover the face. When we went farther [into the snow mountains] we couldn't even find any soil. We'd use a piece of a woven mat and roll the body up in that, bind it and bury it. Later on [in the grasslands] we couldn't even find any woven mats, so we just used grass to bind up the corpse."

After marching for several months, the Fourth Front Army met the First Front Army. When the First continued north, the Fourth turned south, recrossing the grasslands and the snow mountain range. Liu Jian, who was in a cadre working in the headquarters of the Fourth Front Army, had known hardship intimately. Her father had been a member of the Farmers' Alliance, an organization allied with the Communists but with a reputation for banditry. When his work took him away from the family too often, Liu Jian's parents entrusted her to her aunt and uncle to raise, not knowing that the uncle was an opium addict. He promptly sold her for several ounces of opium. She was so badly mistreated by her owner that she contemplated suicide before her father found her and helped her join the Red Army. When the Fourth Front Army was climbing the glacial mountain range, Liu Jian said, they were ill prepared.

> We were having a hard time. We didn't have any grain because we hadn't made any preparations when we went through places where we could have gotten grain. Women comrades carried guns, bullets, stretchers, whether they were leaders or not. I carried stretchers, too. It was very hard to walk carrying stretchers. There were rocks on the road, high piles of rocks. If there were only a twisted, narrow path, how could the stretchers go? Some would go in front crawling down the rocks with the stretcher on their backs. Those behind pulled back on it. We did this over and over again.

Kang Keqing, who had been transferred from the First Front Army by this time, was with Liu Jian's unit when they spent three days crossing a glacier mountain range in the foothills of the Himalayas. She became ill, and Liu Jian's group was instructed to leave her in a ditch. However, they improvised a stretcher made of saplings and their own leggings and brought her safely down the mountain. They eventually settled in Ganzi, in northwest Sichuan, where they met the Second and Sixth Army Groups in July 1936.

Liu Jian continued,

> Our squad went to find the minority people and to do ideological work with the lamas. If we'd done our work well, they'd sell wool to us. We gave them money for it. Some of the money was paper money, some was silver coins. In the places where there were no people, we took the wool and left a note with some money. We did our ideological work very slowly and carefully.
>
> We rested there for three months. We were preparing to cross the grasslands the third time. After we bought the wool, we washed it in the river, then we used a stick to beat it until it was soft. We spun the wool so we could make clothes. Since we didn't have any knitting needles to make sweaters, we used the ribs from umbrellas for needles or we would get the thin branches from trees. If we wanted to make a sweater this long, we'd need several dozens of those twigs because they broke very easily. If they were rough, they couldn't go through [the yarn]. We not only made sweaters for ourselves, but also for people in the 2nd Front Army who also had to cross the grassland. Each of us made one for ourselves and one for them. If you don't have anything to wear, how can you cross the grassland? That would be too much!

While they were in Ganzi, He Manqiu, who at fourteen had run away to the Fourth Front Army in Sichuan "before my grandmother could find a mother-in-law for me," embarked on a new career. Deeply upset by the general lack of medical knowledge of women's physiology and diseases, she trained as a nurse in the general hospital. When the Fourth Front Army was resting and regrouping in Ganzi in western Sichuan, the doctors, each of whom had been allowed to bring one medical text with them on the March, established a medical school. Because she had some schooling before she joined the army, she passed the exam easily. She entered medical school and eventually became an army doctor.

* * *

The Second and Sixth Army Groups had left the Guizhou-Hunan border in November 1935 with about twenty-five women. Two sisters, Jian Xianren and Jian Xianfo, were married to the generals of the army groups, General He Long and General Xiao Ke. The older sister brought her infant daughter, He Jiesheng, with her on the March; her younger sister gave birth to a baby in the grasslands. The two army groups followed parallel routes, rarely converging along the way. After the two groups met the Fourth Front Army, they reorganized to become the Second Front Army.

Four women from the Second Front Army were interviewed. In addition to the two Jian sisters, Chen Zongying, married to Ren Bishi, the highest political leader, worked as a telegraph decoder. She had been chosen for this work because she had demonstrated her ability to stand up under interrogation in a Nationalist prison in the early 1930s and because she was illiterate. If captured, she would not be able to reveal the content of the telegrams she decoded. The fourth, Ma Yixiang, was eleven or twelve when she begged the Red Army to allow her to join a hospital unit as a laundress. She believed that the family she had been sold to would beat her to death. As the Red Army marched along, her duties expanded to include nursing, recruiting, and propaganda work.

Jian Xianren, who brought her newborn baby with her on the Long March, did propaganda work when she was not caring for her child. Her sister, Jian Xianfo, had been trained as an art teacher before she joined the army. Her primary job in the propaganda team was painting posters. All the women who worked in propaganda spoke of the need to convince the peasants that the situation they lived under was neither acceptable nor necessary. Her paintings illustrated the nature and extent of landlord exploitation of the peasants who worked their land.

Both Jian Xianfo and Chen Zongying became pregnant just before they left the Hunan-Guizhou-Sichuan Base Area on the Long March. They delivered their babies in the summer of 1936, when the Second Front Army was in the grasslands. In both cases, a male doctor was in attendance, but during the actual deliveries doctor and husband stayed outside the shelters the women had found while women assisted at the birth. Both women got on horseback and continued the Long March within a day or two of delivery. Unlike the women under the strict discipline in the First Front Army, they did not leave their babies behind but were able to carry them along.

The Fourth Front Army had crossed the grasslands three times. The first time was with the First Front Army. When the two armies disagreed about destination, the Fourth turned south, recrossing the grasslands. After the Fourth joined with the Second Front Army, they again turned north to rejoin the First. Liu Jian couldn't remember whether it took two weeks or nearly three before they were out of the grasslands:

> There was sand and rock to walk on, but you can sink into the quicksand. As you walk along, you just get pulled in. Pools of water here, pools of water there. The road was so narrow. You could walk one way, but not another. If you'd try to run, you'd fall down. If you fell into the muddy quicksand, and someone tried to pull you out, you would sink in deeper. It was like paste, pulling you down. From a distance it looked like wheat, yellow. The grass wasn't very

tall. When you looked in the distance, you could see the edge, but actually after you'd walked three days in it, you still haven't come to the end. Even if there were water, you didn't dare drink it. The water stank.

Walking in the grasslands was like walking on a blanket—one foot goes down and the other goes up. Really soft. We didn't have any more grass shoes by then. The grass was bent down to the ground, so it was slippery to walk on. If you couldn't walk right, you'd fall on your butt! It was like that all around. There were muddy bogs of quicksand, some big and others not as big. If you walked into a quicksand bog you couldn't walk out. There would be one on this side, one on that. No order to it.

None of us thought about whether we would be alive tomorrow if we were alive today. We only thought about getting to a place where we could get some food and have a good sleep. This was our highest hope, because at the end, we didn't have any grain.

Safely out of the grasslands, Jian Xianfo's husband was transferred to the West Route Army while the others in the Second and Fourth Front Armies continued to the Shaanbei Base Area, where the First Front Army was based. She, her baby, and two male soldiers who helped her followed her husband's unit until the fighting became so intense that she decided they would strike out on their own to find the First Front Army in the adjacent province.

* * *

In standard Western histories about the Long March, there are few or no index listings for propaganda, recruitment, collecting grain, or caring for the wounded. In other words, the logistical support work that women and men performed may be assumed necessary but worth little mention in military or political histories. When women are mentioned in standard histories, the usual focus is on the suffering of the women. However, the women interviewed did not view themselves as victims but believed that their work on the Long March was essential. The work they did was the meat of their own stories, a substantial part of the broader history.

Much of the work the Red Army women performed was of a nurturing nature, defined in most societies as "women's work," although it was done under far from traditional circumstances. They procured food, hired help, sewed clothing, gave routine medical care, and delivered babies. The other work they did cannot be as comfortably described as nurturing. Even though Red Army women could interact with village women more easily than male soldiers could, they did the same work as men in the propaganda team. The women did transport work, shouldering packs and stretchers as needed. And in some circumstances they shouldered guns as well. Both men and women decoded telegrams, wrote slogans and painted posters, took notes in meetings, and recruited soldiers.

The lives of the veterans of the Long March, especially those with the First and Second Front Armies, have been significantly different from those of their relatives and friends in their villages who did not participate in the Long March. The large number of women in the Fourth Front Army who were captured by Ma Bufang's troops after the Long March did not fare as well. Since the early 1980s there has been a concerted effort to identify these women, many of whom were given as concubines to their captors, and reinstate them as honored veterans of the Red Army. Many of the First and Second Front Army veterans ended up in Beijing or provincial capitals, retired from positions of prestige, some with power. A large number married prominent men, and although it can be argued that some held their positions because of their husbands, this was not true of all. One, with no important husband, held a powerful position: general secretary of the Communist party in Guangdong province. Many of the others were members of the Chinese Peoples' Political Consultative Conference at the national or provincial level. Most of the Long March participants did not hold up half the sky in the country's decision-making positions, but they are considered national treasures, treated with great respect and honor.

7.   First Front Women

In this chapter, twelve women give voice to their experiences on the Long March in a chorus of voices that is greater than the sum of its parts. The same story told from the different perspectives formed by their various backgrounds, experiences, and personalities emphasizes the collective nature of Chinese Communist society in an immediate way. And because the First Front Army was under the direction of the top Communist party leadership and therefore the most strictly disciplined of the troops that made the Long March, hearing the story from many sources allows readers to assess the differences in the way stories are told. In this way, we can make more informed judgments about how to understand the nature of the women's experiences as Red Army soldiers and Chinese Communist Party (CCP) or Communist Youth League (CYL) members in a predominantly male army.

These twelve First Front Army women came from small villages and towns in Guangdong, Fujian, Jiangxi, Hunan, and Zhejiang provinces. Most grew up with an intimate knowledge of poverty. Those whose families could afford schooling for their children came from traditional families in which only boys were supported in school. Six reached maturity in families that had bought them and, in two cases, abused them; in five of the six families, there were no husbands for the *tongyangxi* to marry. Several came from families with strong revolutionary commitments. They all knew how to work hard, struggle, and survive. In the early years after they joined the revolution, they all rose to leadership positions within the Communist party and Communist government at local, county, regional, provincial, and central levels, typically in the women's departments. Several were named delegates or alternates to the Second National Peoples' Congress held in Ruijin, capital of the

Central Base Area, in 1934. Many had been transferred as cadres or students to the party school before leaving on the Long March in October 1934.

Path to Ruijin

Li Jianzhen: "Children should be wanted."

My hometown was poor,
A three-family mountain village;
We ate sweet potato gruel for every meal,
Had a worn-out stool,
A worn-out wooden bed.
Red-tasseled spear in hand,
Women strive for liberation.
    (Li Jianzhen)

In 1907, the year of the Horse, another daughter was born to a poor family in Fengshun County, in the eastern part of Guangdong province. As the mother returned from drawing water with her baby on her back, she met a carpenter who

Li Jianzhen at home in Guangzhou, 1988.
(Author's photo)

remarked on her good fortune in having children. She retorted that the baby was unwanted. The carpenter looked at the baby's hand and offered to take her into his family, saying, "Children should be wanted." The father, learning that his wife had sold their eight-month-old baby for eight copper coins, insisted on using a matchmaker to have the baby properly married into the carpenter's family. This would ensure that she would not be sold and resold, as sometimes happened. The matchmaker brought a fan, carried the baby to the foster family, held her during the wedding ceremony, waved the fan and she became an official bride. Her name was entered into the family records, but, Li Jianzhen explained, "There was no real marriage. At that time, my 'husband' was seven years old."

Li Jianzhen's path to the Long March originated when she joined the revolution in her late teens. Her first assignment was to stand guard, "red-tasseled spear in hand," while some of the male Communists were having a meeting in her home. She worked in the earliest of the Communist areas, the Hailufeng Soviet in Guangdong established by Peng Pai. She joined the party and held increasingly responsible positions in the party and in Chinese Soviet governments in Guangdong and Fujian provinces. By the time she came to Ruijin shortly before leaving on the Long March, Li Jianzhen had between eight and ten years of experience as an active leader in the revolution. She had held var-

A Long March veteran
in Guizhou province,
1997, wearing the same
kind of straw shoes
worn on the march.
(Author's photo)

ious responsible positions unrelated to women's work before the party decided to involve women directly in the revolution.[1] After that, she worked with
women in Fujian province before coming to the Central Soviet Base Area. Zhou
Enlai and Deng Yingchao asked her to stay in Ruijin as head of the Women's
Department. "I didn't want to be the head," she said. "I cried." Her duties included supervising women making food sacks, straw shoes, and clothing for
the Red Army.

Liu Ying: "Why educate girls?"

In Hunan province to the north of Guangdong,
where Li Jianzhen grew up, Liu Ying's family
was on a downward financial spiral when she
was born in 1905. Her father came from a schol-
arly tradition. Her mother was also literate, but
her father was "rather feudalistic," she said, favoring his sons over his daughters (*zhongnan
qingnu*).

Liu Ying. (Courtesy of Wen
Wu Chubanshe [Cultural
Relics Publishing House],
Beijing)

> We owned land in a farming village. Because of
> the warlord fighting, we couldn't live in the village.
> We moved to Changsha and the peasants took care
> of the land. We were small landlords, but we went
> bankrupt. Since we didn't have enough money to
> support all of the children in school, the family only supported the boys be-
> cause they thought it was useless for girls to be educated. Since they would
> marry and belong to another family, why educate girls?

My mother's family lived in Changsha. She had studied the classics and thought that if girls weren't taught, they would have a miserable life. Since she thought women must be educated, she supported my desire to study, but I still had to fight my family. My father was against it.

Their father arranged for her older sister to marry a man with an active case of tuberculosis. He died within six months of marriage, after infecting his new wife; Liu Ying's sister died several years later. Liu Ying was determined to have more control over her life and to become self-sufficient so that her father could not force her into an arranged marriage. Studying on her own, she passed the entrance examination for a branch of Changsha Normal School that was supported by the county and did not charge tuition. She then passed the exam for entrance into Changsha Women's Normal School, recently established by Xu Teli, a Communist who had returned from studying in France with Zhou Enlai. Liu Ying's memories continue:

This was the most important time in my life, learning revolutionary ideas from my progressive teachers. They were all men—we didn't have any women teachers. They were all either underground Communist party members or Nationalist party members—Sun Yat-sen Nationalists. Their influence was quite strong because they taught us to love our country, instilling patriotism in us. In our history and geography classes, we learned about the encroachment of the imperialists and the Chinese warlords. Our Chinese language teachers also taught us all of these things.

At first when I began Normal School, I didn't have any revolutionary ideas. I thought after I graduated from Normal School I would become a teacher so I could support myself and not have to rely on my family. The idea of that time was "self-struggle," not revolution. After I got into the school and was influenced by the teachers, I realized that self-struggle was a dead-end and the only solution was to join the revolution. So I joined the association set up by some of the teachers and students and the Communist Youth League. At that time I was quite young, eighteen or nineteen years old.

The May 30th movement [*Wu Sa Yundong*] in 1925 influenced the Hunan Students movement.[2] Since Principal Xu Teli didn't stop us and our teachers encouraged us to participate, our school had the most students in the movement among all the women's schools. We wanted to save China. If we didn't love our country, if we didn't fight to eliminate imperialism, British imperialism, the country would die and we would be enslaved. So the students participated in the student movement. In the revolutionary tide, we set up the Student Association [*Quansheng Xuelian*] in Hunan.

Liu Ying's revolutionary path took her out of school and into active work in the Communist party. She worked at the provincial level in trade unions and the women's department, going underground in 1927 when the Nationalists turned against their Communist allies and made the Communist party illegal. In 1928 she was sent to Shanghai and then to Moscow to study in the Chinese Communist Worker's University. "The USSR welcomed students from China who were good Party people, for advanced training in theory," she said. "At that time the USSR was the Communist International and gave us a lot of help." After she returned to China, she came from Shanghai to the Jiangxi Soviet in 1932, traveling much of the forty-day journey on blistered feet, and worked in Yudu, not far from Ruijin, the capital of the Central Base Area.

* * *

Liu Ying's thirst for education was shared by all the women. Li Jianzhen reported that she learned to read and write a little by standing outside the window of the village school, listening to the lessons after she delivered the younger boys in the family to the school. Qian Xijun was more fortunate: Her "husband" arranged for schooling for her. Educated in a missionary school, he came to believe the Christian church to be imperialistic, and he joined the Communist party. Treating his *tongyangxi* as sister rather than fiancée, he brought her to Shanghai and enrolled her in a party school (*pingmin nuxiao*) established for mothers, wives, and sisters of Communists.[3] When the school was disbanded for lack of funds, Qian Xijun enrolled in several different Nationalist schools in Zhejiang province. As a student she was always active in Communist organizations. In 1924 she returned to Shanghai and joined the CYL; the next year, when she turned twenty, she joined the CCP.

Qian Xijun: "Everything was subsidized."

In 1926 Qian Xijun married Mao Zemin, younger brother of Mao Zedong, and worked with him in the organization that published Communist materials. For the next few years in Shanghai, her life paralleled and sometimes intersected with Chen Zongying's.[4] Both had the dangerous job of carrying messages among the CYL and CCP leaders, both married CCP leaders whose release from arrest they helped engineer, and both came into the Jiangxi Soviet Base area along the Red Line through Fujian. Qian Xijun and Mao Zemin arrived in Ruijin in 1931, in time to attend the First Party Congress.

Qian Xijun. (Courtesy of *Liaowang Zhoukang* [Outlook Weekly])

When we arrived [in Ruijin], I helped them with the meeting. I did special work like making the eating and living arrangements because the representatives had come from everywhere. All those people had walked there—there were no cars or horses. When they arrived, Kang Keqing and I took care of them, letting them know when the meetings would be held, what they would eat, where they would sleep. After the Congress, we set up the Soviet Central Government and I did Party work. I was branch secretary [*zhibu shuji*].[5] All of the Party members of the Soviet Central Government were under my management, even Chairman Mao. His party relationship was in my branch. My work was with meetings, problems in the Party, differing opinions from the masses, although in our Organization there were very few masses—they were all party members.

The most important things we did were taking care of people like the messengers, bodyguards and orderlies; doing general political work, and trying to solve problems with illiteracy. . . .

In the Soviet area, everything was subsidized. We didn't have any money, not a single bit. In the Soviet area, we didn't have to worry about anything. That was great!

We lived in an ordinary, single-story house. When you walked in the door there was a little space which was our bank. There were spaces for the office, head of the bank, head of the accounting section, accountants and bookkeepers—more than ten people working and living there. Our family lived in this kind of place. The room was smaller than this room [less than 300 square feet]. People who wanted to get money, people who had other business, all came to this room. We ate in this room. We slept there, too, on a wooden bed with mosquito nets.

There were people in charge of getting water, people who cooked the rice, people who fried the food. Each family had a flat piece of metal for [carrying] food. [The serving people would ask] how many people there were in the family and give you a certain amount. If we had a guest, they would give another helping. Eggplant, sweet potatoes, cow peas, turnips—mostly these vegetables. Chairman Mao ate the same thing. At each meal we had one dish of vegetables, no meat.

Qian Xijun continued working in Ruijin at various jobs with the party organization, party school, and party newspaper until she moved out with the First Front Army in October 1934.

Kang Keqing: "I never thought I would marry him!"

Kang Keqing, who helped Qian Xijun with registration and room assignment for the first Party Congress held in the Jiangxi Soviet, had been born to a poor fisherman's family in 1911. She was *tongyangxi* in another poor family, growing up in a village near the Jinggang Mountains in western Jiangxi near the Hunan border. Mao Zedong and Zhu De had brought their soldiers and established a Soviet Base Area there in the late 1920s before establishing another base area near the Jiangxi-Fujian border in 1931. Describing her childhood, Kang Keqing said,

Kang Keqing. (Photo by Sho Namura, 1944, in the author's collection)

> You can either say I was sold to the family, or sent to the family. It was a very common situation. We didn't know about birth control and kids were born one year after another. There were ten children in my natural family: three boys and seven girls. In my foster family, I was the only child, just waiting for a boy to be born.
>
> What I did in that family was everything a daughter-in-law should do, and I didn't do anything a daughter-in-law didn't do. [For example,] I began to gather kindling when I was five or six. Compared with other daughters-in-law, I had a good situation and the family liked me very much.
>
> In 1926 there was a woman's organization in my hometown, so I did some work for them, such as organizing the women to liberate them. I also joined the Peasants Union, the woman's organization and the children's group. I was a member of the Socialist Youth League in 1926. We all joined the revolution this way.

Kang Keqing was fourteen when the Great Revolution (*da geming*) ended but kept her Communist connection active "even when things were at low tide," she explained. Not knowing that her foster father was also active in the revolution, she was sweeping one day when Chen Yi, one of the early members of the CCP and a protégé of Zhu De, came to see him.

> I swept the floor up to the door and heard them talking. [Later,] I asked my father to tell me what was going on. I told him I would tell other people about it if he didn't tell me what he was doing. My father then told me the [Red Army] troops were trying to make people think they were going to fight a battle, but it was just a feint, and they [planned to] retreat.

The first day the troops were in our area, they distributed the landlords' grain among the poor families. The women organized themselves to get the wagons [to carry the grain]. The army stayed there three days, and then I left with them.

Kang Keqing went into the mountains with a group of about eighty Red Guards (*chiweidui*). As they walked, they talked about their commander, "but I never thought I would marry him!" she exclaimed.

The soldiers were forming up and the commander was inspecting them when we passed by. This was the first time I met him. My first impression was of his thick, black beard and dark complexion. He was wearing the same clothes the ordinary soldier wore and seemed to be just a simple, ordinary soldier.

For a while after that we didn't have any contact. I met his wife, Wu Roulan. She was an intellectual who wrote slogans. Very capable, but quiet. During the year after we met and before we were married, Zhu's wife went down the mountain and was captured. After she was captured, she was killed and [her head] was displayed in public.

Kang Keqing married Zhu De when she was eighteen. In the following years, she proved herself an able fighter who won the respect of her fellow soldiers and held political positions as a member of the CCP, which she joined in 1931.

*　*　*

The intense poverty that compelled families such as Kang Keqing's natural family to sell their own children was typical of the six women who were born into families they identified as "poor peasant" or "worker" families: those of tenant farmers, semiskilled artisans, and fishermen. Although they were all born between 1905 and 1915, they described their families using the classifications Mao Zedong defined in an article published in 1933. In it, he characterized the classes in China in this way:

—a *landlord* lives off of the labor of other people
—a *rich peasant* lives off other people's labor, but also works for himself
—a *middle peasant* does his own work
—a *poor peasant* works for himself and sells his labor as a tenant farmer
—a *worker* lives by selling all of his labor.[6]

Deng Liujin: "How could we live like this?"

Life was desperately hard for all the poor peasants and workers, especially those living in the remote mountainous areas near provincial boundaries. Deng Liujin came from a village in Fujian province near the Jiangxi border, about forty kilometers from Ruijin, where she would begin the Long March twenty-four years later. Her birth father was a tenant farmer who also peddled small household items such as needles and thread to make ends meet, "carrying those odds and ends on a pole from street to lane." When Deng Liujin was ten days old, her parents sold her to a family in another village whom her father had met on his circuit.

Deng Liujin. (Courtesy of *Liaowang Zhoukang* [Outlook Weekly])

Since my parents had six children and were poor, they couldn't feed all these children. Only one sister got married out of the family. The other four of us, the rest of the daughters, were all given to other families when we were babies. They had no choice.

There were no sons in my foster family, only the old couple. My foster father was a barber, a worker not a peasant. He was crippled. I usually helped him carry his equipment as he went from place to place giving haircuts.

At six years old, I became his apprentice, carrying his tools in a box from one township to another, while I learned barbering skills from him. I started off washing hair and later I used a piece of knife to cut hair and shave men's heads.

I learned to plow the ground when I was ten. I also went to the mountains to collect brushwood, carried water from the well, did the housework.

We rented about a sixth of an acre [*yi mou*] of land from the landlord. We depended on the income from this land and my father's barbering for our living. Although we planted two crops of rice a year, we had to give most of the rice we harvested to the landlord. There was very little left over for us to eat. We had to plant some extra things like yams, just to eat. Year after year, day after day, we ate sweet potatoes. Three meals a day, just sweet potatoes!

There were times when we had nothing to eat. When that happened, my foster parents would take a crop bag to the landlord's family to beg some rice. They not only refused to lend us any rice, they set their dogs on us. I still have a scar on my leg from the landlord's dogs. That's the way the landlords were!

Spring Festival was the most important time for us.[7] We worked hard the whole year and when Spring Festival came we would like to buy a piece of meat. Sometimes we used the money my foster father made from barbering to buy a piece of cloth to make some clothing. We usually wore our clothes for three years.

I vividly remember one Spring Festival. The three of us were enjoying our Spring Festival meal together, eating meat, bean curd, and other good things. Several of the landlord's men burst in and demanded that we pay our debts. Of course we had no money. They said, "You had money to buy meat to eat, but you don't have money to repay your debts to the landlord." Then they took away everything on the table.

How could we live like this? How could the poor keep on like this? There were many, many people like us. The landlords were in the minority. All the families were poor except for three or four landlords. I began to think about these things. I lived this way until 1929 when Mao Zedong, Zhu De and Chen Yi brought the army to western Fujian where I lived.

In the areas where the Nationalists and communists were fighting, the word spread of the coming of "Zhumao," a contraction of the surnames of Mao Zedong and Zhu De. One rumor was that Zhumao would kill the people and burn their homes. Other rumors played on meanings of the names: Marshal Zhu's surname is the same word for "red" or "vermilion" and has the same pronunciation as the word for "pig"; Mao Zedong's surname also means "hair" and has the same sound as the word for "spear." People said that Zhumao was a red pig, a hairy pig, that would stab people and kill them.

Most of the townspeople where Deng Liujin lived hid in the mountains until the Red Army propaganda teams persuaded them that they would not be harmed. Deng Liujin was befriended by an advance Communist worker who persuaded her to become a revolutionary. Deng Liujin cut her hair, joined the Communist organizations, moved up from the village level to the county and provincial levels in the women's organizations, and was sent to Ruijin to study at the party school in 1934.

Li Guiying: "Don't abuse tongyangxi!"

Li Guiying lived in the southwestern corner of Jiangxi, in a town about twenty-five kilometers equidistant from the borders of Guangdong and Fujian. She was seventeen or eighteen years old in 1927 or 1928 when she heard that Zhumao had come. Not believing rumors that hairy Zhumao truly killed people, she carried some kindling to sell in town so that she could hear what they had to say.

Li Guiying. (Courtesy of *Liaowang Zhoukang* [Outlook Weekly])

As soon as the Red Army came into a village, they established Communist organizations. Li Guiying joined a literacy class. When her foster mother learned about it, she beat her and threatened to kill her. Protected by the comrades in her literacy class, Li Guiying cut her hair, joined the CYL in 1930, and ran away from the woman who had bought her. She worked at progressively higher levels in the party organization and joined the Red Army while she was working as a recruiter. "I was young, in good health, I worked hard, but I was illiterate," she said. "I didn't learn much in literacy class." She was deputy head of the women's department in the Guangdong-Jiangxi provincial committee when she and her husband were transferred to the Central Organization Department in Ruijin in 1934.

Zhong Yuelin: "Who will fight for the new world?"

Zhong Yuelin, born in 1915 to a family living in a poor area among the foothills of eastern Jiangxi province, was young when her father first became ill with "the yellow sickness," jaundice. With no one to do the heavy work, the family was forced to buy all the rice they ate because they had no reserves. "We had economic difficulties, but life was all right. We had enough to eat and to wear." Her father recovered for a while, and when she was six, her little brother was born. There had been a sister who died when she was a toddler. "There were

Zhong Yuelin. (Courtesy of *Liaowang Zhoukang* [Outlook Weekly])

no doctors or medicine out in the country. If you got sick, you just had to wait and pray," Zhong explained. When she was about eight years old, her father had a relapse. Afraid her husband would soon die, Zhong's mother arranged for her to go to a middle-peasant family living near Yudu. Unlike other *tong-yangxi* who were sold after they were no longer infants, Zhong Yuelin was treated well. Her "husband" was a student, two years older than she.

When Zhong was about fifteen, Zhumao's army of Red guerrillas were in the vicinity, and she heard a great deal of discussion about whether they were good or bad. She listened to the talk and decided the Communists were good. "I believed that the Communists would liberate all of mankind, beat up the local bullies, divide up the land, and provide for equality between men and women," she said. When the Red Army soldiers came into her town, they organized a local government and mass organizations. Zhong Yuelin joined the Young Pioneers. It was at a women's meeting that for the first time in her life she was given her own name. She worked hard with the Young Pioneers during that period of guerrilla warfare, doing propaganda almost inadvertently among her fellow villagers.

> At that time in the countryside, [farm] people didn't have anything to do on rainy days. They would meet and chat, talking about the Communist Party and the Red Army. I was still a child and sometimes I would break in and say something like, "I don't believe in sharing property and sharing wives." To people with old-fashioned ideas who were afraid to join the army, I said, "What's wrong with joining the army?" I opposed those men. We wanted women! That was when I would break in and ask, "Who will fight for the new world?" After that, I was recommended to join the Communist Youth League.

At the time Zhong Yuelin was invited to join, however, the local CYL was in the midst of a campaign to clean out members of Communist party organizations with questionable class backgrounds.[8] When the person who first talked with her about joining the CYL disappeared, the illiterate fifteen-year-old was confused as to who was a true Communist and who was not.

> They were killing people in the Children's Group. They were arresting people every day. One person would come to arrest [someone] and in the afternoon he himself might be caught by someone else. Many who were caught and killed were those who had risen up in revolution. Later, the Center issued an instruction to stop it immediately: "Those who weren't killed must be freed." Then my mind was at peace.
>
> The Communist Youth League came again to talk with me and in spring 1931, I formally joined the CYL. I took an oath, sentence by sentence. It was still secret, not public. If you went to a meeting, you couldn't go with someone else, you had to go alone.
>
> After I joined the League, I took part in all the activities of the Soviet. The

Communist Party members and the Youth League members were mobilized to take the lead [to cut their hair]. You had to go against the old ethical code and it wasn't an easy barricade to overcome. Cutting your hair was considered the greatest outrage against tradition. I wasn't married yet—I wore a single braid, since I was *tongyangxi*. Because it was the right thing to do, I took a pair of scissors and cut my hair. I was the first one in my village and there was a lot of gossip. Was it fierce! I wasn't used to [adverse] public opinion, people pointing their fingers at me. Just imagine, during several thousands of years of feudalism, no one had cut their hair, so if you cut your hair, it's heresy! I didn't care about their gossip about my short hair. I hadn't given them anything else to talk about, I hadn't done anything wrong. I was just a country girl, I was pure and the only idea I had was to join the revolution. I answered the Party's call and the League's call. It was great to join the revolution!

One of the first in her village to commit to the Communist cause, Zhong Yuelin was assigned to work at the county level. When she received the letter with the assignment, she said, "I was so happy to get the letter! It's hard to describe how I felt. There was no telling what [good things] this might lead to!" Her "fiancé," who had joined the Red Army, took her to her new post at the district level, where she worked until she went to Ruijin in 1933, in the Central Women's Department.

Wei Xiuying: "It was harder to hold a pen than a hoe."

Wei Xiuying, born in 1910, was six years old when she was sold, kicking and biting, to a family living in Gaocheng village in Xingguo county, Jiangxi. In 1930, some of the young men she worked with in the fields persuaded her to join the army with them by reminding her of the constancy with which she was maltreated by her foster family. The Red Army was leaving Xingguo when Wei Xiuying and her friends ran away to join. "They said they didn't want a woman. Later, they accepted me and gave me a Red Army cap." She was about twenty years old, the only woman in her unit. She was not treated like a

Wei Xiuying. (Courtesy of *Liaowang Zhoukang* [Outlook Weekly])

woman soldier, she reported: "When they gave people jobs to do, they treated me like a man."

When her unit returned to Xingguo, the Gaocheng village leaders asked her to participate in the local government. She was elected to the Standing Committee of the peoples' government and became director of the committee to improve women's lives. She joined the CCP in 1932 and was promoted to positions in the party and the government, moving from the village level to the county, regional and provincial levels. At the provincial level she worked in the Women's Department under Cai Chang, one of the most revered of the early revolutionary women. Wei Xiuying explained,

> Cai Chang asked me to give her a report about women in the countryside [assessing] what the situation was in terms of production, daily life, and family life. Women must be liberated in all aspects: politics, economics, and social status; women should be equal to men and should work in agricultural production because better cultivation of the fields will yield more grain for the country, the people and the families. Cai Chang told me to go to the countryside to find out if women were participating in labor. After I came back, I reported orally to Cai Chang about what I understood.
>
> Cai Chang Dajie wanted me to learn to read and write because I had never been to school. She taught me two characters every day. There was no paper, no pens. I got down on the ground, used a stick as a pen and wrote in the dirt on the ground.
>
> [The first words I learned were] "Long live the Chinese Communist Party!"
>
> Later, Cai Chang Dajie used her own money to buy pen and paper for me. I didn't know how to hold a pen. I told her it was even harder to hold a pen than a hoe. With a hoe I can pull up about fifty pounds of dirt. Cai Chang Dajie stood behind me and held my hand, guiding me. We did this every day for about two months. Later, when I went to the countryside, she bought me a notebook.
>
> She told me, "Write one word. If you don't know the rest, I'll know what it is you want to say."
>
> Cai Chang Dajie was a real mother to me—like my birth mother. She was about ten years older than me. Food was rationed and if I didn't get enough to eat, she and her husband would give me some of theirs.
>
> In April 1934, the Jiangxi Provincial Committee sent me to the Central Party School to study. Cai Chang Dajie had a wool blanket which she had bought with the money she saved when she was a work-study student in France. She and her husband shared the one blanket. Cai Dajie cut the blanket in half and gave me half.
>
> I didn't want to take it, but Cai Chang ordered me to take it. She sewed a bag for me and found me a bowl. We people from Jiangxi usually use chopsticks, but Cai Chang Dajie was afraid I'd lose my chopsticks, so she gave me the spoon she used in France.

Wei Xiuying was made party secretary and monitor of her class at the party school in Ruijin before beginning the Long March.

Xie Xiaomei: "Because of the requirements of our work, Luo Ming and I got married."

When Xie Xiaomei came to Ruijin to work in the party school, her husband, Luo Ming, was under a political cloud. A report he had written in 1933 about the success of guerrilla action in Fujian province, in which he and his wife had participated, had been used to discredit Mao Zedong. The Communist leaders known as the Twenty-Eight Bolsheviks thought the report had become an international line against the Central Committee: the Luo Ming Line, Xie explained.[9] The Twenty-Eight Bolsheviks, Chinese Communists who had been trained in Moscow, were in close

Xie Xiaomei. (Courtesy of *Liaowang Zhoukang* [Outlook Weekly])

contact with the Comintern, which was advising the abandonment of guerrilla tactics.[10]

Xie Xiaomei came from Fujian province, where she was born in 1913. One of her brothers, who was a Communist, used their home as a meeting place and a safe house for party members. Working as an operator at the local telephone company, she overheard Nationalists planning to raid her home and arrest her brother. She was able to warn him, giving him time to remove incriminating evidence and escape. Another brother was not so fortunate. Not a Communist, he had received a letter from his younger brother asking him to try convert Nationalist soldiers to the Communist cause. "The letter was found by the police during the time of the White Terror. My oldest brother was shot less than three days after he was arrested." Xie Xiaomei was imprisoned for a short time before she and her mother were exiled from their hometown. In 1929 she joined the CYL and the CCP. She explained that her marriage came about when they were assigned to live and work in the same building, ostensibly as husband and wife. "In January, 1931, some comrades [acted] as matchmakers. Because of the requirements of our [party] work, Luo Ming and I got married. I was 20."

They worked in Shanghai for a short time, then returned to Fujian to work at various tasks for the party. In 1933, Luo Ming wrote the report that became the basis for the Luo Ming Line. In April of that year, Xie Xiaomei was sent to work in the Central Party School in Ruijin.

> I worked in the Education Department. When the trainees sent by the Central Organizational Department came, we would arrange when and where they would register, where they would live, and which class they would enter. We

would also decide how fast they would cover the teaching materials, and get the teaching materials reproduced. We also decided how many leaders we should invite to give lectures and have the contents of the lectures made into teaching materials [that we] reproduced before the lecture. When the trainees came to register, we had to make sure that they had letters of introduction from the Party organizations of the units they were attached to. And when they graduated, the Central Organization Department would tell us where the trainees were needed and how many were needed, and then we would assign the trainees to these places. At first, one training class would run three months, later six months. There were several classes altogether.

Xie Fei: "Wherever I went, I clutched this letter of introduction to me."

Xie Fei. (Author's photo)

Xie Fei's revolutionary path brought her to Ruijin in late July 1934. Born in 1913 on Hainan Island off the coast of Guangdong province, she was educated in her village on Hainan Island, the only girl in a class full of jeering boys. Sent to the county seat to study in junior high school when she was thirteen, she became the youngest of the student activists. When the Nationalists turned on their Communist allies in 1927 and soldiers raided her school, she returned home and began teaching literacy and revolution, still in her early teens. Learning they were on the Nationalist's "wanted list," the family fled. Xie Fei went first to Hong Kong, then Singapore, doing confidential work underground for the Communist party until she was brought back to work in Fujian province before being sent to Ruijin along the "Red Line."

> The Party Organization sent me; the Central Committee assigned me in July, 1934. It took me two or three weeks [to travel] on the secret route by boat, by bus, at night. [I was with] two people, one in front, one in back, with two guns for protection. I stayed in a shed in the mountains which they called "Lenin Park." Of course, they were joking. They said, "We'll go with you to the next station. The people at the next station will take you on to the next one. The next station will deliver you to the next station." In this way we got to the Soviet Area, to Ruijin.
>
> I was transferred there with a letter of recommendation, to establish my relationship to the Party. Wherever I went, I clutched this letter of introduction to me. The short time I stayed in Ruijin, I worked in the National Political Security Bureau on important confidential matters.

Wang Quanyuan: "Dynamic organizations, dynamic land reform!"

Wang Quanyuan came from a village near the western border of the Central Soviet Base Area, in an area that was both politically and militarily unstable. Born in 1913 in a mountain town of houses clustered along one road, in Ji'an county, Jiangxi province, she was the youngest child in the Ouyang family.[11] She was the only illiterate girl from a poor peasant family among the women interviewed who was fortunate enough to be able to live with her own family: both parents, two older brothers, and an older sister.

Wang Quanyuan.
(Courtesy of *Liaowang Zhoukang* [Outlook Weekly])

Because the family was so poor, she explained, they did not confine her to the house, away from public scrutiny. On the day the Red Army came to town, she took eggs to market to trade for salt and heard people in the street talking insurrection (*baodong*). She saw strangers coming into the village from every direction, carrying flags, playing drums, and beating gongs. She followed them, anxious to discover what it was all about.

> People were having a meeting. Someone was speaking, saying things like, "We poor people are now liberated! Everybody should stand up and join the revolution. The only road the poor people can take is the revolution." When I heard this, I had some new feelings. I myself was poor. If the poor people are going to turn around, I must join the organization.
>
> At that time, I had not yet been married into my mother-in-law's family, the Wang family. I had been promised to that family when I was eleven.

The Wang family had heard that the revolutionaries promoted the practice of free choice in marriage by opposing the traditional practice of arranged marriages. Learning that Quanyuan was interested in joining the revolution, her future in-laws sent for her, fearing she might decide to reject her betrothed for a spouse of her own choosing. Her betrothed was twice her age, just on the lower edge of what was then considered middle age. At sixteen, she was still called "child" (*xiaohai*).

"Five days after the beginning of the rebellion, I went to my mother-in-law's home." She was married early the third month of the lunar calendar in 1930 and by the end of that month had officially joined the Communists.

As soon as Quanyuan moved into her mother-in-law's house, she persuaded the women in the household to cut their hair.

I told them that we are human beings, but our hair made us look like Buddha. I wore mine in a bun. We didn't like the old hair style because it required so many jade and silver hairpins. People should have what they were born with, but a Buddha looks like what people make it look like.

The Communist Party members trusted me more when they saw that I had cut my hair. They believed that I understood revolution and encouraged me in my work, so I participated even more in the revolutionary activities of cutting hair, unbinding feet.

Soon after her marriage, a neighbor, who was a member of the CCP, asked Quanyuan whether she would agree to be introduced to a local Communist organization.

I asked, "What organization?" They told me it was the Communist Youth League and that a member was a model for young people. She found that I had some revolutionary ideas in my head.

I said, "Okay, I'm willing to be a model."

I had to fill out a form and take an oath. Something like, "We Youth League members are models and will take the lead. We are not afraid of being martyred." I couldn't write, so other people filled in the form for me.

As a CYL member she organized and participated in the work of various groups in her hometown. "The rebellion was really dynamic!" she said. "Dynamic organizations, dynamic land reform!" She devoted herself full time to the heady excitement of social activism, ignoring her duties at home and incurring her husband's wrath.

One night when she had worked late preparing beds for incoming Red Army soldiers, she found that her husband had locked her out of their home. Her mother-in-law came out to unlock the door and found herself locked out also. The women shouted, but Quanyuan's husband refused to open the door until his brother began yelling, "You don't have long to live, you devil! If you don't open the door, I'll break it down and beat you to death!"

The party member next door heard the commotion and the next day put a big poster on the wall criticizing her husband for holding Quanyuan back and deterring her from participating in the revolution. "From then on, my husband never tried to interfere with my work."

She worked at the local, district, and provincial levels of the Communist party organizations, demonstrating courage, honesty, resourcefulness, stamina, and strong leadership ability. She was elected Provincial Committee women's deputy to the Second National Soviet Congress, scheduled to meet in Ruijin, January 1934.

In November 1933, she and other delegates were sent to visit the model county of Xingguo for a month before the January meeting. This was the county in which Edgar Snow described "a populace nearly 80 percent liter-ate" because of the literacy efforts of the Communist organizations.[12]

The delegates arrived in Ruijin, the seat of the Jiangxi Soviet government, in January, and the Congress met for nine or ten days. In describing the people she saw in Ruijin, she used titles for Mao Zedong and Zhu De that were not in use at the time.

> When we got to Ruijin, I can remember seeing Chairman Mao, Marshal Zhu, Bo Gu, Zhang Wentian, and the women: Comrade Cai Chang, Comrade Deng Yingchao, Kang Dajie. Chairman Mao's wife, He Zizhen, was there and she also had her child with her.[13] Chairman Mao's son was more than a year old, not yet two. I held him in my arms. When I held him, he was very, very happy.
>
> Li Jianzhen was there. She was working with the All-China Women's Feder-ation.[14] I saw her at the meeting, but we didn't talk. The meeting hall was large and people from different areas sat in different places.
>
> The meeting began at the beginning of January 1934, and lasted nine or eleven days, I can't remember exactly. There were over one thousand deputies. If we include the visitors, there were about two thousand.[15]

When the Second National Congress adjourned, the deputies who came from the west remained in Ruijin, assigned to study in the Marxist-Leninist School. What was to have been a two-year course was shortened because of the military situation.

The course of study was both political and military. In the first three months, the political classes took precedence. Later, the bulk of the students' time was spent studying military subjects. Originally assigned to the regular class, Wang Quanyuan said she was the only woman moved to a higher-level class. At the same time, her membership was transferred from the CYL to the CCP.

Because she was illiterate, she was allowed to give oral answers on the ex-ams. Her excellent memory served her well in the political classes. On the first exam, she passed the political questions, but she failed the second exam, on military matters. "They drew a turtle on the wall, so I was too ashamed to go to class." (The slow turtle is not a complimentary symbol.) When the CYL secretary told her to return to class, "I thought about when I was at home and we were very poor and I kept asking my mother to let me go to school. She wouldn't let me go for even one year. It wasn't good not to go to class here [because] the Party was training me in this way. So I graduated in five-and-a-half months, and I was number one or number two on the military exam."

The head of the Marxist-Leninist school, knowing that Wang Quanyuan was illiterate, "grabbed a woman student, got me a stool to sit on and said, 'She can teach you two words each day.'" He also told her tutor to make sure Quanyuan learned to both read and write, and to understand the meaning of what she was learning. When she graduated several months later, she was able to recognize most of the words in the text her tutor used, *Soviet Construction,* and to write some of them, she said.

After her graduation in June, Wang Quanyuan was assigned to the CYL Central Committee in women's affairs and was also a committee member in the Women's Department of the Central Party Committee, of which Li Jianzhen was the head. Her immediate task was to collect grain in Ruijin and then recruit soldiers. Although she did not realize it at the time, this work was in preparation for the Red Army to leave the Central Soviet Base Area. The effort to collect grain in August 1934 was followed by a recruitment campaign to expand the Red Army to 1 million soldiers.

Wang Quanyuan was sent to find recruits about twenty-five miles from Ruijin under the supervision of Wang Shaodao, the man she would marry during the Long March. She spoke in detail about the process:

> In September, I was assigned to recruit Red Army soldiers in Xijiang. Wang Shoudao was our group leader and I was in charge of recruiting forty people from one district but after more than ten days of searching for recruits we hadn't found a single person there to recruit. Most of the young people were hiding in the mountains to avoid joining the Red Army.
>
> At midnight, instead of sleeping, we went to visit the families who had sons. We heard a mama and a papa whispering, "Aiya! It's raining and our little devils [*xiaogui*] are up in the mountains, but there's nothing we can do about it. One night seems like a whole year." . . .
>
> When we heard this, we knocked on their door and I said, "Folks, please open the door."
>
> They let us in, but when they asked us to sit down, I told them we wouldn't sit down. We had found out which families had young people and knew what their names were. I asked about their son by name.
>
> "Where has Miaoge gone?"
>
> The parents said, "Our little devil went out after dinner. We don't know where."
>
> I said, "You must know! Just tell us. We won't force your child to join the army, because it's got to be voluntary. Parents have to be happy about letting their sons go to the army. If your son isn't willing to go, we won't force him."
>
> The parents said, "Joining the army isn't such a bad thing."
>
> I told them, "Well then, since you know it's all right, you can tell us where your son is." They finally told us.
>
> We visited two or three such families and heard the same story. Then at dinnertime we went to the Party Secretary's home. The Party Secretary took the kids to the mountains when he thought we would be [busy] eating our own dinners. When I got to his place, his wife said,
>
> "He went to a meeting."

"Meeting? There's no meeting!"

"No meeting? Well anyway, he left this morning."

I said, "In the morning? All right, fine."

We didn't trouble her. We left and went to another young person's home. He had left, also, and had gone up to the mountain. The parents told us the Party Secretary had just called him out for a meeting.

So that's the way things were going. We couldn't do our job. The Party Secretary was terrible! Actually, he was a traitor. Some of the conscientious Party Committee members in that area told us that the Secretary never held meetings with them.

We wrote a report to the county explaining how the Party Secretary was being destructive and we couldn't get going with our work. So the county told us to hold a mass meeting for the whole district. We were supposed to tell the local people the truth about what the Secretary had been doing and let the people make a decision. If the masses wanted him shot, then they should execute him. If the masses wanted him expelled from the Party, then they should expel him. It should all be according to the will of the masses. So there was a mass meeting. They all wanted to shoot him because they thought he was obstructive and anti-revolutionary. It was at this execution meeting that more than forty of the young people volunteered to join the army. The reason is clear: we worked at night, visited the local families, were very nice to them, told them that we weren't forcing them to join the army and that joining the army must be voluntary. Some sent their sons, some sent their husbands, some sent their brothers. [That's why] more than forty signed up on the one day. The very next day, they were sent to the district government [to be formally inducted] and I went back to the county for a summing up meeting [zheng jie hui].

Then I received a letter from the CYL committee telling me to finish up my job and return immediately. So I went that very night—twenty miles all by myself on mountain roads, but I wasn't afraid.

After the enemy bombed us while we were holding the meeting [calling for 1,000,000 recruits], the Central government had moved out of Ruijin to a place about 20 miles from Xijiang.

The department head said [to me], "First, fill in a form."

On the form were questions like "voluntary or not," "family status [jiating chushen]," and "position [zhiwu]." That's what I can remember, but there was more.

After I filled out the form, I was told to go to Ruijin the very next morning for a health examination at the general health department. The department head told me not to take much with me, only necessities for everyday use and a single blanket. Altogether, my things shouldn't weigh over twelve pounds.

Wang Quanyuan and the other women soldiers still had no clear idea of the leaders' plans to leave the Central Base Area that summer of 1934. Deng Liujin, who was to work closely with Wang Quanyuan on the Long March, explained, "We didn't know about this then—only the Center knew." She continued, describing what she did not learn until years later:

In 1934, Chiang Kai-shek and his 1,000,000 troops carried out the fifth offensive against the soviet bases in Fujian, Jiangxi and Hunan. At that time, Chairman Mao was not in the top leadership. He was a great person, and was wise. Though he made a lot of mistakes later on, without Chairman Mao there would have been no new China.

The main reason for moving the Red Army was because of Wang Ming's wrong line opposing Chairman Mao's military tactics. At that time Wang Ming was in the Soviet Union. He sent a German advisor to China, Li De (Otto Braun), to direct the Chinese Red Army.[16] His [Braun's] instruction was to retreat because he wanted to escape encounters with the enemy.

The retreat was like moving house. We didn't call it "The Long March" but we called it "moving house." We didn't say this was the "Long March" until after it was over, after a whole year of experience, a year of lessons learned.

Blockhouses such as this, photographed in Jiangxi province after the Red Army left the Base Area, gave armed soldiers a wide view of the surrounding countryside. (Reproduced from C. W. H. Young, *New Life for Kiangsi* [Shanghai, 1935])

* * *

Xie Fei's understanding of the military situation probably is a combination of what she knew at the time and what she learned later:

> The Nationalist planes were always bombing! At that time, although we didn't know much about it then, . . . Chiang Kai-shek had a German advisor who advocated using the strategy known as "blockhouse warfare" to try to wipe out the Red Army. The Nationalist troops built a blockhouse as soon as they occupied a place, so that the Red Army couldn't retake it. There were blockhouses everywhere! This was the way they reduced the Red Army area.
>
> If the Red Army had been fighting according to Chairman Mao's military strategy, we wouldn't have had to force ourselves to fight recklessly. Mao Zedong's strategy was to concentrate forces to attack one unit, eliminate it, and capture their guns. . . . Our German advisor didn't understand this. Our forces were scattered and their army was larger and better armed, but he advocated keeping the enemy from penetrating even one inch into the Soviet Area. Impossible! We would rather let the enemy troops come in, concentrate our forces to get rid of them, and then attack in another place. But the foreigner scattered our armed forces and if we were attacked here, he would send troops here; if we were attacked there, he would send troops there. The German's strategies caused us to lose one battle after another! Forcing ourselves to fight these fixed battles caused such tremendous casualties that finally we had no choice: we had to break through the encirclement. That was why we were forced to withdraw in the strategic maneuver that was the Long March.

Liao Siguang gave us written material about the Long March from her memoirs. We did not interview her because she was taken to the hospital with severe high blood pressure less than an hour before our scheduled interview. From Guangdong province, she had a difficult childhood. A fortune teller told her mother that Liao Siguang was bad luck and would bring great misfortune to both the family and the village.[17] Both she and her brother joined the revolution. In her written account, Liao Siguang added another insight concerning the leader's decision to leave Ruijin: "It was autumn fifty-four years ago [1934], the second year after I had arrived in the Soviet area from the Shanghai White area. Overhead, enemy planes were bombing indiscriminately, while on land the enemy were attacking savagely. Fighting comrades were falling in droves. Since the enemy still maintained a tight economic blockade, not only was the Red Army short of medical supplies but, most difficult of all, we lacked salt. The whole Soviet area was short of salt."

In addition to medicines and salt, the Base Area was short of most other essentials, especially cooking oil, necessary for the well-being of soldiers whose diet included little or no meat. Under these bleak conditions, in Au-

Liao Siguang. (Courtesy of *Liaowang Zhoukang* [Outlook Weekly])

gust 1934 the leadership sent the Sixth Army Group under General Xiao Ke and Political Commissar Ren Bishi to the Hunan-Guizhou border to test the possibility of breaking through the enemy lines. After suffering severe losses, the remnants of the Sixth joined forces with General He Long's Second Army Group.[18]

Deng Liujin was sent across the border into Fujian, her home province, to enroll new recruits.

> I reported to the [Fujian Soviet] provincial government to ask for their help to mobilize people in our area from county to township to village. I got more than one hundred people in less than fifteen days and immediately returned to Ruijin. We had a big celebration when the army reached one million because everybody was happy that we finished our recruiting successfully.
>
> After the celebration, the Central Organization Department told us to stay in Ruijin instead of going back to Fujian. We didn't know why. We stayed in their guest house for awhile, waiting to be assigned new work. We were worried at not getting new assignments.
>
> Li Weihan,[19] director of the Organization Department at that time, came to

tell us that we women would be sent to the front. We were very, very happy. We thought we would go to the front as real soldiers. But there were three conditions for going to the front: you are able to walk, you are in good health, and you can carry fifteen *jin.*

There was another condition: we had to have a medical checkup.

The medical examination loomed large in the memories of many women in the First Front Army, both those for whom it was required and those who were exempt because of their own position or their husband's. Zhong Yuelin reported, "The women who were examined first came back and told us, 'They check you everywhere, from hair to feet.' Women were really embarrassed at an examination like this!" Deng Liujin explained, "It was the most difficult thing for us, because in the old society nobody ever had a physical checkup. We said we'd rather not." Given the choice of submitting to the exam or staying behind when the army moved out of Ruijin, however, she agreed to have the physical examination.

Li Jianzhen did not have the exam because "I was the head [of the women's department]. I had to go." Women such as Liao Siguang and Xie Fei, who came because they were Army leaders' wives or fiancées, had no requirements to meet. "They just came with the army," Li said, "but the people in my department all had to be able to work." She selected them, she said, on the basis of health and capability. She remembered Wang Quanyuan as tall enough to carry stretchers.

Wang Quanyuan described the exam:

> The building where we had the examination was an old style, local house, made of brick, not very high. There were both men and women doctors, but the one who examined us was a man.
>
> First of all he checked our breathing to see if it was normal. The doctor wanted to know if we had pneumonia. He used a stethoscope to examine us for that. Second, they examined our legs to see how strong they were. Third, our eyesight, and fourth, hearing. The doctors used a tape measure to measure our chests before and after we took a breath. They didn't use a stethoscope for that. When they tested the strength of our legs, they did it like this [hitting her knee], to see if our feet would jerk when they knocked on our knees. To test our eyesight, they gave us five colors: pink, green, blue, white, black. We had to stand back and look at them to see if we could tell which was which in a dark place. For the hearing test, they covered our eyes and asked us to tell which side the ticking of a watch was coming from.
>
> They didn't check for pregnancy to see if your body had a baby in it. The doctor would never ask us if we were pregnant because we were chosen after the Central Government discussed [who would go with the Army]. We were

specially selected from many women Red Army soldiers. None of the twelve of us had that [kind of checkup].[20]

There were fifteen women who had the examination. Three were dropped and the other twelve passed. I remember that Dong Lao's wife had pneumonia.[21] She was dropped. She was a little, tiny woman, very thin. I don't know what was the matter with the other two who were dropped.

Top women leaders, party officials, and the wives who accompanied their high-ranking husbands were exempt from being examined. Thus, Deng Yingchao, Zhou Enlai's wife and a strong leader in her own right, was able to accompany the First Front Army even though she had an active case of tuberculosis. She made the march lying on a stretcher most of the time. Both Liao Siguang and He Zizhen, Mao Zedong's wife, were pregnant before the March began. Yang Houzhen, whose husband, Luo Binghui, was commander of the Ninth Army Group, had bound feet and was the only one of the women whose feet had not been unbound.

The eleven women with the First Front Army whom we interviewed estimated the number of women who had the health examination as ranging from fifteen to a hundred. The total number of women who left Ruijin with the First Front Army also varied in their accounts from thirty to thirty-five. What is clear is that at least twelve women passed the medical examination and at least thirty left with the Army from one place or another in some official capacity.

None of the women realized the scope of their undertaking, and few had any knowledge of why the army was leaving the Central Soviet Base Area. Even the women whose husbands were at the top or close to the top had no prior knowledge. Kang Keqing said simply, "We were told that we would start out, but we didn't know where we would go." Qian Xijun, Mao Zedong's sister-in-law, might be expected to have known more, but she said,

> Let me tell you! Our Party work was very secret. At nine in the morning of October 10, 1934, I was told to go to a meeting organized by Li Weihan, director of the Party Organization Department. He said we were going to break out of the encirclement because there were several million in the enemy army besieging us. Where were we going? We didn't know.
>
> Only the women comrades attended the meeting. Even Mao Zemin didn't know anything about it. The meeting was in the morning. At four in the afternoon, all the women comrades gathered together and sometime in the evening we started leaving.

Liu Ying, in explaining her experience, gives more insight into both the chain of command and the narrow channels of information.

When I was in Yudu, Chairman Mao was also there, studying the roads. He was preparing for the Long March, but we didn't know a thing because it was secret. He told me to return immediately to Ruijin, but I said I couldn't go because my work wasn't finished. I was in a muddle. Chairman Mao was the Chairman of the Central Government, but my direct supervisor was Li Weihan of the Organization Department. Since I reported to him, I thought that I could leave only if he told me to go, not knowing anything about the Long March.

Then Li Weihan phoned me. "Come to Ruijin immediately. There is special work."

I got on my horse and went to Ruijin.

As soon as I got back [to Ruijin], Li Weihan said, "If you had come any later, you couldn't have caught up with us." How could I know that?

Three days after I got to Ruijin, the Long March started.

Li Jianzhen was told only that there would be a strategic troop movement of the First Front Army to the rear of the enemy forces. "Nobody said where we would go. We didn't make many preparations—we only made straw sandals."

Xie Fei, working with the Security Bureau, said, "At that time I heard that the Red Army was going to be shifted out of the area. We heard about the movement, but where we would go and how far away, we didn't know."

Xie Xiaomei had given birth to a baby in September and was still in the hospital for the required month of quiet and rest after childbirth when she received orders from the Central Committee. She left the hospital immediately, returned to the party school where she had been working in administration, and learned that she had three days to make arrangements for her baby daughter.

"Making arrangements for the baby" meant giving her away to someone. After I heard the decision, I began to look for a local family [to adopt] the baby. I felt badly, but there was nothing else I could do. The situation was critical. We often heard gunfire. If I hadn't given her away, she would become a burden and it wouldn't be any good for either my work or for the child.

I located a family within the three days. The husband was a Red Army soldier. They already had a son and the wife was happy to get a little girl. We were grateful because, if she hadn't wanted to adopt her, we'd have a real problem. We left some silver coins and told her, "We have left the child to you and hope that you will be kind to her." She lived in Ruijin, close to the Party School.

After I had settled the problem of the child, another order came telling us to make arrangements for the trainees in the Party School. Some of them would be reassigned and some would be sent back where they had come from. Those who were asked to stay in Ruijin began to sort out documents and files and packed those we needed to take with us in large iron trunks. It took us two or three days to pack up. We had raised some pigs in the Party School. We butchered them and ate pork.

Luo Man [Li Weihan] said to me, "Get prepared. You are leaving with the troops. Don't take too many things with you. Just the necessities—food, clothes, nothing more." Then I knew that the troops would be transferred [*diaobing*].

The Central Committee had selected about three hundred [male] trainees and thirty women comrades. The First Front Army grouped us into the cadres company. Then the Organization Department ordered us to leave, and we set off at about five o'clock in the afternoon of October 14, 1934.

The March Begins

> On the evening of the 10th [of October 1934] at the head of the
> main force of the Red Army along with the organs in the rear area,
> exceeding 86,000 men, the Party Central Committee and the
> General headquarters of the Red Army left Ruijin, advanced
> towards western Hunan and began the Long March.[22]

The discrepancy in the women's accounts concerning when they started off arises from the fact that not every group left from the same area. There is no reason to think they would have known the date they left. Not only was it unlikely that they consulted calendars, but the scope and importance of the "strategic maneuver" that became the Long March did not become clear to them until after it was over.

Like the others, Zhong Yuelin had no understanding of the situation. "We didn't call it the Long March. We called it 'fighting to the rear of the enemy' [*dadao diren houfang qu*]," she said. "We were told it was going to be very, very difficult."

Zhong Yuelin, who said she was among the healthiest of the women who had the medical examination, developed a bad case of diarrhea. She tried to hide her problem, afraid she would not be allowed to go with the army. However, the women were all sleeping together in close proximity, and someone noticed how often she got up during the night and reported it to the leaders. Zhong said,

> They [the leaders] talked to me formally and told me to stay [in Ruijin]. "You are sick, you can't march. We're afraid you'll drop out along the way."
>
> That's what they said. Just imagine how I felt after that! There's no word to describe my feelings. I was as frantic as an ant on a hot pot! I said, "No! No matter what happens, you can't leave me behind! I won't be a burden to the

organization! I don't want any special treatment, like having a horse [to ride]. It doesn't matter how far we go, I can go that far. One step is one step. If I can't keep walking and I die there, then that's it. No one is immortal! I can overcome such a trivial illness."

When they saw that I was so determined, they gave me two small packets of medicine. I didn't know what it was—I had never had any western medicine before then. After I took the two packets of medicine, the diarrhea stopped for a whole night, and I was all right. The next night we officially started out.

Before Wang Quanyuan's unit left, she described how they were given some basic instruction in how to move silently and what to do if they became separated from the rest of the soldiers:

> Everything we brought with us had to be wrapped up tightly so the enemy wouldn't hear us. We had to walk on tiptoe because if we put our heels down we'd make a *dong dong* noise which the enemy could hear. They also told us that if we got lost, we should try to find signs left along the road.[23] In this way, no one would get lost and would always be in touch with the others.
>
> The health examination was at the beginning of October. The day after the health examination, we left for Xijiang. That very night we crossed the Gan River on a floating bridge.

The army units, numbering between 80,000 and 100,000 people in total, began slipping away at night, eluding the encircling Nationalist troops. Qian Xijun explained,

> We lined up. We had a road map to show where we would go that day, how far it was. We women comrades were all together. Deng Liujin, Liu Ying, Wei Xiuying, Wang Quanyuan, Wu Fulian, . . . Li Jianzhen wasn't with us then, but later on she was. There were some other women comrades who joined us on the way because they followed other forces. Different army groups left from different places at different times.
>
> Mao Zemin [her husband] and I left at different times. I didn't know when he left or where he was going. I didn't even know *if* he left. He hadn't told me anything. He wasn't allowed to—not even husband to wife. He knew I had left because I left first, but he didn't know where I was going. Later we met on the road.

Xie Fei explained that the rule was to walk five kilometers an hour, but their pace varied with the kind of road they were on. "We would rather walk one-hundred *li* on a flat road than twenty *li* on mountain roads," she said, adding, "When we were marching, we were too tired to talk."

> Marching at night, the road is long
> Revolutionary thought is the sun. (Li Jianzhen)

At the beginning we walked at night [Deng Liujin said]. We didn't dare walk in the daylight because the Nationalists might discover us. The first night there was a heavy rain. The bearers couldn't go on because of the rain, and those of us who followed couldn't move either. We couldn't have a light, couldn't have a fire. The first night we just went five *li*. Those in front of us couldn't move, so we couldn't move. We were completely stopped. This was the first time we experienced walking at night since we joined the revolution. We fell several times, and hurt our legs.

We all had walking sticks. Walking sticks were very important for everyone: they were our third legs from the time we started in Jiangxi until we reached Wuqizhen.[24] The soldiers who weren't seriously wounded used walking sticks. They often lagged behind because they couldn't keep up the pace.

The First Front Army was made up of both political and military elements, with some leaders holding positions in both. Kang Keqing, who was often with her husband during the march, was a political instructor in the Military Headquarters. Other leaders' wives were attached to the Health Department in the Central Government Headquarters, in a cadres' group. During this part of the Long March, Wang Quanyuan explained, she was assigned to a work unit under the Health Department:

> Three of us organized a work group, called the "Women's Work Group," with Dong Lao at the head. I can still remember the names of some of them: Wu Fulian, Wu Zhonglian, Li Bozhao, Zhong Yuelin, Wei Xiuying, Deng Liujin, me.[25] I can't remember the others. Li Jianzhen wasn't with us. She was with the cadres' battalion [*ganbulian*]. I remember the wife of the political commissar of the 9th Army. She had bound feet.[26]
>
> We started out from Jiangxi with five stretchers and carried them along all the way to Shaanbei [northern Shaanxi province]. Who were on the five stretchers? One was Deng [Yingchao] Dajie because she had tuberculosis and couldn't walk. Another was Chairman Mao's wife, Comrade He Zizhen. Her belly was in danger. She was pregnant before the Long March. When we got to Guizhou, she had her baby and left it there. These two and another, a division commander named Deng Feng, who had been wounded during the third encirclement. There was a soft-nosed bullet inside him. He couldn't walk. And there was a regiment commander who had lost his legs in a battle.

They continued night marches across southern Jiangxi province. At the first morning light, they searched for a place to rest. When they stopped, some could rest, "but the comrades in the women's working group had no time for that," Wang Quanyuan explained. "The only women who could rest were the ones with small [bound] feet, or those in bad health." Before seeing to their own needs, the women worked until they had finished caring for the wounded soldiers and settling them down to sleep. Deng Liujin explained, "We would boil water for them to wash their feet. Then we would clean their wounds and cook their food. After that, we could eat and rest."

The women's daily duties also included constantly replacing the civilians who walked with the army for a day or two, carrying stretchers and supplies. When they went into the countryside to recruit, Wang Quanyuan said, "We did some propaganda. The people should be willing to come, and we would pay them." Her recruiting team included Wu Fulian, Zhong Yuelin, Deng Liujin, and Wei Xiuying. "Wei Xiuying was very short and couldn't keep up with us if there were an emergency, so she didn't come with us to the countryside very often."

They carried cooking pots and cooked for themselves when necessary. If they were in a village, sometimes they ate with the family in the home where they slept.

When the army was able to rest, Wang Quanyuan said, they looked for grain and silver. They worked with the civilians, encouraging them to change their relations with the powerful people in their communities. Li Jianzhen described the situation in a mountain song:

> Bitter people have bitter hearts.
> Landlords do no work, but they still have new clothes,
> Have three meals of meat and drink,
> Three tubs of rice, and half a *jin* of wine.
>
> Bitter people have bitter hearts.
> Have three meals of mush.
> Bitter people, united as one heart,
> Pick up poles and beat the landlords.

Wang Quanyuan described the process of identifying the landlords and "local tyrants" and dealing with them:

> When we saw a very good house several stories high in a village, we would go investigate. Some of the people didn't dare to talk [with us]. They were people looking after the house [*kan fangzi*],[27] or family members who didn't dare say anything, so we had to do our investigation in the neighborhood. First, we would go to the poor people who lived in small sheds, tumble-down shacks, thatched sheds. Even when these people told us something, they wouldn't say much because they were afraid of the landlord. The landlords had people in their households who might try to get back at them. So we had to hide them in a secret place to ask them about the landlord. After the poor people had told us everything, we reported to the district government office, and then we would go and overturn the landlords.[28] Everywhere we went we had to find out what the living conditions were.

Another job we did was to teach the masses. We told them what the Red Army was like, and [let them see] how the landlords and local tyrants treated them. On the way, [we found] some of the masses willing to join the Red Army, so we recruited them.

Deng Liujin remembered how very difficult the first month was. "When we got to the [Jiangxi-]Hunan border, we were exhausted. We rested for a week." And Zhong Yuelin remembered another complication:

> He Zizhen said, "We're going to rest for a day. Take off your clothes and boil them."
> When I boiled my underwear, there were so many lice! As soon as the water boiled, they boiled right out! They were gray. Who didn't have any! If you didn't have lice, you're not a revolutionary! There was nowhere to bathe, no way to change clothes.

By the time the First Front Army had safely evaded the blockaded areas in Jiangxi, the Nationalists had located them and began aerial bombardment. The planes used were one- or two-person fighters, which the pilots flew so low that they could see their targets. Because they had no equipment for night flying, the long line of the Communist forces hid during the daylight hours, and their nighttime ordeal continued.

Wang Quanyuan remembered the march across Jiangxi and Hunan as one blur of forced night marches, as did most of the other women. Deng Liujin spoke of falling asleep on her feet as they marched, then opening her eyes to find the troops had already moved on. Liu Ying's memories of Hunan, despite battles, bombardment, and constant exhaustion, showed another aspect: "Back in the Soviet Base Area, we were hungry. We didn't have enough to eat because we were saving the food for the [soldiers at the] front. You couldn't see a bit of oil in the food, and, even worse, there was no salt. It was miserable. But when we were in Hunan, we fought the local tyrants, killed their pigs and ate the meat. Even though we walked the whole day and it was very tiring, we had delicious fat meat to eat."

The discipline in the First Front Army was strict, and the rules about what the soldiers could take as the army moved through the countryside were explicit. Kang Keqing, political instructor at Military Headquarters, spoke of her daily duties on the Long March within the context of these rules:

> I would get up, and, after the troops lined up, would check how many units there were in the lines, who were in the units, and where each unit should be in relation to the others. While we were marching, I would check to see if anyone had dropped behind, had gotten sick, and decide what to do with them. When we stopped, I would remember where the villagers' things that we used

had been, so that we could return them to their proper places. For instance, if we had taken a door down, we would have to put it back in its place and bundle up the grass, following Mao's Three Rules of Discipline and Eight Points for Attention.[29] I had to make sure these things were properly done. I would make sure that we didn't do anything counter to the villagers' interest.

The Red Army continued west across Hunan province and into the northern tip of Guangxi province, where they suffered great losses. With the increased number of wounded soldiers, the women's work became more difficult.

One of the hardest tasks was locating civilians who would agree to keep severely wounded soldiers in their homes after the army marched out. Finding a family who would promise to care for a Communist soldier was seldom easy: "Only when people promised to protect our wounded would we stop worrying," Wang Quanyuan said. The task was complicated by two factors: The villages they passed through often were empty because the local people had fled from the army, and the soldiers were terrified of being separated from the army. This was especially true of people who had been so severely wounded they could not keep up with the army and would be left with local people, who might turn hostile, or be at the mercy of the pursuing Nationalist army.

Not only were the women responsible for placing the severely wounded in friendly homes, but they sometimes had to carry the stretchers themselves if a stretcher carrier ran away or was wounded. Deng Liujin explained that the stretchers were made of hempen ropes and bamboo poles. Two men could carry a stretcher, but if there were not enough men, four women (or two women in front and one man in the rear) were needed. The rough, mountainous terrain made it hard going for the carriers as well as those being carried, Deng said. "The wounded complained about us and even beat us with their sticks when we couldn't take good enough care of them. They beat us and cursed us; they shouted, 'Fuck you!' but we knew why they acted this way and we didn't blame them."

* * *

The Red Army fought across Guangxi, past the amazing karst formations around Guilin. Often under bombardment from the air, under attack by ground forces, and sometimes surrounded by enemy soldiers, none of the women commented on the strange beauty of northeastern Guangxi.

Reflecting the chaotic conditions under which she was trying to move the sick and wounded on stretchers when they reached the mountains, Wang Quanyuan said, "We were running for our lives with our stretchers. Then we broke through the enemy line and got away."

The mountains in Hunan, Guangxi, and Guizhou were not as high as those she would encounter further west but certainly rugged enough to challenge the ingenuity of the women overseeing the transport of stretchers. Some places were so steep that they swung themselves up pathless inclines by grasping tree branches and roots, helping each other, as Wang described in this anecdote about climbing a mountain in Guangxi:

> When we went over the mountain, it's not to say I'm really good, but I did put out a lot of effort. I could walk fast, run fast, and I was one of the strongest. I weighed 129 *jin* at that time.[30] Up in the mountains, there weren't any roads but there were a lot of trees. [We'd] put one hand on the branch of a tree and swing across. In one running step, I'd swing up on top of the cliff, and say,
> "Comrades, come on over. I'll help you up one by one!" So I got them up one by one. The wounded people in our hospital, how many were there? There were several hundred. We had to get all the stretchers up, one by one. After we got the stretchers up, we got to the front.
> It took two days and one night to get over the mountain.

As the army, seriously depleted after the battles in Guangxi, went into Guizhou province, the soldiers moved through remote, impoverished mountain areas where the Miao minority people lived.[31] Wang Quanyuan reported,

> We did a lot of work in the Miao area. We left a lot of the wounded soldiers with Miao people in their small huts on the tops of the mountains. The wounded soldiers slept in their small huts and we slept outdoors, but we left our clothes and things in the huts where the wounded soldiers were.
> The wounded soldiers knew we would be leaving them behind. One night, when I went to the house where I had left my things, I discovered one of the wounded soldiers had stolen my clothes, my pants, my blanket. I could only find my towel, toothpaste and bamboo hat.
> What could I do? I went to the [field] hospital where the nurses gave me pants and other clothes.

The wounded soldier may be forgiven: He was left behind in an area where the people were so poor even teenage boys had no pants to wear. It was in this area that Liao Siguang gave birth prematurely to the first baby born on the Long March. Liao Siguang explained what she remembered thinking about leaving her baby:

> What a lovable child! But at that time, we couldn't communicate with the minority-nationality people and they didn't understand the Red Army at all. The people had taken all their things up into the mountains and not even a shadow of a villager could be seen. What were we to do? At that time, our first aim was to keep alive in order to accomplish the revolution. After the birth, I

was very weak and had to be carried on a stretcher. If I had brought along the baby, it would have added considerably to the burden of the soldiers.

So I made the decision and endured the pain of leaving the child behind. When the troops were ready to start, I wrapped the child in a towel and in my own hand wrote the birth date of the child. I explained that he was born when the Red Army was in the area and hoped that he would be cared for. Then I started off with the troops again.

In Jiangxi, the Red Army battled the Nationalist forces. In Hunan, they fought the Nationalists and the Hunan Army.[32] In Guangxi they fought provincial troops. After they left the eastern minority area in Guizhou, however, not only were the battles fewer, but in some places the locals welcomed the Red Army as champions of the poor. Said Xie Fei,

> We were happiest in Guizhou. The courageous Guizhou people didn't run away. They were so poor. Guizhou is famous for a saying:
> "There are no three days of sunshine"—it always rains.
> "There is no one with three cents"—everyone is poor.
> "There is no place with three *li* of flat land"—it's all mountains.

After a battle by the Wu River, the Red Army went to Zunyi, the second largest city in Guizhou, about 100 miles north of Guiyang.

Liao Siguang wrote, "The people of Zunyi packed the streets to welcome and greet the Red Army. The comrades were greatly applauded." Li Jianzhen wrote, "Zunyi people's consciousness is high. / Send the grain. Lead the way. Carry the stretcher. / Forests of guns and cannon fire create heroes."

When the Red Army captured Zunyi, they also captured arms and other badly needed supplies. They quickly established themselves in the city and began setting up a Communist government and replenishing the army.

The political and military leaders lived and worked in the former home of a Nationalist general.[33] They immediately convened a meeting of the Political Bureau, attending to their regular work during the daytime and holding their meetings in the evenings. It was during these meetings that the military strategy, and consequently the political leadership, was dramatically reversed, Mao's policies adopted, and his leadership acknowledged. The official party history describes the Politburo meeting: "Saving the Party and the Red Army at an extremely critical moment, it constituted a turning point on which hinged their survival."[34]

The only woman among those we interviewed who said she knew the content of the meetings at the time was Mao Zedong's sister-in-law. Qian Xijun said she knew that the meetings were taking place and that there was disagreement among the top leaders about military strategy and party policy. She knew about the struggle for power, she said, because many leaders' wives were in her group, including the wives of Mao Zedong, Zhou Enlai, and Bo Gu, and she heard their discussions. "We were all in the convalescent corps together, although He Zizhen wasn't with us each day. When she came back from Chairman Mao's place, she told me everything." Qian Xijun gave her understanding of the military situation: "On the way to Zunyi, there were mistakes. We had a forced march every day. There were many people who were lost. Many were ill, and many didn't have enough to eat. When we fought with the enemy, we were always on the defensive, never on the offensive. When the enemy came, we fended them off. We didn't fight when we should have, and we fought when we shouldn't have. Our casualties were great."

Qian explained that before the conference convened, Mao Zedong worked to convince the others to abandon the costly tactics of positional warfare that Bo Gu and Li De (Otto Braun, the Comintern representative) had been using since the Fifth Encirclement of the Central Soviet Base Area. Mao successfully advocated reverting to the guerrilla warfare strategy that had worked so well for the Communists in Hunan, Jiangxi, and Fujian before the Party Center moved to Ruijin and thus strengthened his own leadership position.[35]

Kang Keqing was assigned to share her husband's quarters, where the Politburo meetings were held. In the reorganization decided upon during the meetings, Zhu De retained command of the military forces. However, Kang was not aware of the content of the meetings, including matters directly affecting her husband. "I didn't know anything about the decisions that had been made at that time. They held the meeting in our rooms, but I was out collecting grain. I stayed in the house where the conference was held. The other women, like He Zizhen, stayed elsewhere, perhaps a day's walk away. Where we stayed was decided by headquarters—we stayed where we were assigned."

The women's work team lived together while they replenished grain supplies, recruited soldiers, and worked with the civilians to restructure the local government. Xie Xiaomei, the woman who had left her newborn behind in Ruijin, said,

> We "little devils" were together.[36] We had a rest, and at the same time we spread propaganda among the masses. The Red Army needed additional recruits, as well as carriers because the stretcher team was short of hands. We women comrades spread propaganda among the masses. We told them that the Red Army had come and that in the Red Army were the troops of the poor and that a provisional people's government had been set up. We told them that the Red Army needed people to carry stretchers, and other things. We told them that they could return home when they reached a certain place and that we would pay them. We also told them what we could do to help their families if leaving their home would cause some problems.

Woodcut of a mass meeting in Zunyi, created by the artist from memory. (Courtesy of Renmin Chubanshe [People's Publishing House], Beijing)

Some of the educated women stayed in a girls' school near the political and military leaders. The Political Department set up working quarters in a Catholic church across from the school. The women worked with documents which had been neglected during the Army's flight from Ruijin, assisted by some of the progressive women students in Zunyi.

Wang Quanyuan also worked with them:

> The students came to participate in the work. Then Li Jianzhen, Liu Ying, Wang Shaodao, Cai Chang and I were transferred to work at the civilian level. We held mass meetings in four villages. I hadn't had any education at that time, but they had all been educated. Comrade Cai Chang encouraged me: "I've had [formal] education and you've had revolutionary theory. Don't be afraid."
>
> When we held the meetings in the four villages, we gave the peasants all the things which had been confiscated [from the landlords]. The peasants enthusiastically joined the army. Why did people come to join the Red Army? Because [Guizhou] was such a poor place. We got over five hundred new soldiers.

The short time in Zunyi was a time for work, but it also gave husbands and wives a chance to be together and was the occasion for at least one marriage. The requirement for marriage on the Long March was that the couple report their intentions to the party secretary because there was no time to prepare documents and no way to keep records. In many cases, the couple had been introduced by men or women they worked with, who acted as matchmakers.

Wei Xiuying told about a budding romance between a commander in the Ninth Army Group and one of the women. Her story is remarkable for several reasons. It shows that what constituted marriage to her, at least while the army was on the Long March, was sexual union. Her account also made clear her own agenda, which was to paint the Red Army in pure and glowing colors, in this case stressing the lack of sexual misconduct. "No one got married on the Long March," she said. "There was none of that." Wei Xiuying continued,

> A Commander in the Ninth Army Group took a fancy to Liu Caixiang. When they were in the bivouac area, he took a horse [and they went] away. Li Jianzhen told me, "Xiuying, you go get her and bring her back."
>
> I asked where Liu Caixiang was. "She's at the Ninth Army Group."
>
> When Li Jianzhen gave orders to others, it wasn't as easy as when she gave me orders. I would obey. When she called me, I was very tired. We'd been walking so many *li* each day, and then she asked me to walk some more to get Liu Caixiang back. But I went. When I saw her, they were just sitting on the ground, talking.
>
> I saluted and said, "Commander, Li Jianzhen has ordered Liu Caixiang to return to her own troops."
>
> He said, "All right, Xiuying, she will go."
>
> I said, "All right or not, you have no choice. You've violated military discipline." He just laughed and started off with us.
>
> I said, "If you try to escort us, you'll be caught, too." So he laughed and went back.
>
> I said, "Under these conditions, how can you, a Commander, possibly fall in love? How can you hurt us women? What will you do if she gets pregnant? Leave her behind?"
>
> How could they get married? They were free to fall in love, but they couldn't get married. Marriage was harmful to women. Women would be destroyed, given to the enemy and killed. What do you think: is it good to get married? Our First Front Army of the Chinese Workers Peasants Red Army had only 30 women out of 80,000. Liu Caixiang was among the 30, and she violated the Army discipline. You can fall in love, but you can't get married.

Li Jianzhen wrote,

> Fluttering red flag, five foot rifle.
> The sun hasn't risen, we've already gotten up.
> Sisters of the revolution:
> Don't love boys, love guns!

Perhaps there was a problem concerning marriage between Liu Caixiang and the commander that Wei Xiuying was unaware of or unwilling to speak about, for there was at least one officially sanctioned marriage in Zunyi. Reflecting a common feeling that leaving behind a spouse from an arranged marriage effectively ended that marital relationship for a Red Army soldier, several of the highest-ranking women urged Wang Quanyuan to marry a second time. Wang Quanyuan was considered to be among the prettiest of the women. The man who wanted to marry her, Wang Shaodao, who was head of the political department of the Ninth Army Corps, happened to have the same surname as her first husband. Wang Quanyuan said,

> I married him in Zunyifu. Comrade Cai Chang, Comrade Li Jianzhen, Comrade Ah Jin [Jin Weiying]—these three comrades introduced me to him for marriage. I had known him earlier when he was Xianggan Provincial Committee Secretary, but not very well.
>
> We were together only three times: once when we got married, once when we crossed the Dadu River, and once when we [the 1st and 4th Front Armies] separated at Lianghekou.

When the Army left the Central Soviet Base Area in Jiangxi, they expected to reach the base area on the Hunan-Guizhou border and combine forces with Generals He Long and Xiao Ke. Believing they would soon reach the new base area, the First Front Army brought equipment needed to reestablish the Central Soviet government. However, the Nationalist and Hunan Armies continually blocked their access to the north, preventing the Red Army from consolidating forces.

Both Liu Ying and Li Guiying also described the difficulty of transporting nonmilitary equipment. Liu Ying said,

> One night when we climbed a mountain in Hunan, there was a very heavy rain. The road was muddy, and even if we had been traveling light it would have been difficult. Six people carried a printing press on shoulder poles. How could they walk? One by one, people fell off the mountain and died. We could only cover five *li* in one night. Why did we carry these things which caused so many people to die?
>
> After the Zunyi Conference, Zhang Wentian made a speech at a meeting for cadres.[37] He told us he had criticized the erroneous line. I was very happy when I heard that because then we knew the line we had followed was wrong: the military tactics were wrong, the way we fought wasn't right, trying to move all our things was wrong. Many had died, about 30,000, so we didn't have very many left. The army was reorganized and from then on, Chairman Mao was our commander.

Li Guiying spoke about medical equipment they carried from Jiangxi province until they reached the Guizhou-Yunnan border area:

After the Zunyi conference, the Army was being streamlined. Chairman Mao discovered that eight people were carrying [something] very heavy [that looked] just like a coffin. Chairman Mao asked,

"What's that coffin-like thing you're carrying?" They told him it was an X-ray [machine].

"It's so heavy and there's no electricity where we're going. If you carry such heavy things, the carriers will be tired to death."

So we left it there in the care of a civilian family. It was said that when [our] troops left, the Nationalists got it.

Unable to reach the Second and Sixth Army Groups on the Hunan-Guizhou border, the First Front Army then decided to join forces with the Fourth Front Army in Sichuan after the Zunyi Conference. From mid-January until late April 1935, the First Front Army repeatedly drove north into Sichuan from the Guizhou-Yunnan-Sichuan border area, crossing the Chishui River four times. Rebuffed each time, they suffered great casualties.

The women students who helped the educated Red Army women with paperwork in Zunyi were anxious to be among those recruited into the First Front Army, but the leaders had decided not to induct any more women. The army especially did not want to recruit young women intellectuals who were not physically fit. Li Guiying said,

Originally, there were eight school girls from Zunyi who insisted on joining the Red Army. Cai Chang Dajie, who was doing women's work at that time, persuaded them not to join but to stay and work with civilians. [She told them],

"You won't be able to stand the hardships. It would be better for you to do civilian work."

They followed from Zunyi to Tongzi county [about 50 kilometers north of Zunyi]. They followed us on the first crossing of the Chishui River, and we let them stay with our guerrillas. But they couldn't keep up with us. They'd never had this kind of experience. After half a month, they collapsed and we couldn't find them. They were stragglers!

One of the students was so desperate to stay with the army that she followed the troops, even though she had been told she would not be able to join the army. However, the pace became too much for her. When she became ill with dysentery, she had to drop out and do underground work in Sichuan and Guizhou.[38]

It was during these months of fierce fighting that Li Guiying's and Xie Xiaomei's husbands were seriously wounded, and they were transferred from the army to work locally.[39]

It was also during the months immediately after the Zunyi Conference, while the troops were unsuccessfully trying to batter their way into Sichuan, that Mao's wife, He Zizhen, gave birth. This second Long March baby was born "somewhere around Tucheng," Li Jianzhen said. Tucheng was a pivotal town northwest of Zunyi on the Chishui River.

Zhong Yuelin, the youngest woman with the First Front Army, remembered the night He Zizhen's baby was born:

> It was in a hut, in the mountains. I don't remember if the house had a thatched roof or a tiled roof. I was assisting, but I didn't understand what was going on. I'd never had a baby! I just helped her a little. Once in a while I brought some water. The birth was quite easy. She had already had several babies and it went pretty fast. She had a girl.
>
> Qian Xijun carried [the baby] that night and found a local family. Qian Xijun should know more about this because they were married to brothers.

Qian Xijun said that when the Long March began, no one knew that He Zizhen was pregnant; she continued,

> Her baby was born in a remote area in Guizhou, in the mountains. When we got to the bivouac area, it was already six o'clock in the evening, almost dark. Her stomach starting hurting, and the baby was coming. The birth took a couple of hours. The baby, a girl, was born at about eight or nine o'clock. Li Zhi, a male doctor and a very responsible person, delivered the baby.
>
> Before we left Ruijin, there had been an order from the organization: no one could bring their babies and babies born on the road couldn't be carried along. Chairman Mao and He Zizhen had a child called Xiao Mao. He was three years old then, born in the spring of 1932. They couldn't bring him along. The reason we couldn't bring babies was that if the baby cried, the enemy might hear it and the target would be revealed. Xiao Mao is not in Ruijin any more. We never found him.
>
> We had to start off again at five the next morning, before it got light. It was in winter. We couldn't bring the [new] baby with us, but we couldn't just leave her there, because He Zizhen would be heartbroken. We had to find someone to take care of her. Chairman Mao's bodyguard and I went into the mountains to find the civilians. We looked and looked but there were very few around. Some had run away, some wouldn't open their doors. Then [we found] an old, blind lady, fifty or sixty years old. We knocked on the door and went in. I said to her,
>
> "Lao Dajie, we have a newborn baby but we have to leave to fight. We can't bring the baby with us. We'd like you to have the baby." There, in the minority area, they needed laborers. I said,
>
> "We'll give her to you. You can raise her as your daughter."
>
> She said, "I'm too old [to nurse her]."
>
> "Never mind. You can find some rice porridge for her to eat. She will be your daughter and can help you work."

She agreed, because there was no alternative. "There's no one else around and you're going off to fight. Just leave her here."

Because she was very poor, we left her ten silver dollars.

After Liberation, nobody knew if she were still alive. Nobody looked for her. Chairman Mao already had Jiang Qing, and she didn't want this child of Chairman Mao's.[40] That's how it was. She hasn't been found up until now. Chairman Mao had several children who have never been found. One in Jiangxi, another in Guizhou.

Within a month after giving birth and leaving her baby with the blind woman, He Zizhen was injured. Xie Fei told the story:

> One afternoon, the enemy planes came and started bombing. It was a complete mess. The two of us had been sleeping in the dry grass beside the road. The army was walking on the road. Horses, stretchers, lots of people. Suddenly the enemy planes came. At first the two of us, Chairman Mao's wife and I, were lying down, close to the road. Then she hid herself some distance from us. I wasn't hurt by the bomb at all, but she was wounded in eighteen places all over her back. She was almost dead. The head of the convalescent corps came over to give her emergency treatment. She was a heroine of Jinggangshan and wife of Chairman Mao. They carried her. There was nothing else they could do. The third day, Chairman Mao sent over his own stretcher to carry his wife, He Zizhen. He Zizhen's life was saved.

Injuries, marriage, and babies were not the only events that made these months of maneuvering and fighting in the mountains difficult for the women. Wang Quanyuan discussed what Li Jianzhen called "women's special suffering":

> When women started menstruating, it was miserable. We didn't have any place to dry our pants in the sun. We had to wear the wet ones and let them dry with the heat of our bodies, so it was easy for us to get sick.
>
> When we were in Guizhou, the doctors from the hospital gave us some lectures. They told us that we shouldn't say it's dirty. The women comrades say it's dirty, but the doctors said actually it's very clean. Menstruation comes from the uterus, the most important part of the body, so it is very clean. In those days, we didn't have any sanitary equipment. The doctors said that we would get sick from using a cloth, and that we should use clean paper.

Deng Liujin told a story that may have been apocryphal or may have happened more than once, to different women:

> It was a lot of bother. At that time we didn't have anything to use. Sometimes we had to use leaves from the trees.

In the book, *Nubing Liezhuan,* Wei Xuiying told a story.[41] She said she was behind me when we were crossing a river and saw that the water was bloody. She thought I was injured. She shouted at me,

"Liujin, Liujin, you're wounded, you're wounded!" She kept shouting, "Hurry up, hurry up," and pulled me out of the water to see where I was wounded.

Actually, it was my period, though I didn't realize it had started.

When she was a girl, Li Guiying's daughter had heard her mother describe a similar incident. She later read the story in a magazine article, and thought it must have been about her mother. "It was me," Li Guiying admitted.

Women and [men] soldiers were together crossing a river. When soldiers saw a woman who was menstruating, they thought she was wounded. In the past, when we menstruated, we didn't have any way to wash, we didn't have any paper, so we just tore off a piece of our pant legs. When we were fighting and crossed a river, the blood flowed down our legs. Once when we waded across a river the water was up to our waists—there were so many rivers I can't remember which one—the blood spread in the water. But those young soldiers didn't understand, and they shouted,

"You're wounded! You're wounded!"

I said, "I'm not wounded." I deceived them. I just told them a story. I couldn't explain that it wasn't anything extraordinary.

After Li Guiying and Xie Xiaomei left the First Front Army, the attempt to cross the Chishui River continued into April. Then the Red Army suddenly feinted south in Guizhou, diverting the Nationalist troops and bringing Chiang Kai-shek to Guiyang. Then the First Front Army moved swiftly into Yunnan, stopping briefly in a Muslim village near Kunming,[42] before driving north to cross the Jinsha River into what was then Sikang, now Sichuan.

The women told stories of the crossing of Jinsha and Dadu Rivers and of climbing a glacial mountain, using these now legendary landmarks as chronological and geographic anchors. They may not have had their own actual memories of their own experience on the rivers and mountains of western Sichuan. There are many accounts in the Chinese Long March literature about these feats, which may have become embedded in their own memories. They had crossed so many rivers under difficult conditions, their memories of specific places blurred. They did not necessarily recognize a particular river crossing as a heroic high point of the epic journey until after they reached the Soviet Base Area in Shaanxi and heard the male leaders speaking about what the Long March represented in terms of the soldiers' endurance, bravery, and sacrifice.[43]

Li Jianzhen recited the mountain songs she had written about the places that later became so well known, bringing the women into the stories of crossing the Dadu River on the chain-link bridge at Luding:

> Waters of the Dadu River swift and deep,
> Hand in hand, heart to heart,
> Class brothers tightly united
> Unafraid of 80,000 enemies.

> The red army quickly crossed Luding Qiao:
> Cannon fire everywhere in the sky, iron chains swinging,
> Feet on the iron chains, heart did not race;
> Women soldiers vied to carry the medicine boxes.

The women told us about the arduous terrain, so different from the provinces they previously crossed; they explained that after they crossed the Dadu River, the fighting had decreased and the Nationalist troops were no longer the threat they had been. They remembered eating poisonous mushrooms and recovering and told more stories of dealing with the ubiquitous and egalitarian lice. They spoke of their difficulty in finding food for the wounded in their care, exacerbated by communication problems arising from the different language and customs of local Tibetan people.

Fragmentary and confused as these memories often were, their memories of the day Zeng Yu gave birth to her baby in an empty stone house in Sichuan were quite clear. They particularly remembered their own participation in the event, although they did not always remember which other women were directly involved. They mentioned two things that made it especially difficult for Zeng Yu. First, she did not have the full month of postpartum rest considered essential by Chinese women at the time because she had to begin a strenuous march almost immediately after the baby's birth, with neither a stretcher to lie on nor a horse to ride. Second, she was not able to follow the stricture against bathing during that crucial first month.

Li Jianzhen said, "I not only saw it, but I felt like I had a baby myself! There were three women comrades, two supporting Zeng Yu, one on each side. One put her hand down, under the baby, and pulled it out." Xie Fei said that Zeng Yu had the most difficult time because her baby was born in a minority area, where there was no food available. "Three days after the baby was born, she had to go on. There was no horse for her," Xie said.

* * *

Deng Liujin was climbing a mountain with Zeng Yu when her labor pains began:

We kept looking for a house. Liu Caixia and I were on either side of her, pulling her up the mountain. We reached the top and started down, but her pains were so strong that she couldn't go on. I tried to carry her on my back, but it was impossible, so we half supported her, half pulled her along. She had the baby that night. Just two of us who knew nothing helped her pull the baby out. We used a knife to cut the cord and found some old clothes to wrap up the baby.

There was nothing there, not even food. We picked the leaves of some pea plants. When Cai Chang heard about it, she gave us some flour, and we mixed it with water and made a soup. [Zeng Yu] was bleeding a lot.

We left three days later. What else could we do? We just put the baby on a pile of dried grass in the house. The mother had to leave, too, still bleeding. Maybe the conditions were better for the other three [who had babies on the march] because they were senior leaders' wives.

Qian Xijun described Zeng Yu's ordeal this way:

> Let me tell you!
>
> Zeng Yu's baby was born in the minority area, a miserable place, in a very remote area in Sichuan. We were climbing a mountain, not a very big one. I walked along with her. We walked and walked. When we were almost at the bivouac area, she said,
>
> "Xijun, hurry! Please go ahead and find some toilet paper for me. My stomach hurts. The baby is coming."
>
> When I got to the bivouac area in the minority area, there was nothing to be found in the place we were staying. I couldn't find any toilet paper. I couldn't find anything. I put some dry grass on the floor to make a bed and told Zeng Yu to lie down there. She had the baby that night. There was absolutely nothing to use to wash the baby. I tried to clean it, but actually, there was no way to be clean.
>
> I didn't know what to do. I had a baby, but I didn't raise it. It died just after it was born. I never saw it. I didn't know how it was born, but I'd seen others having babies.
>
> We stayed there for three days. After Zeng Yu had her baby, she was able to rest for three days. When we left, the baby was left behind. There wasn't anyone there [to care for it].
>
> Three days after the baby was born, we crossed a river. The water was so high! A woman comrade did this!

Qian Xijun apparently was struck anew by the conditions that made it impossible for women to follow the traditional safety precautions that required a new mother to avoid getting wet during the first month after childbirth. Zhong Yuelin described crossing the river with Zeng Yu:

Zeng Yu—she had the hardest time. She wasn't in the same house with us. She was with Deng Liujin, but the day we crossed the river we were together. She had just had her baby. We happened to be crossing the river at the same time. The water was up to our waists. When we crossed the river, we held each other's hands. We were afraid of being carried away by the strong current. We used the horses, holding tightly onto their tails. We women together, held each other's hands. No one crossed by herself. I've forgotten the name of the river.

After the First Front Army crossed the Jinsha and the Dadu Rivers, their next ordeal was crossing the Jiajin Mountains in Sichuan. Stories the women told of crossing the snow-covered mountain range may have been individual memory combined with what they later heard or read, but the experience was significant for many of them. Kang Keqing, who was to cross glacier mountains two more times after she was transferred to the Fourth Front Army, described her first encounter with the Jiajin Mountains:

When we got to the snow mountain, we didn't know how high the mountain was, nor what the conditions were. There was no enemy behind us but there was some sporadic gunfire by the local Tibetan minority bandits. Also, people were rolling stones down on us from the top of the mountain. One of the soldiers was hit in the face by a stone and it knocked out all of his teeth. We were also being shot at from behind. I saw a bullet go all the way through a soldier's body.

We didn't make any preparation the first time we climbed the mountain. I didn't have any special shoes. I put on all the clothes I had. When we got to the foot of the mountain, we just climbed it. The front units had already gone and my own unit had already gone, too. My husband was in the front and I was in the rear. Once we started climbing, we couldn't stop because there was no way to go back. I held the tail of the horse in front of me. That's how it was.

It was the natural conditions which made it so hard. When we were climbing, there was rain, snow and hail. We only had umbrellas made of oiled skin.[44] The umbrellas were slowly destroyed by the hailstones hitting them, making one hole after another. When I had climbed to the top, I rolled my padded coat around me and slid down the mountain like a child on a slide. But at that time, I didn't know what a child's slide was! I felt better after I got down further. I wasn't dizzy any more and all the discomfort was gone. It took us one day to get over the mountain.

I didn't realize at the time that we were climbing such a snow mountain until after we climbed over it. It was the first time I had seen so much snow.

Liao Siguang, in her written account, said,

After crossing the Dadu River, we continued to cross many wooden bridges and marched about two or three days. As we looked up, we could only see the

Woodcut of climbing Jia-
jinshan, the snow moun-
tains. (Courtesy of Ren-
min Chubanshe [People's
Publishing House],
Beijing)

silvery-white peak poking into the gray misty sky. It was summer then and we perspired from the heat at the bottom of the mountain. Half-way up the mountain, we were beginning to get cold. We reached the peak at noon-time. We were hit by large wind gusts and after that a hailstorm. When climbing the mountain, we couldn't climb fast and on reaching the top, we couldn't slow down or stop. It was different going down the mountain; we couldn't stop even if we were fatigued.

Some of the women comrades in our convalescent unit, the wounded and sick, just couldn't walk. They hung onto horses' tails to climb the mountain. Deng Dajie at that time was suffering from TB and had difficulty breathing. She just hung on the horse's tail to reach the mountain top. The air at the top was thin and it was planned to descend the mountain quickly. Some comrades just slid down; sliding was much faster than going down step by step and I just slid down behind them. Crossing the snow mountains required a whole day. They could not be crossed at night.

Wang Quanyuan explained that they rested for a time after they crossed the glacier mountain, which gave them a chance to learn: "We had to know the local customs or we couldn't do our work well." They attended a meeting where they were advised to eat lightly of the local grain "because our stomachs couldn't take it."[45]

The Tibetans, she said in explaining local customs, did not use chopsticks when they ate from their bamboo bowls. When they traveled they carried bowls of food in one of their sleeves left empty for the purpose, so they could take the bowl out and eat whenever they were hungry. She also told how she used a mirror to display the difference after she washed the faces of people who did not customarily wash. Wang Quanyuan continued her explanation of Tibetan living conditions:

> [Their houses] had three stories. The ground floor was for horses, oxen, sheep. The second floor was for sleeping and eating. The stairs to the second floor was only a board with some notches on it but the stairs to the third floor were regular stairs. The third floor was for storage. If we were working [in a Tibetan village], we had to sleep with them because we couldn't go back to the troops to sleep. They didn't know how to fix beds. They just put a rug on the floor and everyone, young or old, male or female, slept together. Some families had a ragged blanket, others didn't have any, and just put clothes over themselves. I can say that I became accustomed to all the Tibetan ways. We [the women's working group] lived in villages for over 20 days.

Wang and Wu Fulian went to find food to buy from the civilians each day. "That was the time when we were eating grass and tree bark," she said. On one of their forays they met Zhou Enlai, who was quite upset to find the two, unarmed young women alone, roaming the countryside for provisions.

Premier Zhou really cared about cadres. He took out a piece of paper and wrote a letter to our Political Commissar criticizing him.

"You have sent two people out to work like this! Why don't you send people with them as guards? What are your armed people doing? Are they all protecting you? You will be held responsible if anything should happen to these two comrades."

Our Political Commissar wasn't very happy. He thought we had reported him to Premier Zhou. Actually, we hadn't [made a report]. We just told him the truth when he asked us [why we were alone].

This incident may well have played a part in the series of events that would make Wang Quanyuan's life so different from that of the other women in the First Front Army. When they reached Lianghekou, she and Wu Fulian were again parted from the First Front Army troops, assigned to the group that collected those who had become separated from their own units. It was at Lianghekou, before crossing the grasslands, that Wang Quanyuan and her husband, Wang Shoudao, saw each other for the last time.

* * *

While meetings between the leaders of the First and the Fourth Front Armies continued, the soldiers prepared to cross the grasslands that lay between them and the Sichuan-Gansu border. Qian Xijun remarked on the difference between the two Front Armies when they met in the summer of 1935. The First Front Army had been moving and fighting since November. With badly depleted forces, worn out from forced night marches, they were a sorry sight. They were thin from having inadequate provisions for too long, and their clothes were in tatters. The Fourth Front Army, four and one half times larger than the First, had left their Soviet Base Area in Sichuan in late March. The soldiers in the Fourth were strong, in good health, and their morale was high.[46] However, the women in the First Front Army thought the Fourth lacked the discipline of the First. Deng Liujin said, "There were all kinds of people in the 4th Route Army—women with golden lilies, kids." Li Jianzhen wrote,

> Ten thousand *li* Long March.
> Crossing the grassland,
> Iron feet flatten the mud lands.
> Conquered in seven days and seven nights:
> Red flags climb straight up Liu Pan Mountain.

Getting across the grasslands was the last major environmental ordeal for the weakened First Front Army. In Xie Fei's view,

The unchanged wet grasslands, the final challenge for soldiers on the Long March. (Courtesy of Waiwen Chubanshe [Foreign Languages Press], Beijing)

That damn place was really strange! Just grass, no trees. It wasn't mountainous, just flat land. It rained every day and the sun came out every day. The ground was all wet. At first, the vanguard troops sank into the bog. If you tried to pull them out, you would sink, too. They couldn't climb out and they couldn't be rescued, either. You could only watch them die. Once we learned this lesson, we let the animals walk first. If the animal sank, then people wouldn't die. What a weird place!

Li Jianzhen's description typically was focused on the logistics of crossing rather than the feeling the place evoked:

Each of us brought our own food. We all carried at least fifteen *jin* of grain. In the 1st Army, we were prepared for it. Before we crossed the grassland, we bought or collected grain, roasted and ground it. Some of the grain wasn't ground, and we just ate it as it was. The hardest time was when there wasn't any water. We couldn't drink the water on the grassland, so we had to carry water. Some people used buckets, some used gourds, some had canteens. Today, every soldier has a canteen, but then it was impossible for us to each have one.

Many men were lost in the swamps or died from infection, malnutrition, or exhaustion. Deng Liujin explained, "Some of the people who died during the Long March died from the fighting, but most died from lack of medicine, lack of food, and the terrible hardships." The women came through the ordeal unhurt, perhaps from privilege, perhaps from carefully following instructions. Having access to information about the terrain ahead of them often meant the difference between death or survival for them on the Long March. As Deng Liujin said, "We had been told how to cross the grassland, and we were very lucky." The women also knew the value of mutual aid, as Qian·Xijun emphasized:

> After we crossed the snow mountains there was a short rest before we crossed the grassland. We had ideological preparation. We needed to prepare some things because there were no houses on the grassland and everyone's clothes were too thin. The Organization [Department] instructed us to use every possible means to make some clothes, and get some rations. He Zizhen found a piece of sheepskin with the wool still on it. She took several pieces of red cotton [that were] around the Mausers belonging to Chairman Mao's bodyguards, found some more cotton, and with the piece of sheepskin, she made a padded vest for Zhong Yuelin who was the little sister, the youngest in our Army.

> The most help I got [Zhong Yuelin said] was from He Zizhen and Qian Xijun. We helped each other however we could. Qian Xijun helped with the simple everyday things. She had a lot of trouble, herself. Her feet weren't big, but they weren't bound. She's ten years older than I am. He Zizhen could get some good things to eat from the Chairman, like yak butter and beef jerky. The Chairman got special treatment. When the army got some cattle, he would get some beef. She would try to get some from him and we would all share it.

> It was going to be very cold crossing the grassland, and she [told me], "You can't cross the grassland in the clothes you are wearing." She got some pieces of silk that had been used to wrap around the guns. I remember that it was rose red and a little bit gray. I don't know who she asked to help her, but she [also] made me a wool vest.

> She had Chairman Mao's stretcher because she had been wounded. Marching during the day, He Zizhen wasn't on the stretcher. She walked with a stick. At night we propped up the tarpaulin from the stretcher to keep the rain off. All of us—Qian Xijun, Xiao Yuehua (I don't remember if A Xiang [Xie Fei] was there or not)—slept under that shelter.

> And we used the basin we carried with us. That basin was so useful! A treasure! We used it for carrying food, cooking food, boiling water, washing feet and it could also be a stool. There was no where to sit down in the grassland, so we just turned over the basin and sat on it.

Deng Liujin also remembered the worth of the basins, as well as the care and kindness He Zizhen showed to the younger women:

> We women comrades were very careful when we crossed the grasslands. We went very slowly, little by little each day because it was such hard going. Some of the grass was tall, some short. It rained a lot and there was no shelter for us to rest in. Sometimes we would find something to burn and would make a fire to keep warm. At night we just sat on our basins to keep dry. Several of us would sit together. Some of the leaders, like He Zizhen, the Chairman's wife, were concerned about us. She would give us some food—flour or beef jerky. Sometimes she would spend some time with us, sitting on the basin with us, chatting. She empathized with our hardships. At that time most of us wore pants without any legs. Short pants was all we had. Our legs were in bad condition—rotten, full of cuts, wounds, bleeding.

Liu Ying said, "When we were crossing the grasslands, everyone talked about how terrible it was. When I went back to see it, I didn't know how we had done it. It was horrible! It was so big. We didn't see any people, or any houses. Day after day we walked. It took us seven days to cross."

When they reached the other side of the grasslands, differences between the leaders of the First and Fourth Front Armies came to a climax. The question that had been discussed as the First and Fourth traveled north through Sichuan was the ultimate direction the two Red Armies should take: whether to return south to Sikang and establish a new Soviet Base Area there, as Zhang Guotao from the Fourth advocated, or continue north to establish a new base from which to fight the Japanese troops, then firmly entrenched in Manchuria in the northeast, Mao Zedong's position. Zhang Guotao was one of the founding members of the Communist party and the political commissar of the Fourth Front Army. He neither acknowledged the decisions made at the Zunyi Conference as valid nor accepted Mao Zedong's new authority. After the Long March was over, he joined the Nationalists and later emigrated to Canada. Qian Xijun's explanation of the disagreement between the leaders, Mao Zedong and Zhang Guotao, is a combination of what she knew at the time and what she learned later:

> Zhang Guotao didn't want to go north. He wanted to go south, but the Central [Committee] and Chairman Mao had already made the decision to go north. At the end, [Zhang Guotao] ostensibly agreed with Chairman Mao and the Central leaders, but when we were in the bivouac area in the evening, he sent a telegram, saying that he was going to go south. Ye Jianying, the Chief of Staff, received the telegram and immediately reported to Chairman Mao. Chairman Mao discussed it with a few people. If he [Zhang Guotao] wanted to go

south, he would go south because we couldn't force him. He had never said that he wanted to be under the leadership of our Central leaders. What could we do? If we forced him, we would be fighting against ourselves.

Originally, we had decided to start out at seven o'clock the next morning, and then we were told that we would start off at 3:00 A.M. Everyone wondered why. Some said that it was because Ma Bufang's cavalry was coming, that the enemy was catching up to us.[47] When we got to the bivouac area, I told He Zizhen to go to Chairman Mao and ask him what was at the bottom of this. The answer was that the 4th Front Army had separated from us.

The next day, we were informed by someone in the political bureau that the reason we started out at three o'clock was that we were separating from Zhang Guotao, that Zhang Guotao was going south and we were going north.

Zhu De joined the Fourth Front Army, partly to do ideological work [on Zhang Guotao] and partly to keep an eye on him. When we separated, Zhu De couldn't get away because he was with Zhang Guotao at headquarters. Now that we were separated, he couldn't come back. Both Kang Keqing and Yang Shangkun's old companion [his wife, Li Bozhao] went to the 4th Front Army.

The First Front Army, accustomed to the discipline of leaving quickly and marching fast, left the Fourth Front Army behind. When they crossed the Minshan Mountains in Gansu province and occupied Hadapu, the Han Chinese soldiers had a sense of homecoming, of returning to a familiar civilization after three or four months in the Tibetan areas. Li Jianzhen recalled it as one of the happiest times on the Long March, a time when they could eat familiar food and discard their tattered clothes. "[When we reached Hadapu] I looked like a male comrade. My hair was very short and I wore a military hat. I wore a pair of shoes made of leather. The sole was sheepskin with the wool on the inside. The uppers were made of leather and tied onto the sole with a piece of rope. I couldn't have gone on without them, but in Hadapu we got shoes made of cloth and the civilians made clothes for us."

It was in Hadapu that the leaders of the Central Army held a meeting and formally announced the decision "to make northern Shaanxi the headquarters for leading the Chinese revolution."[48] They knew there were other elements of the Red Army already based in northern Shaanxi and were determined to fight their way out of Gansu and across Ningxia to join them in Shaanxi and establish a new Soviet Base Area.

Just as the women soldiers had no perception of a grand beginning when they left western Jiangxi in October 1934, they also had no feeling of a triumphant ending when they arrived in northern Shaanxi. Their work of provisioning the army and recruiting new soldiers continued, although they did have a greater sense of security than they had on the Long March. Liu Ying described the difference:

[On the Long March] when we arrived in a resting place, we didn't even want to eat. We just wanted to sleep. The minute we lay down we were asleep. And we were always on edge. As soon as we heard the bugle, we jumped up immediately, folded up the quilt and went. If you were late, you'd be left behind and would get lost and be captured by the enemy. After we walked for a year, we really wanted to find a house where we could sleep for a day or two. When we got to Shaanbei [northern Shaanxi province], we could sleep. We were completely worn out.

* * *

Zhong Yuelin was married when the March was over. Emphasizing the immediacy of the mammoth task of creating a self-sufficient base area in one of the poorer areas of China, she said, "One day I got married. The next day I went to the countryside to recruit for the Red Army."

8. Left Behind

THREE OF OUR First Front Army women did not complete the Long March. Li Guiying and Xie Xiaomei, whose husbands were wounded in fierce fighting after the Zunyi conference, were left behind with their husbands to work in the civilian sector. Li Guiying and her husband were sent into southern Sichuan to join the guerrilla troops. Xie Xiaomei and Luo Ming were assigned to work underground in Guiyang, capital of Guizhou province. The third, Wang Quanyuan, stayed with the First Front Army until they met the Fourth Front Army in western Sichuan several months later. Wang became ill, was sent to a hospital unit in the Fourth, and stayed with the Fourth when the First Front Army pulled out. The accidents of life that led them away from the First Front Army had serious consequences for these three women.

Their stories demonstrate the basis of the fear all of the soldiers, men and women, had of being left behind. After they left the First Front Army, they were all captured, jailed, and physically abused for various amounts of time. Escape was made exceedingly difficult by the prevailing attitude toward mobility: Ordinary people, especially women, who could not show a valid reason for traveling were suspect in the China of those years. All three were captured outside their native provinces, where the provincial spoken language unintelligible to them and a hostile attitude to outlanders was common.

Li Guiying's husband was wounded in battle after the Zunyi Conference. In February 1935, to prepare those ordered to stay behind, Zhou Enlai held a meeting in which he reported on the decisions made in Zunyi that led to their reassignment. "The military situation was tight," Li Guiying said they were told, "and the safety of the Red Army had to be assured." To make the army a more efficient fighting unit, the leaders decided to transfer the wounded to local units. In Li Guiying's case the transfer was to the Red guerrilla units fighting in the Sichuan-Guizhou-Yunnan border area. She, her wounded husband, and a woman comrade, Gan Shiying, were given the task of creating a larger, united, organized communist guerrilla unit strong enough to divert the Nationalist troops from the First Front Army as it continued to the west. Li Guiying, reflecting the common feeling among the women, said, "I didn't want to stay [behind], but my husband was also staying. He was the head of the Organization Department. We had to adapt to the needs of the situation. It would have been better for all the Dajie to be together, but Gan Shiying and I stayed."

Gan Shiying's father was a landlord with a large holding in Sichuan and apparently quite feudalistic. However, she had managed to attend university in Shanghai before going to the Communist Base Area in Jiangxi province. She was party secretary of the Central Women's Department during the first part of the Long March, Li Guiying said. Li was not sure why Gan Shiying had been sent to join the guerrilla forces because she was unmarried and therefore not assigned to accompany a wounded husband. Perhaps, Li said, it was because Gan was a Sichuan native: She spoke the Sichuan dialect and had contacts. And perhaps it was because her feet had been bound and then let out, leaving her somewhat crippled.

About 200 male soldiers remained behind with them, about half of whom were wounded. They were able to recruit an additional 800 or 900 men and women, bringing the guerrilla forces initially to about one thousand. Li continued,

> The Nationalists wanted to pursue and attack [the First Front Army] but they couldn't catch up with our troops. Now they would have to deal with our guerrillas. The guerrillas fought fiercely for more than two years, running over one hundred *li* each day. It was even harder than the Long March.
>
> My husband was killed in battle in February, 1935. With my own eyes I saw him fall down, hit by bullets. I tried to grab his leather bag and his gun, but a Red Army soldier dragged me away. Otherwise I would have died, too, or been captured. Because of the leather bag, the enemy knew he was a leading cadre. They cut off his head and displayed it in public.
>
> The more we fought, the bigger the battles. There was a squadron which fought for three years in the mountains at the Sichuan-Yunnan-Guizhou border. They got a lot of recruits very quickly. They got defeated quickly, too! Most of the ordinary people smoked opium. I'm just telling you what I experienced. Sometimes we fought three or four times a day. We ran and fought. We would run more than one hundred or two hundred *li*. You couldn't keep your eyes open. Gradually the army was worn down. The Nationalists had several million people and we only had several thousand.

After Li Guiying's husband had been killed, a political commissar with the guerrillas asked the party organization to introduce him to Li and to give them permission to marry. His first wife had been killed many years before. When Li became pregnant and came close to term, her husband sent her to his family home in Sichuan to have the baby. Gan Shiying accompanied her.

It was during the very hot season when I went to Yu Zehong's home to have the baby. The baby was about to be born, so I couldn't walk fast. It was awful being pregnant. I had to urinate so often!

The fighting was very intense. At that time the Nationalists were trying to catch women Red Army soldiers, but they couldn't catch any. The District Committee Secretary brought us to a family who were tenants of [my husband's] family. His family was a landlord family. The tenants had only one bed. They gave the bed to Gan Shiying and me. They waited for me to have the baby. Waited and waited. The couple and their child slept on the straw in the cowshed.

When the enemy came, [the tenants] were afraid. . . . The enemy came and searched and searched. They looked everywhere in the shack and in the cowshed. They couldn't find anyone. They said,

"Are you hiding anyone from the Red Army? Why has someone been sleeping upstairs?" We had slept upstairs in the thatched shack.

"I have a lot of children. Three children, my wife and I. The children sleep here."

We were below in a cellar which was used to store sweet potatoes. The enemy was searching. They upset the urine bucket. Drip, drip, drip on our heads.

They might shoot at any time and we would die right here. We had made up our minds.

There was a sudden silence. We were prepared. . . . It was intense. . . . But in the end, the enemy fired two shots and left. After the enemy left, the old lady came and said,

"You Red Army women soldiers! You live a charmed life!"

This was in Sichuan, [near] Yunnan. Later when this event was investigated, they even went to see the cellar where we hid.

The masses had a lot of ways to protect us. Several times when we were in dangerous situations the enemy didn't catch us. When we were with the guerrillas and the enemy came after us during the daytime, there was no place to hide. We went to a peasant's home. No place to hide there, either. They told us to climb into the stack of sheaves of drying rice and then they toppled it. The enemy searched and searched and when they couldn't find us, they left. [The peasants] were afraid, too, but they protected us. If we didn't get wounded, we wouldn't get captured.

While Li Guiying and Gan Shiying were waiting for the baby to be born, Li's husband was killed. Leaving her newborn baby with her husband's family, she and Gan Shiying returned to the army. They found the guerrilla forces in collapse, with only about thirty people left. "Some had died, some were captured, some returned home," Li explained.

> I was still headquarters political instructor and [Gan Shiying] was the Party Secretary. We recruited three or four hundred people. The enemy thought they had wiped us out. How could several hundred appear again to fight back? So the enemy started to encircle us again. That was the third encirclement.
>
> I was wounded. I had stepped on some bamboo and a piece went through my foot—I was wearing straw shoes. I walked over 130 *li* before I could wash my foot. My foot swelled up and I couldn't walk fast. [When we stopped] I told everybody to wash their feet—use some salt and boiled water and soak their feet—and after dinner we would start off again. It was foggy and we couldn't see clearly. Gan Shiying and I were washing our feet. The others had finished. My feet were still in the basin.
>
> Gunfire! Our [local] guide had run away. He met the Nationalist forces and led them to our headquarters and our political committee. When the fighting started around us, I didn't have time to put my straw shoes on, and I didn't wrap my feet. Usually we wrapped our feet with a piece of cloth and then put on a pair of straw shoes, but I didn't have time. It was raining. Barefoot. So slippery. I ran out of bullets. A squad encircled me with bayonets.
>
> That was how I was captured. Gan Shiying was taken at the same time. They took us under escort to Zhaotong [in Yunnan province]. I just limped along. At first, they treated us badly. Later there was food. They interrogated us twice. Most of the time Gan Shiying argued with them because she was a student and she has broad knowledge. They just asked me where I was from, why I had joined the Red Army, and what I did in the Red Army. I told them that I was a propagandist. They said,
>
> "You're illiterate. How could you do propaganda?"
>
> "I carried the lime bucket for people to use to write slogans."

Thus, Li Guiying was able to avoid telling her interrogators about the responsible position she held, although she was beaten during the interrogations.

In December 1936, while Li Guiying and Gan Shiying were being held in the Nationalist prison in Zhaotong, Chiang Kai-shek was captured in Xi'an by warlord troops who held him until the Nationalists agreed to suspend fighting the Communists. The two parties formed a United Front against the Japanese who, by that time, were firmly entrenched in northeast China.

> Fireworks went off in the streets, just like the Spring Festival at Lunar New Year. Gan Shiying and I were really suspicious [because] it wasn't Spring Festival or any other festival. Later we learned that Chiang Kai-shek had been released and [the Nationalists] were talking about national cooperation. We didn't understand.

They propagandized about the national cooperation, [saying that] Communists wouldn't fight against the Nationalists, and the Nationalists wouldn't fight against Communists, either. We would unite and fight the Japs. [They said they] wouldn't kill us or torture us, but would send us back to where we had come from, but that was only talk. Gan Shiying was sent back to her province, Sichuan [because] her father was well-known, and rich. She was bailed out, but I wasn't.[1] I was to be sent back to Jiangxi but they locked me up again. They wouldn't let me out. I didn't know why.

The United Front had a condition that all political prisoners were to be taken to Chongqing and imprisoned there. I walked all the way under escort to Chongqing. The Nationalists and Chiang Kai-shek hadn't come there yet. There was no interrogation in Chongqing.

I was taken to Baxian, to a single-story house [*pingfang*].[2] The prison guard was a very short old woman. Some of the prisoners were from the local area. Their husbands often came to see them and some of their relatives brought them food. They would give some money or other things [to the old woman] and she would let them visit. I had no relatives or friends. Nobody came to see me.

There were about two hundred prisoners, about seven or eight in my room. Four were from the Army. The others weren't political prisoners. The Nationalists could say anything. . . . Some were opium sellers, some were arsonists, some were wives who had been caught because they had run away. They were all poor. Some were people who had infiltrated the government.

The enemy didn't torture us. Over one hundred students and representatives struggled. They wrote me a note, but I couldn't read it. There was an old man, over fifty, who asked me to join in a fast. I asked what a fast was. [He said] you don't eat, only drink water. We'll fast until they set us free. I told them I would join in. We political prisoners refused to eat for eight days. We turned over the tables, threw the benches out of the way, threw the bowls into the latrine. It was reported in the press. The Communist underground struggled inside and outside to get the political prisoners released. The Center negotiated and they set us free, group by group. The first group were civilians. The second group was from the Fourth Army. I was among the thirty-odd in the third group.

After I was released from the prison in September 1937, the Chongqing Communist Party underground found me. I didn't know any of the Party members. I was frightened. [I had been in prison] nine months. They had beaten me in prison.

A male comrade asked me what I was going to do. I told him I would go back home, go straight home. There was nothing else I could do. I had no money, no place to live, no food to eat. If I go home to Jiangxi, I can find the guerrillas, find the Red Army. We all know each other.

He asked me, "Can you teach?"

"I can't read or write. I don't know how to teach."

Then he helped me. He said, "Go to the New China bookstore tomorrow.

Go to the restaurant several doors away and help the woman who runs it. Help her chop food, wash dishes, sweep floors. I'll send someone to see you there."

Three or four days later, someone from the party came to the restaurant to see Li Guiying and verify her story.

He said, "You came from Jiangxi. You had a physical check-up."
I said, "Yes, I did."
He said, "Don't you recognize me? I am the doctor who gave you your examination. You were very healthy."
I thought it was really strange. An army doctor? Was he a traitor? No, he wasn't. He sent me to Luo Suwen [head of the Sichuan Communist party in Chengdu]. The doctor gave me travel money, bought me busfare—there was no train, just a bus. It took me two days by bus to Chengdu. No one took me, I went by myself. Luo Suwen met me. We had originally planned to go to Yan'an, but we couldn't go. Tai Yuan had been occupied by the Japanese devils and we couldn't get through, so we had to go back to Chongqing.

Li Guiying took the long bus ride back to Chongqing, where she met Luo Suwen's wife, who helped her make travel arrangements. The party leadership had decided to send her by train to Wuhan to find Dong Biwu, the man who had been in charge of the women soldiers in the First Front Army during the Long March. Because Li Guiying had never been to Wuhan and could not read or write, she found a child to help her as soon as she got off the train.

I had an address rolled up in my pantleg. I took it out and asked my little friend if he/she knew this place.
"Yes, I know it. It's not far away. I'll take you there."
That child brought me to Dong Lao's home. It was early in the morning, before Dong Lao had gotten up. His rickshaw puller opened the door. He didn't have a private car: his car was the rickshaw. When Dong Lao got up he said,
"That Little Devil is still alive!"

Li Guiying met Li Jianzhen, Wei Xiuying, and other First Front Army comrades in Wuhan. From them Li learned the details of the ending of the Long March and their subsequent work in Yan'an. They advised her not to try to get to Yan'an but to go to Nanchang in Jiangxi, where the New Fourth Army was in process of being established by many of her old comrades.

They celebrated the New Year at a dinner given by Zhou Enlai for cadres from the New Fourth Army who had come from Yan'an. Li Guiying was delighted to see many old comrades, people she had never thought she would see again. "We all talked quite freely. They welcomed me, even though they knew that I had just come out of prison."

In 1938 Li joined the New Fourth Army as head of the women's division in the New Fourth Army's front line service regiment and held other responsible positions as political director and party secretary of various military organizations. In January 1941, she was with the New Fourth Army in southern Anhui province when the Nationalists, erstwhile allies under the United Front, surrounded some of the New Fourth troops and wiped them out in the Wan Nan Incident (*Wannan Shibian*). She was the only one of three women comrades in Wannan who broke out.

> For eight days and nights, nothing to eat. The enemy encircled us everywhere. There were some people who had nowhere to live, no food to eat, nowhere to run, not enough strength to break the encirclement. I was working with the civilians, trying to help them break the encirclement. Later [after they broke out] we found a peasant who was a cadre in the Farmer's Alliance. He had a pig, [weighing] about 30 *jin*. He was afraid the Nationalists would snatch it away and eat it so he killed it and buried it in the ground. He also had several dozen *jin* of rice which was also buried in the ground. When we made it clear that we were in the New 4th Army, he brought out the pig and the rice. He cooked a big pot of rice and the 30+ *jin* pig and some vegetables. His family and eight or nine of us finished it in one sitting! I ate five bowls of rice. My husband ate eight bowls of rice. We ate too much and that wasn't good. Before that we had just had cold water and horse urine.

During the war of liberation, Li Guiying was director of the political department of the health department of east China military district. After 1949 she held responsible positions in various departments of military districts in east China. Her third husband died in 1968.

"I've had an unfortunate life—three husbands. I had children with each husband. Some died, or I couldn't keep them and then couldn't find them." She became diabetic but was denied medicine and medical care during the Cultural Revolution, when she was under investigation as a former prisoner of the Nationalists. She retired in 1981. When we interviewed her in Nanjing in February 1989, she was living in a home for retired veterans and had been blind for five years.

*   *   *

Xie Xiaomei, who recounted her life in a flat, matter-of-fact voice, told a continuing story of misfortune and missed opportunities. In 1933, the year before they left on the Long March, her husband, Luo Ming, wrote a report on successful guerrilla operations in Fujian. The party leaders who disagreed with Mao Zedong's guerrilla warfare tactics used this report in a campaign against the Luo Ming Line to attack Mao and his policies. At the beginning of the Long March, Luo Ming had been relegated to the job of collecting the wounded and stragglers in the Rear Service Department. After being reinstated as a result of the shift in leadership at the Zunyi Conference, Luo Ming was attached to the Third Army Group, in charge of liaison with civilians.

Xie Xiaomei, who had herself fought with the guerrillas in Fujian, described fighting in the Guizhou-Yunnan-Sichuan border area:

> We crossed the Chishui River a second time and reached Maotai.[3] We drank Maotai and washed our feet with Maotai. Then we launched a second attack on Loushan Pass. The first attack was after we had taken Zunyi. It was much easier then, because the enemy in Zunyi had already been defeated and we weren't stopped until we took Tongzi [north of Loushan Pass]. The second time we went back to attack Zunyi, the enemy there was very tough.
>
> When we were attacking Lo Shan Pass, the 3rd Army Group was the vanguard. The fighting was hard and fierce so it was important for morale to be high. All the cadres in the department for civilian work went to the headquarters to do propaganda work, raising the morale of the soldiers and writing slogans. At that time a few people in the department knew where the slogans were and were in charge of covering up anything that the bombers might spot as a target. The slogans were written in red and green, easy for the bombers to find. The Nationalist planes came and bombed us. Luo Ming and Hu Yaobang were hit before they could take cover.[4] Hu Yaobang was injured in the leg, and Luo Ming in an artery [in his arm]. Hu Yaobang's injury wasn't serious, so after he had received emergency treatment, he went back to the troops. Luo Ming was seriously wounded and had lost a lot of blood. He was sent to the Convalescent Corps for further treatment and did not return to the 3rd Army Group.
>
> The Central Committee decided that my husband and I should stay behind because Luo Ming was too seriously injured to march. They wanted us to stay behind and work with the peasants in Guiyang. The Central Committee had also ordered two others to stay behind with us. We were told just one day in advance.
>
> From the beginning, we thought that there would be a lot of difficulties if we stayed behind. Our troops had recently passed by [Guiyang]. We spoke different dialects and we looked different from the people in Guizhou. But the Central Committee told us that this was an important job and that the Party needed us to do it. So we accepted because we were Party members. We had to do it at any cost, even if we were faced with a lot of difficulties. It was April 1935 when we left the army.
>
> A small unit of armed soldiers were sent to march with us for one day, then they told us to head toward Guiyang. They said, "You four people are to walk to Guiyang." The four people were my husband and me, Zhu Qi the Trade Union organizer, and an old man from Sichuan who was our guide. The armed soldiers stayed in the mountain area while we continued the journey.
>
> We walked a whole day and got to what is now Guanlin, a county town. It

was about five in the afternoon when we got to the town gate. It happened that warlord troops from Guizhou who were pursuing the Red Army had just arrived. They stopped us. They said that we didn't look like Guizhou people and they were suspicious. We told them that we four were business partners. We told them that we were from Guangxi and that we were doing business in Guizhou. We didn't dare say that we were Guizhou people. We told them that it was a difficult time for doing business here, so we wanted to go to Guiyang and were just passing through.

They didn't believe us, but the troops were leaving soon and they couldn't bring us to trial, so they put us into the county jail. That night the county judge questioned us. When the judge asked me where I came from, I told him that I was from "Pig Farm." In that area, many places were named "Pig Farm," "Cattle Farm," "Sheep Farm." The judge said, "Nonsense! Give her twenty slaps on the face." Then I was taken away.

The judge began questioning the others. When it was Zhu Qi's turn, the judge seemed to have been lenient, because Zhu Qi came back soon after he was taken away. He packed his things and prepared to leave.

He said, "I'm leaving now, but you have to stay here for a few more days." We didn't know what had happened.

When Luo Ming was questioned, the judge said, "Luo Ming, you are Communists." Luo Ming said, "No, we're not. We four are doing business together." The judge said, "No, you're not." We suspected that Zhu Qi had betrayed us. We wouldn't admit that we were Communists and insisted that we were business people.

The judge asked, "Can you use an abacus?" When Luo Ming was given an abacus and demonstrated that he could use it, [the judge] still wouldn't believe him. He knew there were a lot of educated people among the Communists so Luo Ming couldn't prove his innocence with the abacus.

My husband and I had no money. When we had left our troops, the leaders in the Central Committee put Zhu Qi in charge of the group and gave him responsibility for the funds. Zhu Qi was kept in the men's cell and I was in the women's cell. When Zhu Qi was leaving with the old man, Luo Ming asked him to leave us some money, but Zhu Qi refused.

The old guard at the jail felt sorry for us. He said [to Zhu Qi], "You four people came here together and now you are leaving. If you don't leave them any money, what will happen?"

My husband and I were kept and questioned for more than ten days, but they still couldn't decide that we were guilty, because they had no evidence.

The judge told Luo Ming, "You say you are a businessman. Do you have any money with you?"

Luo Ming answered, "You know I don't. When the man named Zhu left here, I had asked him to leave me some money, but he wouldn't. He has taken all the money."

Then [the judge] asked, "Do you have anything made of gold?"

"How could we have any gold?"

The judge asked my husband, "Is that woman your wife?"

And Luo Ming answered, "Yes."

"Does your wife have any gold?"

Luo Ming said that he didn't know. The judge wanted him to ask me about it. We thought that Zhu Qi must have given the judge some money and now the judge wanted money from us. We thought that we might be able to buy our freedom. Luo Ming wrote me a short note, asking if I had any gold rings and if I had, would I give the judge one gold ring. I didn't have any gold ring of my own but, when we were asked to stay behind, I was given two gold rings to be used as reserve funds if there were trouble. I had them because a man couldn't carry rings. We women wouldn't be searched. I tied them up inside my coat. I read his note and gave the judge one ring.

Then the judge said, "A new magistrate is coming here. He is sure to inspect the prison and question the people kept here. He'll ask you why you are here. When he comes, you must shout that you are being held unjustly. You must do that."

The next day, the new magistrate came and he went from one cell to another, inspecting them. When he came to our cells, we shouted,

"Injustice!" We told him that we had been doing business with our partner, but he had taken all the money. We said that we were business people and were innocent. We were caught by the troops.

The magistrate asked, "Why did they shout, 'Injustice'?"

The judge said, "Those four people are business partners, but two of them have left, without leaving these two any money. The troops didn't know that, so they sent them here."

The magistrate asked, "It that true?"

We said, "Yes, that's true."

The magistrate said, "All right. I'll let you go."

It was around lunch time. The magistrate said, "I'll let you go, but you can't stay in Guanlin county any longer. You must leave right away."

Then the two of us grabbed our clothes and left in a hurry.

We had a lot of troubles. We couldn't afford to stay in an inn. Whenever we found an old, ruined house, we would go inside and spend the night there. Often we didn't have anything to eat. We just kept walking. Sometimes we were too weak to go on. When we couldn't go any further, we would sell some of our clothes to get something to eat. The next day we would walk on. This is how we got to Guiyang.

When they reached Guiyang, security was extremely tight because Chiang Kai-shek had come to supervise military operations there. They slipped into the city with people who were returning from a market outside the city wall.

When they found a small inn, they made arrangements to stay there, not letting the innkeeper know they had no money.

> One night, after we had been there over ten days, troops came to check every-
> one's registration. Luo Ming asked me to deal with them, because he was sick.
> They asked, "What are you doing here?"
> I replied, "We are Guangxi people doing business. We are just passing through
> on our way back to Guangxi."
> They searched our things. They didn't find anything except a small box of
> ointment.
> They said, "Why do you have to have this with you if you are business peo-
> ple? You don't look like business people."
> They didn't dare arrest us because they didn't have any evidence, but one of
> them said, "I'm suspicious of you. If you really are innocent, I'll let you cut off
> my head! You have three days to leave Guiyang."
> But our Party Organization had told us to work among the peasants in the
> outskirts of Guiyang. How could we leave? We had to fulfill our task assigned
> by our Party.

Needing money, they looked for jobs in Guiyang. Xie Xiaomei agreed to
work for her room and board as a housemaid in the home of a minor Nationalist official but found herself a virtual prisoner of the family who hired
her. To try to allay suspicion, she played the part of a peasant.

> I had been in the army so I was lean and dark, and I didn't comb my hair.
> Sometimes [the boss] would bring back some newspapers. I could read, but I
> pretended that I was illiterate. When he asked me how old I was, I told him that
> I was thirty-eight. Actually, I was in my twenties, but he believed that I was even
> older than his wife. I changed my surname to Zhang and my husband's to Lin.
> So he called me "Lin Dasao [older brother's wife]." I did the housework well.
> Everyday I had two meals with them, but they didn't give me any money.

Luo Ming, still recovering from his wounds, stayed on at the inn. He was
waiting to hear from a cousin in Shanghai and another in Vietnam whom
he had written for help, but decided he must get a job. "What else could we
do? We had no money, we hadn't found Zhu Qi, and our task was to stay
there," Xie Xiaomei said. Luo Ming found employment as a street cleaner
until, overworked and underfed, he began spitting blood and was fired from
his job. For the next two months he slept with the beggars in a Catholic
church until he was again told to leave because of his illness.

They decided that under the circumstances it was impossible for them to
carry out their assignment in Guizhou. Security was still tight because Chiang
Kai-shek was in Guiyang. Luo Ming was too ill to work and, because they were

unable to locate their original comrade, they had no resources. Then the Shanghai cousin sent fifty *yuan* to the couple in care of Xie Xiaomei's employer, who helped himself to thirty *yuan* before giving the letter to her.

> What could we do with twenty yuan? I bought a black *qi pao* and Luo Ming bought some men's clothes. The first time we tried to leave the town gate, we were caught and sent back. Then we learned that in Guiyang the women ride in sedan chairs while the men walk. We did this and passed through the gate.
>
> After we left Guiyang, we walked until February 1936. We went back to my husband's home town [in Guangdong province]. Luo Ming became a teacher in the local middle school.

After the War Against Japan began in July 1937, Xie Xiaomei and Luo Ming went to Longyan in Fujian province, ostensibly to visit her mother but actually to find the Communist guerrillas. "We wanted to report our experiences to the organization and to have our relationship with the Party reestablished." They found the party organization and were told that "the problem" of their party membership would be reported to the Central Committee. They were ordered to return to Luo Ming's home in Guangdong to help with the work of resisting the Japanese. "When the CCP organization in the south was destroyed in 1942, we lost contact with the leaders again. . . . We took part in the anti-Japanese war—the Middle School did very well in its anti-Japanese work—but some people were still suspicious of us and it became very difficult for us. When things got desperate, we went to Hong Kong in 1946 to look for the [Party] Organization. We asked them for instructions."

Xie Xiaomei and Luo Ming went next to Singapore, where she taught primary school. They returned to China in 1949 when the People's Republic of China was established. She worked as a teacher and librarian in Guangzhou in schools and universities until she retired in 1973. After she retired she worked with Luo Ming to edit and write about party history.

> As for the question of Party membership, Luo Ming was not reinstated as a Party member until the 3rd Plenary Session of the Central Committee in 1980 and I, not until 1981. The Central Committee approved complete [retroactive] Party membership. Luo Ming had become a Party member in 1925. I started working for the Party in 1929 and joined in 1930, so I have a membership starting from 1930. Now I'm just an ordinary old red soldier [*lao hongjun*] again. We have gone through a lot of hardships.

We interviewed Xie Xiaomei in Guangzhou in early 1988. When Wang Weihua arranged the interview, Xie Xiaomei asked her to come alone to pick her up and bring her to our hotel for the interview. Xie Xiaomei did not want me to see how poorly she and Luo Ming were living—the worst conditions, Weihua said, of any of the women we had interviewed thus far.

* * *

The third First Front Army woman we interviewed who did not complete the Long March and reach Shaanbei was Wang Quanyuan. When the First and Fourth Front Armies met, five First Front women were transferred, by intent or happenstance, to the Fourth Front Army. Thus, while their comrades in the First Front Army were building the new Soviet Base Area in Shaanxi, Kang Keqing, Li Bozhao, Wu Fulian, Wu Zhonglian, and Wang Quanyuan were still marching with the Fourth Front Army.

Wang Quanyuan explained the situation as she understood it:

> We all went to Songpan with Chairman Mao, and joined up with Zhang Guotao. After we joined him, there was a meeting and Zhang Guotao split with Chairman Mao. We wouldn't have known about it if some people from the 4th Front Army hadn't made up a song against Chairman Mao. They called marching north to fight the Japanese "opportunism" [*jihuijuyi*].[5] We never sang this song.
>
> I was with Kang [Keqing] Dajie because Chairman Mao sent Wu Fulian to the cadre's company. Because Kang Dajie was waiting for Commander-in-Chief Zhu [De], she was sent to the Fifth Army Group of the 1st Front Army to work. The Fifth Army Group was in the rear. Our Convalescent Corps of the Cadres Company was also in the rear. Zhang Guotao took the rear of the 1st Front Army to the south. They didn't force us [to stay], but Zhang Guotao took away the Commander-in-Chief's horse.

Kang Keqing explained,

> The 1st and 4th joined at the first Nationalist blockade line on our way to Jiajin Mountain, and my husband and I were assigned to the 4th Front Army. When Zhang Guotao led the 4th south, we couldn't do anything [to prevent it], even though we didn't endorse it. Commander Zhu said it could only please the enemy. He persistently tried to persuade Zhang Guotao to change his ideas, but at that time, Zhang Guotao was Political Commissar. Zhu Laozong[6] was the Commander of the entire [Red] Army, but the Political Commissar had the final word.

When the First Front Army left, Wang Quanyuan was with the Fourth in Aba. She was quite ill, unable to see clearly and unable to stand. When she began to recover, she wanted to catch up with the First Front Army. However, her political commissar, whom Zhou Enlai had criticized for sending unarmed women into unfriendly territory, ordered her to stay behind.

He told me to rest in the 4th Front Army hospital. When I thought of the song I wasn't happy. I didn't want to go to the 4th Front Army hospital. I said, "We have a general hospital. Why should I go to the 4th Front Army hospital?" He left without saying anything.

What kind of attitude is this? He shouldn't treat his comrades like this! This is the way you treat enemies.

The head of the Health Department persuaded her to stay and rest in the Fourth Front Army hospital by promising to come back for her in a few days. She told the health minister, "Since you have told me in this way, I agree. I didn't like the attitude of the Political Commissar." In less than a week she was discharged from the hospital but was too late to rejoin the First Front Army. She marched south with the Fourth, crossing the Jiajin Mountains a second time.

The Fourth Front Army established a regional and provincial Soviet government in four counties east of the Jiajin Mountains. "At that time," Wang Quanyuan said, "Zhang Guotao was trying to split the Central Government and set up his own Organization."

Wang Quanyuan and Wu Fulian were transferred from the Health Department to the Women's Department, under Zhang Qinqiu. Zhang was head of the Women's Regiment and was described by one of the Fourth Front women as "the best. She had studied in Moscow and most of our education came from her. She often told us about her travels and work and how to take care of our own bodies."[7] Wu Fulian worked at the regional level, and Wang Quanyuan was made head of the provincial level women's department under her. They celebrated the New Year of 1936, Wang said, "doing propaganda, women's work and mobilizing the people." She learned from her comrades that Fourth Front Army Headquarters had received a telegram from the First Front Army saying they had reached northern Shaanxi province in November and were consolidating forces to establish soviet regions there.

The Fourth Front Army then crossed the Jiajin Mountains a third time and worked their way up to the Ganzi area in west Sichuan. Wang Quanyuan, by this time inured to hardship, did not describe this trek in detail.

They crossed another glacier mountain before reaching Ganzi, at an elevation of 15,000 feet. Wang Quanyuan said they were led across the mountain during the three hours when it was safe to cross. "During the other hours, the wind will sweep you and the snow to another mountain."

Wang Quanyuan was assigned to work with the civilians in Luhuo, not far from Ganzi, because "I knew some of the local Tibetan customs." During the next two months, she worked with an interpreter who was the son of a Han

Chinese father and a Tibetan mother, fluent in both languages. She was successful in recruiting forty new Communist Youth League (CYL) members, and when she returned to Ganzi, she was elected CYL party secretary.

While they were in the Ganzi area, they learned that the Second and Sixth Army Groups were approaching after marching from Hunan. Wang Quanyuan explained her role in greeting the troops.

> Three times we sent troops to meet them, but they were all killed by the Tibetans. So we had a meeting. They knew that I had good relations with the Tibetans so they told me to go and take the interpreter with me. Before I left, Comrade [Zhang] Qinqiu had a talk with me.
>
> She said, "The 2nd and 6th Army are short of food and we must do our best to find a way to buy some food to help them, but be careful."
>
> So we left—the interpreter, a groom for the horse who was an eleven year old Han Chinese, and I. I told the interpreter,
>
> "We have a lot of people in the rear who are coming here to protect you and let you be your own master."
>
> "Good."
>
> Then I said, "Three times we sent people [to meet them] but they were all killed by your people. Today just the three of us will go into your region. Please let your people know."
>
> "Secretary, don't worry. I guarantee you'll be safe."
>
> At the foot of the mountain, he sent a signal by yelling three times: "Ah! Wei! Oh!" Afterwards, we went into the mountains. Nothing happened. It was very safe. On our way down the mountain, we saw two houses where local families lived. We told them why we were there. We told them that more troops were coming to protect the Tibetans, but were short of food. We just want to buy some food for the army in the rear.
>
> The Tibetans said, "All right. They are welcome."
>
> "Okay. So tomorrow you help us go. Okay?"
>
> We found a place to rest for the night. The next morning, at daybreak, the two people left. We wondered if they had gone to find food for us, or if they had gone to find people to surround us. The three of us didn't know what to do because the Tibetans had left without a word. We figured that if they had gone to get food from the local people, we should be there to receive it. If they had gone to get the local people to surround us, we should block the door.
>
> I sent the groom into the mountains to be a lookout. I told him to watch the four or five paths on the mountain opposite: if only a few people come, we don't need to be afraid because they would be coming to talk; if a lot of people came, he should let us know immediately.
>
> At about 9:00 A.M., the *xiaogui* shouted: "Four or five people coming from the other mountain are carrying baskets."
>
> We ran toward them and helped them carry the baskets. We asked them their

names so we could record them and weighed their grain. On that day more than forty people brought baskets of wheat. We recorded their names and put their baskets on the side without touching them.

The next day we had a meeting for these people. We told them that we had bought food from them to supply our rear army. I told them that our rear troops would be there soon. Would they welcome them? They said, "Of course."

We prepared small triangle flags made of red paper. We used a sliver of bamboo to cut the paper and put slogans on the flags. Each person should have two small flags in their hands.

When the 2nd and 6th armies arrived, Comrade He Long, who led the army, saw me and said,

"*Xiaogui*, why are you here?"

I said, "Things have been hard for you in the rear. We came here to buy food from the civilians to welcome you."

I had never met him before. I'd seen comrades Wang Zhen, Ren Bishi and Xiao Ke in Xiang-Gan province [Hunan-Jiangxi Soviet Base Area]. Comrade He Long was [elsewhere]. These leaders were older, so they liked to call us "*xiaogui.*"

We piled the baskets [of wheat] along the road so that the army could distribute it themselves. We led some of the [Red Army] leaders to a place where they could eat some *dianxin,* and then they left.[8]

With the arrival of the Second and Sixth Army corps and the news that the First Front Army was establishing a large base area in Shaanxi, the Fourth Front army was persuaded to go north. They crossed the grasslands for the third time, then climbed the Minshan Mountains into Gansu province, where Wang Quanyuan and Wu Fulian were transferred to the newly formed West Route Army.

"We fought in Gansu for about three months," Wang Quanyuan reported. When their ammunition ran out, they retreated into the Qilian Mountains on the border of Gansu and Qinghai provinces. The Women's Regiment stayed in the mountains to cover the westward movement of the main forces. The regiment divided into three parts, with Wang Quanyuan as political commissar of the first part, Wu Fulian in charge of the middle section, and Hua Tiansong head of the third.

The enemy attacked and surrounded us. Since we had run out of bullets, we could only fight hand-to-hand. The enemy realized we were all women and shouted,

"Don't fire! Catch them alive and make them your old ladies!"

So they stopped shooting. One enemy came close to me. I socked him onto the ground. Another came up, a short one. I tripped him up and he fell on the ground, too, and I slugged him several times. As I tried to run away, the enemy crowded around. At that kind of moment, either you'll be caught, killed, or you escape.

Wang Quanyuan escaped and caught up with the West Route Army. Fearing their troops made too large a target, the leaders decided to disperse the soldiers to fight as guerrillas in the mountains. Wang Quanyuan's guerrilla group consisted of five women and five twelve- and thirteen-year-old boys from the vanguard regiment. "The vanguard regiment all knew that the women's regiment liked kids," and had begged her to take them into her group.

They hid in the mountains, dodging the enemy cavalry who were searching for Communists. She killed her horse and the little group made the meat last a month. Whenever they heard hoof beats on the road, they faded into the brush after sweeping away their telltale footprints in the snow. "We were on one mountain one day and another mountain the next day. We ran every day for a month and we still didn't run out of the Qilian Mountains." When they finally found signs of civilization, they were able to ask about the disposition of enemy troops. Assured that there were no troops in the Nanshan foothills, they walked there at night and found a row of caves.

We five women went into one [cave], and the five boys went into another. Just as we were falling asleep, the enemy surrounded us. Two enemies came to me. One held my arms and the other took my gun. I had two pistols: one Mauser and a hand gun.[9] I carried the Mauser and Li Kaifeng carried the pistol.[10]

They [the enemy soldiers] took me outside and began to search me to see if I had any bullets or other weapons. Li Kaifeng put her gun in the grass. We didn't see the boys captured, and I don't know whether or not they were captured later.

We were sent to the headquarters of the first regiment of Ma Lu's brigade. Ma Lu was the brigade commander under Ma Buqing.[11] After we rested in the regiment headquarters, we were sent to the brigade headquarters. When we got to brigade headquarters, I found dozens of our women comrades. We felt bad because they were our comrades and we had all been captured by the enemy, but we pretended that we didn't know each other. We didn't say anything—just "Hello" with our eyes. After we rested awhile, we lined up. I said to Li Kaifeng, "We'd better go to the end of the line. If we are at the head of the line, the enemy will know we are the leaders."

Then the enemy commanded, "About face!" and we became the head of the line. The commander of the brigade had captured a young girl who told them who the leaders were. All my front teeth had been knocked out and the little girl said the one without any front teeth was the regiment commander. As soon as we got to the bivouac area, I was called in and questioned.

During the initial interrogation, Wang Quanyuan insisted she was a common soldier, not the regiment commander, that she had found the guns in the mountains, and that she was unable to read and write. The questioning continued until her captors showed her a picture drawn from the description given by the little girl. "I got ready to die. [I told them], 'If you want to kill me, then kill me! A soldier isn't afraid of death!'"

> The enemy said, "There's nothing wrong with being the commander. This is the time of the United Front, the time of cooperation between the Nationalists and the Chinese Communist Party. Why didn't you tell us your rank before? We won't beat you or abuse you. It would have been better if you had told us earlier."
>
> Then we went to the division headquarters and a lot of officers came around when we got there. There were seventy or eighty women soldiers.
>
> Ma Buqing was there and he ordered us to line up because he wanted to make a speech. "Now that you're here, don't be afraid. We're in the same family because now we have a United Front. Don't worry."
>
> After the speech they wanted to take a picture of us, but we didn't want them to because we were in rags. Besides, they were our enemies and we didn't want to have our pictures taken with them. We all put our heads down and wouldn't look up. Then the officer poked me again with his stick, and when I looked up they took the picture. Afterwards, the enemy checkpoints all had this picture.

Wang Quanyuan, Wu Fulian, and the others were put into a prison in Wuwei, Gansu province, with about 130 other women prisoners. The women were divided up among three Nationalist regiments: engineering, artillery, and security. "They were forcing us to be their wives," Wang Quanyuan explained. "All of us women were dragged, pushed, pulled and carried," she continued. "I stamped my foot and said, 'We can't be married like this! When your commander caught us, he said he wouldn't kill us, or abuse us. Since we're the same family, why are you forcing us women to marry you? Even though we're here today, we all have husbands back in Jiangxi and Sichuan. We came here because we were fighting for our country. If you try to force us women in this way, I object!'" The army commander, perhaps deliberately misunderstanding her objections, promised to match her up with someone of her same rank.

The women discussed their predicament and decided their only alternative was to try to escape after they were separated and "married" to the Nationalist soldiers. They agreed the only thing to do was to steal a gun from the "husband," kill him, and then escape. If they were unsuccessful, they would turn the gun on themselves and be martyred, they decided.

Wang Quanyuan apparently thought she was in a position to make demands of her captors in return for capitulating.

The commander of the 3rd Battalion and the Imam came. They were all Moslem. The battalion commander told me to go to the regiment commander's home. I said I would, but before I went, the regiment commander would have to meet my requirements. I would go if he agreed, but if he didn't I wouldn't go.

He asked, "Tell us your requirements and we will tell the regiment commander."

I said, "Your regiment commander has to come here."

The only thing they could do was go to the battalion headquarters and bring the regiment commander. They didn't dare beat me. When the regiment commander came, he put his hands on his hips and asked me,

"What are your requirements? What do you want to say? Talk!"

I said, "My first is that Wu Fulian must stay with me because she is very sick. I'm the only one who understands her sickness. I have to take care of her."

He said, "Why not send her to the hospital and let the nurses take care of her?"

I said, "No. If you don't meet my request, I won't go with you."

He said, "All right. I'll do it. Wu Fulian can be with you."

"The second is that Li Kaifeng will stay with me." The reason [I wanted] Li Kaifeng was she could read and write and I was uneducated. Since I planned to escape later, it would be better to be with a person who could read. The man said that Li Kaifeng had to go to her own "husband" [*zhongsheng banlu*].[12]

I said, "No, she must be with me."

He said, "Okay, okay, I agree."

"The third [requirement] is freedom of religion. I won't become Muslim." [I said this] because the local people had told us that when a Muslim wanted to marry a Han, the Imam would punish him. The person must become a Muslim before she can marry a Muslim.[13]

He didn't dare agree because the Imam was right there, but the Imam tried to trick me by saying, "Okay, okay." So they met my three requirements.

I went upstairs to rest awhile. By then it was 4:00 A.M. What should I do? The Imam and the two battalion commanders went downstairs. Only the regiment commander and I were left in the room. What could I do if he tried to rape me?

When I asked where the toilet was, he told the orderly to take me. I stayed in the toilet until morning.

On the same day they married me to the commander of the engineering regiment, they sent Wu Fulian to the hospital.

The next morning when we were eating, the hospital people came to tell us that Wu Fulian had died. When I heard that, I couldn't eat. I didn't know whether or not she committed suicide or just died. I'm still not clear about it.[14]

When she heard that Li Kaifeng had been sent away and her second requirement thus disregarded, Wang Quanyuan tried to commit suicide by jumping off a wall. She was revived and then sent to the home of a Nationalist company commander who had been given a political commissar of the Fourth Front Army as his concubine. Wang was again moved to a home where another of her comrades was living. As soon as she got there, she slipped outside to scout out an escape route but was seen by her "husband."

The regiment commander saw me from the gate tower city wall. He, the Imam and five aides-de-camp came on their bicycles. The regiment commander said,

"Your mother's cunt [*Ni ma le ge bi*]! What are you doing here?"

I stood there, ignoring them.

The regiment commander said, "Huh," just that noise, and then said, "Get her inside."

The five aides pulled me inside. Two took my hands and two took my feet and dragged me inside the yard. They closed the door and they also closed [the other woman] in her own room. The seven of them pressed me to the ground. Two pushed down on my hands, two my feet and one my head. The Imam took a piece of firewood and beat me until it was broken. He beat me with more than twenty pieces of firewood, taking skin off with each stroke.

They beat me to death. I was dead for over an hour.[15] I didn't know anything. Twenty sticks of firewood and a bundle of willow twigs were all broken. My back was bleeding and the lower half of my body was black and blue. Later they spat corn liquor over me and I started breathing again. Then they stomped on the lower half of my body.

I came back to life completely deep in the night.

I called out, "I can't move. I can't turn over!"

My comrade came in. She hugged me and cried. She said, "How could you move! There's no unbroken skin [on your back]. You've got five dozen herbal compresses on your back to stop the bleeding. They locked us up when they were beating you, so we couldn't do anything [to help you]."

I said to myself, "You can beat me and kill me as you like. I'm not afraid. If I were afraid of death, I wouldn't be a soldier. I would rather die than be your wife."

I was beaten [for trying to escape] five times altogether in his home.

Wang Quanyuan had been a captive in Gansu for two years when a man in charge of provisions, Han Chinese, befriended her. He warned her that she would be killed if she did not escape. He knew he was being transferred to another province and therefore would not be subject to reprisals if she were caught. When she said, "Where can I go? I'm just like a piece of meat on the butcher's block," he suggested that she dress as a young man and pretend to be his brother-in-law because her picture had been given to each of the checkpoints. He gave her some identifying documents and told her to go to Lanzhou, the provincial capital of Gansu province, where she could find an office representing the Red Army. When she protested that she had never been in a city before in her life, he instructed her to hire a cart, assuring her that the driver would be able to find the office.

Acting on the advice of the Han man, Wang Quanyuan persuaded the regiment commander's wife to help her find the men's clothing she needed and to steal the official seal from the county section chief for a forged pass. She chose a time for her escape when most of the troops were away. She alerted her own regimental orderly, a thirteen-year-old girl whom she had been able to keep with her, and together they slipped out the back door after the guards had gone to sleep.

> I threw her over the wall first and told her to wait for me outside in the ditch by the road. Then I climbed over the wall. We started walking at 11 o'clock that night, and we had walked 90 *li* by daybreak.
>
> In the morning we caught a ride on a cart after the driver investigated us: "Do you have a pass?"
>
> I said, "Yes, we have," and I took out the note [the Han man had given her].
>
> "Okay, okay, you can get on," and we got on the cart.
>
> On the way there was a checkpoint set up by local security. The regular army had gone somewhere else for review, and I took that opportunity to escape. The guards shouted,
>
> "Do you have a pass?"
>
> "Yes," and I took out the [forged] pass. My handwriting wasn't very good, and he said,
>
> "Why does a section leader have such bad handwriting?"
>
> I said, "Hey, what haughty manners you have! Isn't his writing better than yours? You're not so great!"
>
> "Okay, okay. Take it, take it. Go on. Go on."
>
> So I passed the checkpoint and got to Lanzhou.

Wang Quanyuan and her orderly made arrangements to stay at an inn whose proprietor was known to be sympathetic to the Communists. She hired a cart to go to the Eighth Route Army office, believing, "If I could find that, everything would be all right." There was no one she recognized in the office, however.

She was interviewed by Wang Dingguo, who was working to identify and gather together the Red Army soldiers who had been held captive in Qinghai and Gansu. "The situation at that time was so complicated," Wang Dingguo said.[16] "You couldn't tell from the uniform who was trustworthy and who was not."

When Wang Dingguo learned that Wang Quanyuan had been held captive more than two years, over a period spanning the three years from 1937 to 1939, she asked the center for instructions. Wang Quanyuan remembered being told, "When someone returns during the first year, we welcome them back. The second year, we will investigate. [Into] the third year, we won't take them."

Wang Dingguo then telegraphed Wang Quanyuan's husband, Wang Shaodao, to see whether he would accept her, but he refused because she had been forced to marry a Nationalist officer.[17] In despair, Wang Quanyuan asked,

> "What can I do? This is the third year away for me. What can I do if you won't take me back? I beg you to explain about me to your leaders." I told them all about my history and situation. "You have to take me back! I don't know anyone here. What'll I do? There are two of us."
>
> That was our entire discussion. Three days later she sent us five *yuan* and a message: "That's all we can do now. We can't take you back. This five *yuan* is for you to live on."
>
> Two of us with only five *yuan*. What could we do?

Her hopes of returning to the army and regaining her status as a Red Army soldier shattered, Wang Quanyuan returned to the inn to find two aides-de-camp from the Ma family waiting for her. She threatened to jump into the Yellow River if they forced her to return. The innkeeper reported them to security as army deserters. This prompted the security people to investigate everyone at the inn, and they turned their suspicions onto Wang.

She hid in the inn until their money was gone. "We were so hungry that we were skin and bones! Every day we had only five *zhongzi* and three leaves of cabbage to eat with water." *Zhongzi* is made of glutinous rice filled with vegetables, or meat if the times are good, wrapped in a broad leaf, and steamed.

Successfully eluding the Nationalist soldiers and local security forces, she located some of her West Route Army comrades and learned that, in order to survive, many had married soldiers or local men. Because they were starving, she instructed her orderly to do the same, explaining, "She didn't have any choice except to marry a local barber in Lanzhou." When the husband of one of Wang's comrades introduced her to a chauffeur originally from Jiangxi, she agreed to marry him and go with him to Yunnan province, where his mother was living. "There was nothing else I could do but go to Yunnan with this person named Wen. Did I marry him? That's right. That's how it was. When we got to Yunnan, his mother had died, and he didn't have any people in Yunnan."

This was in 1942, during the anti-Japanese War, when the United Front between the Communists and Nationalists was still operative. When Wang Quanyuan heard that the Nationalist army was looking for drivers to go to India for training, she encouraged her husband to sign up, effectively ending that marriage.

She then sent a message to her brother in Jiangxi and from him learned that her mother was dying of tuberculosis. Her brother urged her to return home as quickly as possible. She arranged for a ride to Jiangxi with a friend of her husband.

She stayed in her brother's home for the next six years, through the end of the War Against Japan and during the civil war between the Communists and Nationalists. In 1948, when the civil war was still raging, the local landlord drove her out because she had been a Red Army soldier. "They were going to kill my brother's pigs and take away his cattle, so my brother couldn't do anything but make me leave," she said. Reminding her that she had married out of her natal family, he told her she couldn't live with them forever and besides, after serving in "her" Red Army and joining "her" Communist party, he said she was likely to be arrested.

She went to Taihe, where a maternal aunt lived. Her brother tracked down her fourth husband, only to find that he was in Sichuan, remarried with five children. Wang Quanyuan married her fifth husband in Taihe. After the Communists came to power, her husband's family was labeled counterrevolutionary during land reform, and her husband was jailed for five years. "That was an unjust case," she maintained.

Later, when Wang Quanyuan's own past came under investigation by a work team, they asked her whom she knew in the Central Government. She replied that she knew almost every leader. They suggested that she write to those she knew for help in clearing her name. "I had a [step-]grandson who was studying in Hubei in 1961. He asked me why I never went out. I told him I didn't have any choice because I am from a counter-revolutionary family. My grandson wrote a letter to Kang Keqing. She wrote back to me, telling me to go to the Jiangxi provincial government [to appeal to the party secretary]."

Her situation still unresolved, she began working in an old peoples' home that doubled as the local orphanage after her fifth husband died during the 1960s. Working at every kind of job from janitor on up, she eventually became director of the home where she worked. In 1980, when she was sixty-seven, she retired and returned to her hometown. She had been given her younger brother's son to raise and had brought a *tongyangxi* into her small family as his future wife. Her foster children married each other and they and their children lived with her, farming a small bit of land.

After she retired, Wang Quanyuan resumed her appeals to the authorities. Zhong Yuelin spoke of meeting her in Beijing:

> Wang Quanyuan was very beautiful when she was young. When she came [to Beijing], I didn't recognize anything about her. She had changed completely. When she mentioned Jiangxi, I recognized her [but there was] nothing left from the past. She used to be smiling whenever she met anyone or said anything. She was so enthusiastic, so vivacious.
>
> We don't know how she got into the 4th Front Army. Wu Fulian was the Political Commissar and she [Wang Quanyuan] was the Commander of the Women's Regiment. When our troops were scattered during a battle some place in Qinghai or Gansu, she was captured by the Ma cavalry. Later on, they [the Red Army] refused to accept her because they said she had betrayed them. Actually that hadn't happened at all. She tried hard to find the Party organization as soon as she could. When she found the office in Lanzhou, they wouldn't accept her because she had been captured by the Ma cavalry. They said she became the wife of Ma someone, and they said she betrayed. So she went back home as just one of the ordinary people. She was married to Wang Shoudao on the Long March, but now she's a peasant.

Wang Quanyuan's life changed again, finally for the better. In February 1989 when we interviewed her, she was glowing because her application to officially adopt her foster son had been approved. In August 1989 she was formally acknowledged as a Red Army veteran, no longer classified as a peasant, and entitled to a veteran's pension and privileges. This meant that her children and grandchildren were no longer tied to the land but could move around more freely and pursue careers other than farming.

Conclusion

WHEN WANG QUANYUAN's sister soldiers from the First Front Army reached northern Shaanxi province in autumn 1935, their welcome sense of relief at being with their comrades in a place that seemed safe was tempered by the hard conditions facing them. They immediately joined in the business of enlarging the Shaan-Gan-Ning Soviet Base Area, developing it into a military base and a social, economic, and political base in one of the poorest areas in China.[1] As the only remaining Chinese Soviet Base Area, Shaan-Gan-Ning became the seat of the Communist government. Shortly after their arrival the leaders held a Politboro meeting. It was after this meeting that Chairman Mao made the speech in which, for the first time, he described their ordeal as "the 25,000 *li* Long March."[2]

The Long March veterans, men and women, were in poor physical condition from months of intense physical exertion and poor nutrition. Leaders such as Chen Zongying's husband, Ren Bishi, went to the Soviet Union for medical treatment. Others simply rested when they could, relying on traditional Chinese remedies and their own tough constitutions to regain their health.

When the women from the Second and Fourth Front Armies ended their Long March and joined their comrades in Shaanbei in the fall of 1936, their lives settled into patterns familiar from earlier times in previous Soviet Base Areas. Women from all three armies were sent to school for training in literacy, military affairs, and political theory. They continued working for the party. Some married and had children, whereas others, such as Jian Xianren, were divorced.

After they all settled in Shaanbei there was some reshuffling of spouses, especially when an influx of young, educated women from the cities came in the late 1930s and early 1940s. Jian Xianren, who told us nothing about her divorce, was better educated than her husband, but many of the educated men were leaving their illiterate and heroic wives for young women with a background more similar to their own. Another complicating factor was the fact that people scattered and some lost contact with each other as they moved around during the war years. For example, Deng Liujin said, "Our political commissar, Li Jianzhen, married our team leader during the Long March, but then [her husband] went to the West Route Army. Afterwards, they each thought the other was dead or lost, and both married someone else."

* * *

The women continued their revolutionary work through the Anti-Japanese War (World War II) from 1937 to 1945 and the civil war against the Nationalists, which culminated in 1949 with the founding of the People's Republic of China. Chen Zongying, Wang Dingguo, Zhong Yuelin, and Liu Ying were assigned as confidential secretaries to assist husbands who were aged or in fragile health. Some left the army, and many were assigned to civilian positions at the national, provincial, or local level.

During the Cultural Revolution years from the mid-1960s to mid-1970s, all the women suffered to some degree, especially those whose prominent husbands or ex-husbands were under attack. Xie Fei, for example, spent two years in prison primarily because of her close association with Liu Shaoqi, even though they had been divorced in 1941 after just six years of marriage.

It wasn't until the late 1970s and early 1980s, when many of the women were reinstated in official posts after the Cultural Revolution, that they had the opportunity to renew friendships made during the war years before and after the Long March. Deng Liujin explained how women veterans living in Beijing interacted:

> Sometimes we see each other when we go to the hospital and sometimes we attend meetings or listen to reports together. We live in different parts of the city so we don't get together very often. I have a close relationship with Wang Dingguo, because we are in the same work unit. We call each other, chatting about our work, our families.
>
> Last night [July 7, 1986] we got together at the Capital Theater where two plays were put on in memory of Li Bozhao. I saw Li Zhen and Liu Ying. Earlier, we were organized to get together at Beihai kindergarten in commemoration of the Fiftieth Anniversary of the Long March. During the Spring Festival, we gathered at the Great Hall of the People and all of us from the 1st, 2nd, or 4th

Front Armies saw each other. Some of us hadn't seen each other for several decades.

Most of us have retired, but we still work because we can still walk and talk. I'm now working for children's welfare, fund-raising for the Chinese National Children's and Youth Fund and working with juvenile delinquents. I'm also busy with interviews. Wang Dingguo is busier than I am. She holds several titles. We don't want to just stay at home—we still want to contribute to our society.

It is significant that Deng Liujin's remarks about renewing friendships with old comrades from the Long March ended with an explanation about the work she and others were doing at the time of the interviews. The strongest ties of friendship and comradeship, the feelings of solidarity among the women, seem to spring at least as much from working together as from sharing difficult experiences on the March. It is within this context that Liu Ying said, when asked about friendships made on the Long March, "We were all close. Whoever I was with in the local work department were my closest comrades, both men and women. There was no one I was especially close to. We were just comrades, working together, sleeping in the same place. Everyone slept together on the ground. When we ate, we all cooked in a huge pot, everyone got a bowl, would fill it, and then eat. Very simple."

In addition to the bonds established by working together, there was another important aspect of their experience. The young women, especially, experienced the nurturing element in their relationships with older women, which Ma Yixiang described in great detail in chapter 3. Zhong Yuelin appreciated the vest He Zizhen made for her before they crossed the grasslands, but He Manqiu, in describing the relations she had with the older women, added another insight:

> The others [women] showed us how to wear our uniforms and at night would make sure we were covered by our blankets. I felt more warmth from them than I had in my own family. Although it was more comfortable at home with other people to cook and care for you and with parents and grandparents to love you, when I was among the army people I felt as if I were in a brand new world. I thought this new environment was exactly right for me, [because it] suited my ideals and personality. It didn't seem at all strange to me. All the others liked me very much.

By distinguishing between being loved within the family and being liked by her comrades and superiors, He Manqiu emphasized the difference between the comradeship forged during the Long March and Chinese family feelings. Many women stated that the Red Army and the party had become their family. The party and the army did replicate some of the functions of the family, such as arranging marriages, giving women names, and caring for the ill and elderly. In addition, the secret nature of their membership in Communist organizations, the confidential information they were privy to, and their status and relationships within the Communist party and army hierarchy in some way replaced the "insider" knowledge of family secrets or private family affairs within the patriarchal family structure. After all, the family, the party, and the army were male-dominated institutions.

The party and the army could not totally replace the family as an institution, however. That the Jian sisters were unique in their attachment, understanding, and support for each other was undoubtedly because they were sisters. The closeness of family members is seldom equaled by other friendships, even those formed under such extreme conditions as the Long March.

When the women chose to join the revolution, they moved out of their place within the traditional boundaries of what had been considered public and private. In traditional Chinese families in the early twentieth century, women stayed within the walls of the home if the family could afford it or, if not, in the family fields or inside another family's home. The men attended to "outside" affairs. One of the old terms for "wife" is "the inside person" (*neiren*). When for the first time in her life Zhong Yuelin received her own name, she learned that joining the revolution opened a space where she and other women could have an identity beyond that of someone's daughter or someone's wife.[3] And when the women announced their progressiveness by cutting their hair, they not only made their commitment to the revolution public but also removed the visible symbol of their "inside" marital status.

Furthermore, women soldiers had more visibility than men in comparable positions in the Red Army. In *To Change China*, Jonathan Spence makes the point that people who might not be particularly important in their own society can become people of consequence when they are a tiny but visible minority in another country.[4] In a similar way, within the male culture of the military, the women stood out, for better or worse. Although they may have been targets for gossip about their relations with men, about bickering among themselves, and about taking able-bodied men away from the real job of fighting in order to protect them, they were also able to forge a positive identity beyond the Chinese traditional ideal of women as fragile, modest, timid, and submissive when they proved themselves to be hardy and tough soldiers.

The women were used, in much the same way that all soldiers are used, to further the military and political aims of their superiors, but with a difference: They were used in a gendered way. Marriages often were arranged for party purposes, primarily to answer needs of the prospective husband or of propriety. When they were doing underground work, both Xie Xiaomei and Wang Dingguo were instructed to marry colleagues. Their husbands needed the physical care a wife could provide, and as a couple they allayed suspicion from the community. Wang Dingguo, in her teens when she joined the army, married one of the oldest men who made the Long March, Xue Jiezai. They were working together in Gansu after she had been released from captivity by Ma Bufang's forces. When asked about their courtship and marriage, she said succinctly, "There was no courtship. It was a Party matter." After the Long March the women's status and the work they were assigned often, though not always, depended on whether they were divorced after the March, on their husband's rank, and on his success at political survival.

The work they performed in nursing and gathering grain had gendered aspects as extensions of the work women traditionally did. When recruiting soldiers, women were sent to persuade wives and mothers to let their men join the army. One reason for using girls and women in propaganda work was to help villagers recognize their own exploitation when listening to the stories of abused *tongyangxi* or women at the mercy of landlords. Another reason was that a woman was assumed to be less threatening to local people and could more easily talk with them and go into their homes.

The women for the most part spoke of joining the revolution, then of joining Communist organizations such as the Communist Youth League and the Chinese Communist Party. For many of these women, joining the army was not an event. They were simply subsumed into the military as political soldiers, cadres, working in jobs in a military setting. The line between party and army was muddy in several ways. During the Long March, the soldiers did not wear uniforms; at best, they had a soft military hat with a red star sewn on it. The military aspect of the Communist party structure emerges in words such as *cadre* and can be seen in attitudes of unquestioning obedience to orders from party leaders. The military nature of the Chinese Communist society created by the party still persisted during the time of the interviews and translations. For example, it was no accident that during the Democracy Movement in 1989, students from each college and university organized themselves into encampments (*yingdi*) in the square at Tiananmen. They established chains of command for disseminating information and for setting and implementing policy decisions. As schoolchildren, they had learned revolutionary behavior and military organization and had grown up on stories of the Long March and other heroic military feats.

One of the things people who write women's history have learned is that when history focuses on women, traditional historical boundaries may change. Susan Mann speaks of transforming "the content of the frame" of conventional history by bringing women into it but adds, "We may also destroy the framework itself."[5] History from the perspective of the women who participated in it often is not a series of discrete events but a continuing process. Dates that historians have traditionally assigned to events become less emphasized, not because of inaccuracies but because a date may signal a turning point in political or military history, which is not necessarily the way people understand their own experience at the time.

It is quite clear that the women did not then perceive the end of the Long March as a singular event but simply saw their experience as a series of memorable moments while performing their assigned tasks during the year-long troop movement. What they did was extremely difficult. It was one of the hardest years, perhaps, but only one of many hard years. Their perceptions may not reinforce the legend of the Long March, nor do they diminish the heroic nature of the March; they add a human face to what has passed into mythology.

By choosing revolution, by being with the army and the party when and where they were, these women irrevocably changed their lives. They have been the beneficiaries of the mythical proportions the Long March has assumed in Chinese modern history. Although they may not have been thought of as important or outstanding when they were in their hometowns, after the Long March and the establishment of the Peoples' Republic of China, those who completed the March attained national recognition, held prestigious positions at national, provincial, or local levels, and enjoyed the fruits of being among the revolutionary heroes, "national treasures."

Deng Liujin perhaps summed up the common feeling when she ended her interview by saying, "We women cooperated very well, we were united, all of us were one heart. At that time, we women had to be united. We couldn't quarrel or fight. At that time we shared everything from food to clothes— we suffered together, enjoyed together [*tonggan gongku*]."[6]

Notes

Introduction

1. Mao, *Selected Works*, 1:160. Mao was speaking at Wayaobao, Shaanxi, December 27, 1935.

2. The Chinese Communists used the Russian term *soviet* to describe the socialist nature of the government established in their Chinese Base Area.

3. Snow, *Red Star*, especially part 5, "The Long March," 171–96.

4. Wilson, *Long March*.

5. In addition to the standard histories, which usually include at least one chapter on the Long March, two more recent full-length books on the Long March are those by Salisbury, *Long March, the Untold Story*, and Yang, *From Revolution to Politics*.

6. Smedley, *The Great Road*, 308.

7. In a broader profile of women Long March veterans, Li Xiaolin charts 231 women who participated in the Long March. See Li, "Women in the Chinese Military," 240–71. Much research is needed to compile a comprehensive profile of all the women who were Red Army soldiers on the Long March.

8. Guillermaz, *History of the Chinese Communist Party*, 3–15, gives a concise overview of Chinese history during the period between 1911 and 1921 in his first chapter.

9. The May Fourth Movement takes its name from the day in 1919 when students in Beijing, outraged by provisions of the Versailles Treaty at the end of World War I, gave vent to their frustrations in a large demonstration against acceptance of the treaty. Under the treaty, the European powers granted Japan the Chinese territory in Shandong province previously designated a German concession rather than allowing it to revert to China. Although the provision was later dropped, many Chinese people felt their interests had been betrayed because the Chinese government had joined the Allied Powers by declaring war against Germany and sending troops to Europe. As Chinese students in many other cities began to join in demonstrating against the treaty, the May Fourth Movement swept the country, making visible deep cultural, social, and political changes

that had been fomenting since before the end of the Qing dynasty. The standard work on the May Fourth Movement is Chow, *The May Fourth Movement.* Wang Zheng examines the role of women during that time in *Women in the Chinese Enlightenment.*

10. John Service was one of the many dedicated officers whose loyalty was impugned during the McCarthy era. Although he was reinstated in the Foreign Service, his career was curtailed.

11. Both Harrison and Charlotte Salisbury wrote about their trip. See Salisbury, *Long March Diary.*

12. The First Front Army started out from the Central Revolutionary Base Area on the Jiangxi-Fujian border in southeast China in October 1934. The Fourth Front Army departed from the Sichuan-Shaanxi Revolutionary Base Area in spring 1935, meeting the First Front Army in western Sichuan. The First Front Army went alone to Shaanxi province, arriving in November 1935. The Fourth Front Army stayed in Sichuan. The Second Front Army, formed from the Second and Sixth Army Groups, left from the Hunan-Hubei-Sichuan-Guizhou Revolutionary Base Area in November 1935. They met the Fourth Front Army in western Sichuan, and the Second and Fourth Front Armies traveled together to join the First in Shaanxi in November 1936.

13. During this period I first read Joan Kelly's discussion of how she changed her thinking about the Italian Renaissance when challenged by Gerda Lerner to include women in the content of her history course at Sarah Lawrence College. See Kelly, *Women, History, Theory,* introduction.

14. In an oral history of revolutionary women in India, the editors observed, "There is for us . . . the knowledge that history as it is written now may well turn out to be the history of a sub-group" (Stree Shakti Sanghatana, *We Were Making History,* 32).

15. An English-language translation of the Marriage Law of 1950 may be found in various texts, including Croll, *The Women's Movement in China,* 107–12.

16. Li Zhisui, *The Private Life of Chairman Mao,* 57–58.

17. Gail Hershatter deals at length with the use of government language in the introduction to her outstanding history of prostitution in Shanghai. She states that the language "cannot be dismissed as sinister Newspeak. What emerges . . . is not only the creation of language by the state, but also its adoption by 'the people' to name an oppression that previously could not have been articulated" (Hershatter, *Dangerous Pleasures,* 22).

18. I discussed the phenomenon at length with Edith Gelles, a fellow member of the Stanford Biographers Seminar when she was in the process of writing her excellent biography of Abigail Adams. Reaching the conclusion that she must write the book topically rather than chronologically, she says, "It has become clear to me that John [Adams] is at the center of her [Abigail's previous] biographies because of chronology. As long as Abigail's life is told against the background or context that emphasizes events in which John took a major role . . . the story tends to slip into his world, making his life work the fulcrum of her biography" (Gelles, *Portia,* xv).

Chapter 1: Newborn on the March

1. Children who showed promise as scholars studied the classics; as young adults, they took examinations that qualified them for various levels of government service (which were abolished in 1905). The traditional social ranking at the turn of the century in Chi-

na was first, scholar, official, and gentry; then, farmer; next, artisan, merchant, and businessman; and last, soldier.

2. The Four Books (*Si Shu*) are *The Great Learning* (*Da Xue*), *The Doctrine of the Mean* (*Zhong Yong*), *The Analects of Confucius* (*Lun Yu*), and *Mencius* (*Meng Zi*). The Five Classics (*Wu Jing*) are *The Book of Songs* (*Shi Jing*), *The Book of History* (*Shu Jing*), *The Book of Changes* (*Yi Jing*), *The Book of Rites* (*Li Ji*), and *The Spring and Autumn Annals* (*Chun Qiu*).

3. The "begonia leaf" map of China at the time included Tibet and Mongolia.

4. Qiu Jin, 1875–1907, Hunanese by marriage and therefore claimed by Hunan province as one of their own, is considered to be the first woman revolutionary overtly working for the overthrow of the Qing dynasty. As a student in Japan, she joined a secret society dedicated to overthrowing the emperor. In her writing and lectures she advocated both education and economic independence for women. When she was teaching at a women's school in Zhejiang province, she organized an army and planned an uprising against the Qing, was captured, and was executed at age 32. Ono Kazuko ends her short biography of Qiu Jin: "Her execution pierced the hearts of others as an act of propaganda far more powerful than any written works" (Ono Kazuko, *Chinese Women,* 65). See also Gilmartin, *Engendering the Chinese Revolution,* 155–57. In addition to the example of Qiu Jin, young girls of Jian Xianren's generation also were captivated by Hua Mulan, known to Western readers through Kingston's *The Woman Warrior* and the Disney movie *Mulan.* Wang Zheng, in her fine book on women activists in the first part of the twentieth century, discusses the influence of Hua Mulan on the women she interviewed. One, Huang Dinghui, even changed her name to Mulan when she joined the Communist Youth League (Wang, *Women in the Chinese Enlightenment,* 347).

5. In several places in *Engendering the Chinese Revolution,* Gilmartin characterizes the *Xiangdao Zhoubao* (*The Weekly Guide*), published in Shanghai between 1922 and 1926, as a "Communist theoretical journal" (80) and a "Communist organ" (83) and states that by 1927 the circulation had reached 50,000 (247n.33).

6. Mao Zedong and other young Communists established many schools for workers, which served the dual purpose of teaching literacy and training future leaders. See Shaffer, *Mao and the Workers,* for descriptions of schools during the early 1920s similar to those Jian Xianren's brother attended.

7. May 20, 1927, the Horse Day Incident (*Mari Shibian*) was one of the few politically important historical days known in China by name rather than date.

8. Garavente ("He Long," 23) reports that He Long was portrayed by westerners as "a popular hero who, though not a knowledgeable Communist himself, accepted the guidance and leadership of the CCP. They compared him to such well-known western figures as Pancho Villa, Robin Hood and Rhett Butler . . . in order to present their readers with a clearer picture of this man." James Bertram states that "tales were told of him [He Long] in half a dozen southern provinces that made him into a sort of modern Chinese Robin Hood" (*Unconquered,* 188). Helen Foster Snow has a section heading, "He Long, China's Red Robin Hood" (*Chinese Communists,* bk. 2, pt. 1).

9. See Ch'en, *The Highlanders,* 226.

10. The discrepancy between Jian Xianren's figure of 1,000 in the army and the 3,000 Ch'en says were recruited by He Long when he first returned to Hunan may be explained

by the nature of the army. Ch'en's figure probably includes peasants and workers who joined the army but perhaps returned home from time to time to farm, earn wages, and take care of their families. Jian Xianren's figure may more accurately reflect the core number of committed and trained soldiers.

11. In his dissertation, Garavente states, "Everybody saw He Long as a physically attractive, tough extrovert who harbored, underneath his boisterously loud exterior, deep feelings of sympathy for the plight of China's downtrodden" (citing Bertram, 1939, 211; Garavente, "He Long," 23). Later he says that one of the charges made against He Long during the Cultural Revolution (1966–76) was that He Long was "a notorious womanizer who formally married nine times (seven times before he joined the Party and twice thereafter) and . . . [had] an untold number of concubines" (25).

12. She is referring to his choosing to join the Communist side after Chiang Kai-shek turned on his Communist allies in April 1927.

13. Dayong is now part of a resort city, Zhangjiajie. The building where the base was established, a former Catholic mission, at this writing is a museum next door to a five-star hotel. The museum includes three rooms used by the three leaders, He Long, Xiao Ke, and Ren Bishi. The largest room is identified as the "honeymoon suite" for Xiao Ke and Jian Xianfo. The author could find no record of where the other wives, including Jian Xianren and Chen Zongying, stayed.

14. Ch'en, *Highlanders,* 225.

15. Other armies relied on conscripts.

16. *Jiesheng* means "victorious." She was born just after the Red Army won a battle.

17. Jian Xianren used the words *horse* and *mule* interchangeably when describing the animal that carried her pack, which she sometimes rode.

18. Benjamin Yang describes it this way: "They marched southeast, crossed the Wan River, and entered the affluent central Hunan area of Xupu and Xinhua. This maneuver distracted the enemy's attention to the southeast and allowed the Communists to gather material supplies and manpower" (*From Revolution to Politics,* 203).

19. "Doing propaganda work" (*xuanchuan qunzhong*) is a direct translation of the phrase all the women used to describe how they explained Communist ideals to the ordinary people, the masses. The phrase "mass work" (*qunzhong gongzuo*) includes propaganda work as well as organizing and obtaining support from the peasants for recruiting soldiers and carriers and procuring food.

20. The four big families were Jiang, Song, Kong, Chen. The Jiang family is the family of Chiang Kai-shek (Jiang Jieshi). Song is the part of the Soong family with strong Nationalist ties: Soong Mei-ling (Song Meiling) was married to Chiang Kai-shek, TV Soong (Song Ziwen) was Chiang Kai-shek's finance minister, and Soong Ai-ling (Song Ailing) married H. H. Kung (Kong Xiang Xi), also a Nationalist finance minister. (The third Soong sister, Soong Ching-Ling [Song Qingling], married Sun Yat-sen, sided with the Communists against the Nationalists, and was posthumously named Premier of China.) The fourth family, Chen, is the family of the Chen brothers, Chen Lifu and Chen Guofu, who were known as the C-C clique and were powerful in the Nationalist government. See Chesneaux et al., *China from the 1911 Revolution to Liberation,* 186–87, and Eastman et al., *Nationalist Era,* 27–32.

21. "A lot of circles" means that words or passages were marked, in the same way we might underline or highlight a word or phrase in a thorough reading.

22. The Communists were already discussing combining forces with the Nationalists to fight the Japanese, although the official call to form a united front was not made until August 1937.

23. The *changpao* is a long, silk, padded gown traditionally worn by intellectuals and officials, the male counterpart to the *qipao* worn by women.

24. A transliteration of Vaseline.

25. See Yang, *From Revolution to Politics,* 202–4. He explains that telegrams came not from Mao Zedong's headquarters in the First Front Army but from Zhang Guotao, commander of the Fourth Front Army. After the First Front Army met the Fourth, the First continued to Shaanbei. The codes were left with the Fourth, and it was Zhang Guotao and Zhu De who responded in the name of the military council and General Headquarters. Yang's source suggests that the telegram exchange actually took place before they reached Bijie and after they left the Wumeng Mountains. Jian Xianren was reciting from memory the notes she had made before our interview. Because she said that the telegram ordered them to "cross the Wu River and go north to fight the Japanese," it seems possible that she was confused about time and place. The Wu River is in Sichuan and Hunan, not in Guizhou. However, I do not think we should dismiss her report out of hand because she undoubtedly had access to written sources and to her brother-in-law's memories. In addition, there may well have been more than one telegram.

26. Jian Xianren was expressing a common reluctance to speak of or predict death.

27. In June 1997 the author talked with two Naxi sisters in Lijiang who remembered seeing the Red Army. The sisters were sitting by the road selling peanuts because, they said, their father was a teacher and therefore very poor. Their clothes were full of holes, and, out of pity, one of the soldiers gave the older sister a mirror as a present. They said they had no chance to talk with the soldiers because they were marching so fast. They described the soldiers as ragged and dirty, not nearly as well turned out as the Nationalist troops. The sisters said they knew of no one who actually joined the army from Lijiang, but they did hear about people who went with the army as guides. When asked how they felt when they saw the women soldiers, they said they thought, "Wow! Look at that! They have both men and women soldiers!" They did not think it particularly strange: "We just thought of Hua Mulan." Interview with Zhou Guichuan and her younger sister, Zhou Guiying, at their home in Lijiang, Yunnan province, China, June 25, 1997.

28. When the author visited one of the ferry crossings northwest of Shigu in June 1997, the river was about 100 yards wide. However, because the river drops so precipitously and moves so fast and the river banks constantly change configuration, one can only guess how wide the river was where Jian Xianren crossed it. For a vivid description of the upper reaches of the Yangzi River, the Jinsha River, see Winchester, *River at the Center of the World,* 331–33, and Bangs and Kallen, *Riding the Dragon's Back,* especially pt. 1.

29. "While the army was in Shigu, some stayed with families, others slept and cooked in the streets. Everyone was cooking rice. There was never time to clean the pot before cooking the next batch and the crust of rice [*guoba*] in the bottom of all the pots grew thicker and thicker. There were soldiers all the way from Shigu to Judian." Interview with Wang Shen, an exceptionally clear-minded 104-year-old former school teacher. Shigu, Yunnan, June 26, 1997.

30. Sikang was a province from 1928 to 1955 that comprised what are now parts of the provinces of Sichuan, Yunnan, and Tibet.

31. Although she did not realize it at the time, Jian Xianfo was already pregnant when she left Sangzhi on the Long March in November.

32. Qi Dajie was an older woman who was also pregnant.

33. Jian Xianren said only that her brothers had "died a martyr's death" during the Long March. She did not elaborate.

34. Unlike the pioneer women who crossed the prairies of the western United States, the Red Army soldiers did not have the privacy offered by long skirts.

35. This was the only time Jian Xianren mentioned having had another child. She did not elaborate.

36. *Bao,* meaning "protect," has the same pronunciation as the word *bao* meaning "precious." *Sheng* means "born" and also means "life." Thus his name means "born in a fort" but also implies "precious life."

37. Li Bozhao had begun the Long March with the First Front Army, but, along with Zhu De, Kang Keqing, and others, she had stayed with the Fourth Front Army. Both she and Jian Xianfo were known for their effective propaganda work. Li wrote and directed street drama; Jian created illustrations to make her point.

38. Tibetans in this area offer a ceremonial bowl of the barley flour to guests, who dip their fingers into the bowl to taste the flour, which somewhat resembles whole wheat in color, texture, and taste.

39. The concept of the United Front was that all the Chinese military forces—the warlord armies, as well as the Nationalists and Communists—should cooperate in fighting the Japanese invading army. From Jian Xianfo's story, it seems that the bodyguard she encountered had no idea that she was the wife of a commanding general and treated her as he would a woman who followed the army. Her demonstrated knowledge of the concept of the United Front probably was enough to convince him that he had better not treat her roughly.

40. In December 1936, the troops of one of the Northern warlords, Zhang Xueliang, captured Chiang Kai-shek near Xi'an and held him until the Nationalists agreed to form a United Front against the Japanese. See Van Slyke, *Enemies and Friends,* chap. 5, "The Sian Incident, and After."

41. See Kristoff, "After Half a Century." The article describes Japan's germ warfare experiments in China, including Changde, the area where Jian Xianfo's parents lived at the time: "Planes dropped plague-infected fleas . . . over Changde . . . and plague outbreaks were later reported."

42. Huaxia Composition Committee, *Dictionary,* 1119, 1120.

Chapter 2: Revolutionary, Mother

1. Chen Zongying told me her birthdate was 1903. It is given variously as 1902 and 1904 in Chinese publications.

2. Bound feet, the "golden lilies," as some of the women called them, are the result of a process in which a little girl's toes are bent under her foot and held there by bindings until the bones are broken and her foot deformed. For a description of this process, see Pruitt, *Daughter of Han,* 22. The binding of girls' feet, which dates back hundreds of years, is only incompletely understood. It was long thought that the practice continued because the resultant erotic walk could enable a young woman to marry above her family status

and because bound feet kept a woman housebound. However, recent scholarship by Dorothy Ko and Susan Mann suggests that foot binding may have persisted because it became a symbol of respectability and possibly an integral part of woman's identity. Hill Gates adds an economic dimension to the understanding of foot binding, suggesting that women did not need mobility when engaged in textile production; it may have been a way to keep young women and wives close to the spinning wheel and the loom. See Gates, "On a New Footing," 115–35; Ko, *Teachers*, 147–51, and "Rethinking Sex," 79–105; and Mann, *Precious Records*, 26–28.

3. Cusack, *Chinese Women Speak*, 188.

4. Andre Malraux wrote a compelling novel, *Man's Fate*, about the Nationalists turning on the Communists in Shanghai in April 1927.

5. There are few physical details available about Longhua prison. In his memoirs, Wang Fanxi, who was jailed during the same time period Chen Zongying was imprisoned, says only, "There were three cell blocks in the Woosung-Shanghai Garrison Headquarters, each containing twenty cells, and the gaol normally held some five to six hundred prisoners. Within each block the cells were opened in the morning and locked again at night, and during the daytime only the main door of the block remained locked. Detainees therefore had a certain freedom of movement, and the prison developed a social life of its own" (Wang, *Chinese Revolutionary*, 163).

6. See Yang, *From Revolution to Politics*, 89–93, for military history details on the Sixth Army Group during this period.

7. See Yang, *From Revolution to Politics*, 89–93, for more background on the Sixth Army Group during this maneuver. Yang believes the Sixth was sent west into these provinces to pull Nationalist troops away from the encirclement of the Central Soviet Base Area and to prevent the provincial troops from joining the Nationalist troops in battling the Communist forces in Jiangxi.

8. The Tibetans are one of the fifty-five minority peoples in China. In 1997, the author visited Zhongdian and other villages in the Tibetan area in northwest Yunnan and climbed the ladder-stairs to the living quarters above the animal pen in a Tibetan home. The largest lamasery outside of Tibet was in Zhongdian. It was there that the Second and Sixth Army Groups reassembled after crossing the Jinsha River. Generals He Long and Xiao Ke met with leading lamas to negotiate safe passage for their armies through the area to the north.

Chapter 3: Little Devil

1. Ch'en, *Highlanders*, gives an overview of the changing economy, especially in chapter 1. His book is an excellent source for details about the time and place Ma Yixiang spent her childhood.

2. Ma Yixiang, *Chaoyang Hua*. The title, which I loosely translate as *Sunflower*, describes the quality of a good revolutionary who is similar to a flower that always faces the sun, never turning away in disloyalty from the light of the CCP.

3. The precepts the Red Army soldiers followed at the time were "Three Rules of Discipline: (1) Obey orders in your actions; (2) Don't take anything from the workers and peasants; and (3) Turn in all things taken from local bullies. In the summer of 1928 he [Mao Zedong] set forth Six Points for Attention: (1) Put back the doors you have taken down for bed-boards; (2) Put back the straw you have used for bedding; (3) Speak po-

litely; (4) Pay fairly for what you buy; (5) Return everything you borrow; and (6) Pay for anything you damage. After 1929 . . . Rule 2 became 'Don't take a single needle or piece of thread from the masses,' and Rule 3 changed first to 'Turn in all money raised' and then to 'Turn in everything captured.' To the Six Points for Attention he added two more: 'Don't bathe within sight of women' and 'Don't search the pockets of captives'" (Mao, *Selected Works*, 4:156n.1).

The "Three Disciplines and Eight Points" was made into a song that every soldier learned to sing and children were still singing in school in the 1990s.

4. Sweeping up Nationalist arms and ammunition after a battle was one way the Red Army kept itself armed.

5. A CCP organization.

6. Meaning that the women with the Nationalist army wore elaborate hair styles and makeup.

7. Having a letter of introduction establishing one's credentials often was crucial to survival during those times of guerrilla warfare, but with her childish behavior and determination, Ma Yixiang apparently bluffed her way into the unit.

8. See Yang, *From Revolution to Politics*, 202: "As the Red Army Headquarters had already consented to the plan for strategic transfer and, more decisively, as the KMT [Nationalist] troops were quickly approaching, a joint conference of the Party and Army of the combined 2nd and 6th Corps was held in early November 1935. They decided to break through the encirclement and fight out of the Soviet base. Initially, their idea was to move only as far as the Hunan-Guizhou border or eastern Guizhou . . . but the gravity of the present situation gradually forced them onto another Long March."

9. Ma Yixiang was born in May 1923 according to the Western calendar and would have been twelve years old by Western reckoning.

10. The Revolutionary Committee of the central organization of the Second Army Group.

11. The recruiting process was constant all during the march. See Yang, *From Revolution to Politics*, 204: "After three months of expedition, the 2nd and 6th Army Corps still maintained their original force of 18,000 soldiers. Their losses on the way were just offset by their recruitment."

12. Ibid., 206.

13. There are no reliable statistics on the number of Second and Sixth Army Group soldiers and transport workers who died crossing the first snow mountain.

14. For an English-language version of the story of the Flaming Mountain, see Yang and Yang, *Classical Chinese Novels*, 133–99.

Chapter 4: From Soldier to Doctor

1. The New Life Movement was officially initiated in 1934, too late for He Manqiu to have unbound her feet. The meetings she and her father attended probably were antecedents to the New Life Movement.

2. Zhongba, now called Jiangyou, is in north central Sichuan province.

3. He Manqiu used the idiom *qisile* (literally, "died of anger"), which is similar to the English idioms, "I'm dying of hunger" or "I'm starving to death." When we questioned

her about the phrase, she assured us she literally meant that the reason they died was because of their anger.

4. To oppose imperialism, to eliminate feudal influence, and to overthrow feudal separatist rule (of the warlords).

5. One *liang* equals fifty grams. Students now consider two or three *liang* of rice with meat and vegetables an ample lunch.

Chapter 5: Why We Joined

1. There are many good sources that give a clear picture of women in the male-dominated China of these years. See Gilmartin, "Gender, Political Culture," 195–225; Johnson, *Women, the Family*; Stacey, *Patriarchy*; and Wolf, *Revolution Postponed*, especially chap. 1.

2. "At the First Congress of the Chinese Soviet Republic in November 1931, a provisional constitution was written and adopted for the areas administered by the Communists. It held: 'It is the purpose of the Soviet government of China to guarantee the thorough emancipation of women; it recognizes freedom of marriage and will put into operation various measures for the protection of women, to enable women gradually to attain the material basis required for their emancipation from the bondage of domestic work, and to give them the possibility of participating in the social, economic, political and cultural life of the entire society'" (Brandt et al., *Documentary History*, 223).

3. Even today, the top-down policy statements and laws concerning women's liberation have not greatly changed the basic attitudes of male superiority in China, especially in the rural areas. During the period of economic reforms in the 1980s and 1990s, many of the practices resulting in violence against women and male control of women's lives that were in existence in the earlier years of the century reemerged in China.

4. According to a soldier who sat in on the interview because she was collecting the mountain songs created by Li Jianzhen, the songs were all original. It seems more likely that Li Jianzhen remembered many songs to which she added her own twist or her own verses. Ono (*Chinese Women*, 144) quotes a version of this poem from a collection of mountain songs, without attributing authorship to any particular person.

5. Yi Haining, who helped with this translation, said peasants in Sichuan used a large wooden bucket to store urine for later use as fertilizer. This was where a girl baby would be drowned if the family couldn't afford to raise her. In a conversation in Beijing in 1988 with Isabel Crook, who grew up in Sichuan, she explained that the bucket was about ten inches in diameter. She said in theory people didn't approve of killing baby girls. The neighbors would bang on the door and shout, "Save the child! Save the child!" but they wouldn't actually go inside to prevent the drowning.

6. Wolf and Huang, *Marriage and Adoption*, gives mortality statistics on adopted daughters in Taiwan. Although the statistics are from Taiwan, there is no reason to believe that the trend was different in the provinces the interviewees came from during the same time period.

7. For studies of more institutionalized marriage resistance, see Stockard, *Daughters*, and Topley, "Marriage Resistance," 67–88.

8. The Sixth Chinese Communist Party Congress, held in Moscow from July to September 1928, passed the following resolution: "It is of the greatest importance to absorb

the masses of peasant women into the struggle for victory in the revolutionary movement in the rural villages. As they directly participate in the economy of the villages, occupy an important place among the troops of the poor peasants in the villages, and have enormous influence in the life of the peasants, they must participate in our movement. Our experience of peasant movements in the past teaches us that peasant women are the bravest of all fighters. . . . The main task of the Party is to consider as a positive fact that the peasant women are positively participating in the revolution and that they must be absorbed into the peasant organizations, particularly into the Peasant Associations and the Soviets, to the fullest extent" (Meijer, *Marriage Law,* 38).

9. Maxine Molyneux develops the argument that political strategies linking gender interests with revolution must include practical gender interests to appeal to women. She states that "it is the politicization of these practical interests and their transformation into strategic interests that women can identify with and support which constitutes a central aspect of feminist political practice" (Molyneux, "Mobilization without Emancipation," 234). Certainly the promise of equality between men and women had special appeal in Sichuan province, where many of the men smoked opium, leaving the women to do the bulk of the agricultural work without being able to own property or participate in political decisions.

10. Hill Gates suggests that desperately wanting to find security in a "government" job may have been a compelling force for these women, as it was later for Latina revolutionaries who called it "employamania" (personal communication, Stanford University, August 1995).

11. Linda Kerber suggests that joining the army and the revolutionary war in the United States resulted in a kind of citizenship to which women previously had no access: "Sometimes women considered themselves to be citizens and sometimes the nation referred to them as citizens in the same way as men, but not always. The notion that there are alternative forms of citizenship, not just the right to hold public office and to vote, but the right to engage in certain kinds of public activities, indicates a broadening of the definition of citizenship" ("May All Our Citizens," 87).

12. Jiang Jieshi was leader of the Nationalist army, more familiarly known as Chiang Kai-shek. She is referring to 1927, when the period of cooperation between the Nationalists and Communists ended and the Nationalists instituted the "White Terror" against Red activists.

13. The Japanese invaded Manchuria on September 18, 1931.

14. Kerber, "May All Our Citizens Be Soldiers."

15. Molyneux, "Mobilization without Emancipation."

16. "However, despite the economic circumstances of a woman, before or after marriage, individual assertiveness was rare indeed. This was not because she did not desire it, nor because it was lacking in her personality, but because there was not place for it within the highly structured social order" (Semergieff, *Changing Roles,* 8–9).

Chapter 6: Women at Work

1. Deng Yingchao, Zhou Enlai's wife. *Dajie,* literally meaning "older sister," is a term of affection and respect.

2. Wang Dingguo published an article about this in 1997. See Wang, "Fight to Ban Opium," 43–44.

Chapter 7: First Front Women

1. The Chinese Communists began putting their most able women in positions of leadership in the Women's Department to help develop the peasant women as revolutionary supporters. As Li Jianzhen's response to her appointment as head of the Women's Department suggests, this resulted in women being sidetracked from positions of importance in the CCP as a whole. For more background and analysis, see Gilmartin, *Engendering the Chinese Revolution*.

2. On May 30, 1925, the foreign concession police in Shanghai, led by a British officer, opened fire on students and workers who were demonstrating outside a Japanese-owned textile factory. About ten students were killed and many more wounded. The demonstrations spread quickly to other cities and gave impetus to the revolutionary movement around the country. See Chow, *The May Fourth Movement*, 5–6n.b, and Guillermaz, *History of the CCP*, 391n.10.

3. Established in 1922, the school also served as a convenient meeting place for male party members, who could come and go from their female relatives' school without arousing suspicion.

4. See chapter 2.

5. She was branch secretary (*zhibu shuji*) of the Soviet Central Government Organization Branch (*suwei ai zhongyang zhengfu jiguan de zhibu*). See Stranahan, *Underground*, especially chapter 2, for organization and duties of Communist party members in Shanghai, 1927–30. The CCP functioned in a similar way in the Soviet Base Area in the 1930s.

6. For the full text, see Mao, *Selected Works*, 1:137–39.

7. Spring Festival is the first day of the Lunar New Year, falling in January or February and often coinciding with Ash Wednesday on the Christian calendar. During Spring Festival, it was the tradition for the family to have one good meal together, and it was often the only time of the year when poorer people had meat to eat. It was also the traditional time to settle debts.

8. This was the same kind of campaign from which both Ma Yixiang (chapter 3) and Lin Yueqin (chapter 6) suffered.

9. James Harrison discusses the Luo Ming Line: "After formally moving its work to Juichin [Ruijin] in January, 1933, the Central Committee . . . called for a further intensification of the revolution and stepped up its attacks on Mao, accusing him of 'persistent and serious errors of right opportunism,' guerrillaism, sectarianism, monopolism, peasant mentality, conservatism, and narrow empiricism. Beginning in February, 1933, the criticism of these errors became the basis for the most extensive public purge of the period, the campaign against the 'Lo [Luo] Ming Line'" (Harrison, *Long March to Power*, 230). See also Guillermaz, *History of the CCP*, 222–23. Many historians view the Luo Ming Line as a political weapon used both in the leadership struggle and in the conflict over military strategy.

10. Comintern, the Communist International, was an organization based in Moscow that directed policy for all Communist parties around the world.

11. Most Chinese surnames are one syllable. *Ouyang* is one of the very few two-syllable family names.

12. Snow, *Red Star,* 172. Snow does not describe what constituted literacy in that time and place. Literacy could well have been defined as being able to write one's name and read Communist slogans.

13. Mao Zedong and He Zizhen's son was one of the children left behind with other families in Ruijin when the army left on the Long March. When efforts were made to locate these children after Liberation, none was ever found.

14. The All-China Women's Federation is the modern name. Li Jianzhen was head of the Women's Department in the Central Soviet Region when she came to Ruijin.

15. Benjamin Yang describes the Congress: "The Second Congress was in all ways a showy demonstration of the Soviet movement. A giant auditorium was constructed and decorated specifically for this occasion; the ceremony included a military parade and a salute of gunshots; the schedule was designed to promulgate the constitution, the code of laws, the government with various ministries, and so on. In sum, no effort had been spared in depicting the Soviet as a formal national state rather than the shaky rebellious base it actually was. The Soviet organ, *Red China,* reported that as many as 693 delegates and 83 alternate delegates came to attend the Congress from all over China, in addition to 1,500 guests from the world. However, the last figure at least was ridiculously exaggerated, or it must have pertained to those curious peasant watchers. To make this national state more authentic, the Congress stipulated formation of a ministry of foreign affairs in the government and nomination of all the Soviet bases as provinces, though none of the few Soviet bases had ever been so large as one third of an average province and all of them were encircled by vast KMT [Nationalist] territory and superior KMT troops" (Yang, *From Revolution to Politics,* 78–79).

16. Wang Ming was the CCP representative in the Comintern (Communist International) in Moscow, one of the group known as the Twenty-Eight Bolsheviks, Chinese men who had studied in the Soviet Union. Otto Braun, whose Chinese name was Li De, was sent by the Comintern as a military advisor. His memoir gives his own understanding of the situation as well as his experiences on the Long March. See Braun, *Comintern Agent.* For details about the leaders and events leading up to the Long March, also see Guillermaz, *History of the CCP;* Harrison, *Long March to Power;* Yang, *From Revolution to Politics;* or other standard histories of the Chinese Communists during this time period.

17. Guo Chen, a journalist for the *Worker's Daily* newspaper in Beijing who has been interviewing women Red Army soldiers since the late 1970s, said in a 1986 interview, "Whenever there was illness or death, she was held responsible for it. She was discriminated against all the time." Guo Chen, interview June 1986, Beijing.

18. See chapter 3.

19. Li Weihan was also known as Luo Man. His wife, Jin Weiying, or "Ah Jin," who was previously married to Deng Xiaoping, also made the Long March and was mentioned positively by the other women. After the Long March, she went to Moscow for medical treatment and apparently died there during a German attack.

20. Five women in the First Front Army gave birth during the year-long March: Liao Siguang gave birth in Guizhou in February or March. She reported that she did not know she was beyond the first trimester of pregnancy when the Long March began. He Zizhen

delivered a baby girl in Guizhou, late in March; Zeng Yu, whose husband was not a high official, had her baby in the mountains of Sichuan, in June or July just before crossing the snow mountains. Chen Huiqing, wife of Deng Fa, who was head of security on the Long March, had her baby in Sichuan, after climbing the glacier mountains sometime between June and August. The fifth, Li Jianhua, stayed with her husband in the radio team and did not travel with the other women. Her baby was born in Huining, near the end of the Long March. She brought the baby to Shaanbei in a basket.

21. "Dong Lao" is Dong Biwu, then head of the party school. The use of "Lao" after a name expresses affectionate respect for a person of high status who is usually an elder within a group. At forty-eight, he was one of the oldest who made the Long March. He was also a founder of the CCP and one of two of the original fifty-seven founding members who stayed with the CCP. The other was Mao Zedong. See Guillermaz, *History of the CCP,* 248 and chapters 4–5; also see Party History Research Centre, *History of the CCP,* 9–10, for a description of the founding congress of Communist revolutionaries who met in July 1921.

22. Party History Research Centre, *History of the CCP,* 93.

23. Li Yong, a graduate student at the Beijing Foreign Studies University, 1989–90, grew up in a village near Wang Quanyuan's home. He helped with the translation of Wang Quanyuan's interview tapes because he could understand her very colloquial local dialect. He said that when he was in primary school in the 1970s, he and his classmates went to the mountains every year for a day of the same kind of training. The teachers went ahead to leave signs on the paths to show the children which way to go. They placed pieces of wood or grass in the shape of an arrow to indicate the right path and made an "X" on the paths they should not take.

24. Wuqizhen is in northern Shaanxi, where the First Front Army stopped at the end of the Long March.

25. Wu Fulian was the wife of a high-ranking leader, Liu Xiao, and worked with Wang Quanyuan after they reached the Tibetan areas. Li Bozhao was married to Yang Shangkun, who became president of the Peoples' Republic of China in the 1980s. Li wrote many of the plays for propaganda teams.

26. She was remembering Yang Houzhen, the wife of Luo Binghui, commander, not political commissar, of the Ninth Army Group.

27. *Kan fangzi,* literally "watching the house," is used in a way similar to *kan haizi,* "watching a child" or "babysitting." People who *kan fangzi* usually lived outside the house, fulfilling a function somewhere between a security guard and a house sitter.

28. "Overturn the landlord" meant confiscating the landlord's clothes, bedding, and food supplies and sharing them between the army and the local people. See chapter 5 for a more detailed description of the process. Li Jianzhen was especially good at ferreting out the location of landlord homes, which were often deliberately unimpressive on the outside to deceive bandits.

29. Mao, *Selected Works,* 156. See note 3, chapter 3.

30. Wang Quanyuan, at about five feet, six inches, was tall for a woman of her generation.

31. The Miao people are one of the fifty-five Chinese minorities.

32. According to Benjamin Yang, the Nationalists did not know initially "whether the

Communists were making a feigned attack or a wholesale evacuation" when the Red Army marched out of the Jiangxi Soviet Base Area. After a battle that resulted in the first defeat for the Red Army, the Nationalists realized that the Communists were transferring large numbers of troops. The Hunan warlord, He Jian, "became the [Nationalist] commander-in-chief of the 'Bandit Pursuit Army.' Under He's leadership were not only the entire Hunan army, but also twelve divisions of the former [Nationalist] Northern Route Army led by Xue Yue. From that time until the autumn of 1935, Xue's troops of the KMT [Nationalist] Central Army served as the spearhead which chased the Red Army's rear all the way while local troops of each province which the Red Army reached served primarily as the checking force" (Yang, *From Revolution to Politics,* 103).

33. This former home of General Bai Huizhang, a Guizhou man who was commander of a Nationalist Division, is now a museum in Zunyi.

34. Party History Research Centre, *History of the CCP,* 94.

35. There are many military and political history books about the Zunyi Conference and what took place after. A concise, readable account appears in Ch'en, "Communist Movement," 94–97. Also see Yang, *From Revolution to Politics,* 100–128.

36. Not only were boys and girls between eight and fifteen who came on the Long March called *xiaogui,* or "little devils," but also mothers in their early twenties such as Xie Xiaomei.

37. Zhang Wentian, also known as Luo Fu, was the man Liu Ying married after the Long March. He replaced Bo Gu as general secretary during the Zunyi conference.

38. Interview with Li Xiaoxia, June 1997, Zunyi, Guizhou.

39. See chapter 8.

40. After the Long March, Mao Zedong sent He Zizhen to Moscow for medical treatment, divorced her, and married Jiang Qing in Yan'an.

41. *Nubing Liezhuan (Biographies of Women Soldiers),* vol 1.

42. The author visited the village, Kedu, in June 1997. The house where Mao Zedong and Zhu De briefly set up headquarters had been made into a museum. The curator told us that He Zizhen had stayed in a house about a kilometer away, but "there is no record of the other women" who were on the Long March. "There is no record of the women" was a response we heard repeatedly when tracing the Long March in Yunnan.

43. These stories of heroic men are vividly told by Snow, *Red Star,* 182–96; Smedley, *Great Road,* 318–28; and Wilson, *The Long March,* 151–84. Wilson quotes extensively from Snow, Smedley, and Chinese sources.

44. In his unpublished memoirs, John Service described sleeping bags his mother had made in Sichuan in 1921 using cotton sheeting permeated with tung oil (*China Hand,* 151). Using oil to waterproof cloth, animal skin, or paper must have been fairly common in the wet Sichuan climate.

45. The grain was either wheat or highland barley, *qingke.* Many women mentioned how difficult the barley was for them to digest.

46. In volume 2 of his autobiography, Zhang Guotao states that General Zhu De "told me that eight months before, when the 1st Front Army set out from Kiangsi [Jiangxi] to go west, there were about ninety thousand men. After innumerable hardships, only ten thousand of them arrived at Maokung" (Chang, *Rise of the CCP,* 379).

47. Ma Bufang, one of the Ma brothers from a Muslim warlord family that was aligned

with the Nationalists. For a deeper understanding of the history of the Chinese Muslims and their armies, see Lipman, *Familiar Strangers*.

48. Party History Research Centre, *History of the CCP,* 99.

Chapter 8: Left Behind

1. Guo Chen said that Gan Shiying was captured in battle: "When she was in custody, she learned that the guerrilla leader had hidden himself with a local family. By some gestures, she directed the leader to escape. She was insulted [*sic*] by a Nationalist Company Commander and was put into prison. Later she was set free because of her county magistrate father's influence. But she was locked up inside the family home and was rather badly treated by her father. Then she managed to get out and married the guerrilla leader whom she had helped to escape. But not long after, he was killed in a battle. She always thought about him. One day, walking on the street in Chengdu she came to a bookstand and read in a magazine about Luo Shiwen, the Party Secretary of the Sichuan Provincial Committee. Luo recommended her to Pan Hannian who was then leading the underground work in Shanghai. Pan recommended her to Yan'an to study and to recover from her poor health. In Yan'an, she got married to a man who was later the vice-commander of the Inner Mongolia Military Region" (interview with Guo Chen at Radio Beijing, June 1986).

2. Baxian was a county seat a few miles south of Chongqing, on the Yangzi River.

3. Maotai is a town in Guizhou famous for the excellent grain liquor produced there.

4. In January 1988 when we interviewed Xie Xiaomei, Hu Yaobang had already been deposed as secretary general of the Communist party, the highest-ranking party official. Because she stressed his name, we wondered whether he were the one who had helped Luo Ming and Xie Xiaomei become reinstated in the party in the early 1980s. Beijing students mourning Hu's death in April 1989 marked the beginning of the Democracy Movement, which ended in the Tiananmen Incident, June 1989.

5. The Fourth Army soldiers were accusing Mao of a serious political deviation from the main political line when they labeled his actions opportunism.

6. Kang Keqing is referring to her husband by the respectfully affectionate "Lao," combined with the first syllable of his title, *Zongsiling,* commander-in-chief.

7. Interview with Liu Jian, a Fourth Front Army woman cadre, Guangzhou, January 1988.

8. *Dianxin* are snacks and pastries, better known in the West by the Cantonese rendering as *dim sum*.

9. For years, the Red Army had been arming itself by capturing guns from the Nationalists, who were supplied in part by the Germans.

10. Li Kaifeng was a soldier with the Fourth Front Army.

11. Ma Buqing was one of the Muslim warlord brothers who were cooperating with the Nationalists.

12. Literally, "lifelong partner."

13. According to Islamic practice, a child born to a mixed couple takes its religious identity from the mother.

14. Deng Liujin, who worked closely with Wu Fulian when they were in Ruijin, told us, "There are many stories about the death of Wu Fulian. Some people say that she was

wounded and couldn't move on, so she used the pistol to kill herself instead of being captured. Others say she was captured by the enemy and died in a hospital. It's unclear how she died." Because Wang Quanyuan was not with Wu Fulian when she died, the actual circumstances of her death remain a mystery.

15. Wang Quanyuan insisted that she had actually died, not just lost consciousness.

16. Wang Dingguo, a Fourth Front Army soldier, was working for the party organization in Lanzhou, trying to place all the Red Army soldiers who had survived captivity. She said she had tried her best to get Wang Quanyuan reinstated in the army (interview with Wang Dingguo at China International Radio Beijing, June 1986).

17. Guo Chen interview, 1986.

Conclusion

1. In her dissertation, Patricia Stranahan describes the area:

On October 25, 1935, the first contingent of the battered Red Army arrived in Shensi from the Long March. Led by Mao Tse-tung, Chou En-lai and other party officials, the troops sought refuge in the last Communist strong-hold in China. What they found was a desolate and poverty-stricken area ravaged by war and famine, and abandoned by any kind of recognizable government. The devastation the Red Army encountered as it entered Shensi was not solely the result of the political, economic and natural disasters of the early twentieth century; the breakdown of social and other institutions had begun generations before the upheaval of the early part of the century merely hastened a deteriorating situation.

Shensi province, which eventually became the center of the Border Region, had once been the site of major dynasties. But when China's economic and political center shifted to South and Central China during the Sung Dynasty, the area declined. Surrounded on three sides by mountains and lacking its former social and governmental vitality, the region became increasingly isolated from the rest of China. By the 1930's, the province had only a few public roads and just one railroad line." (Jackal, "Yenan Women," 58–59)

2. Mao, *Selected Works,* 1:160, speaking at Wayaobao, Shaanxi, December 27, 1935.

3. Rubie S. Watson discusses the naming and not-naming practices in a village near Hong Kong. Although the site of her study is quite narrow, she offers a broader perspective in her discussion of the subject ("The Named," 619–31). Francesca Bray also discusses the gendered aspects of naming in Chinese families in a footnote (*Technology and Gender,* 240).

4. Spence, *To Change China.*

5. Mann, *Precious Records,* 8.

6. Literally, "share comforts and hardships, joys and sorrows." This phrase is one many people who came of age in the Communist revolution from the 1920s to the 1950s use when describing their feelings of closeness to their comrades.

Bibliography

Bangs, Richard, and Christian Kallen. *Riding the Dragon's Back: The Race to Raft the Upper Yangtze.* New York: Atheneum, 1989.

Bertram, James. *Unconquered: Journal of a Year's Adventures among the Fighting Peasants of North China.* New York: John Day Co., 1939.

Brandt, Conrad, Benjamin Schwartz, and John Fairbanks, eds. *Documentary History of Chinese Communism.* Cambridge, Mass.: Harvard University Press, 1952.

Braun, Otto. *A Comintern Agent in China, 1932–1939.* Stanford, Calif.: Stanford University Press, 1982.

Bray, Francesca. *Technology and Gender: Fabrics of Power in Late Imperial China.* Berkeley: University of California Press, 1997.

Chang Kuo-t'ao. *The Rise of the Chinese Communist Party, 1928–1938.* Lawrence: University Press of Kansas, 1971–72.

Ch'en, Jerome. "The Communist Movement 1927–1937." In *The Nationalist Era in China, 1927–1949.* Ed. Lloyd E. Eastman, Jerome Ch'en, Suzanne Pepper, and Lyman P. Van Slyke. Cambridge: Cambridge University Press, 1990. 53–114.

———. *The Highlanders of Central China.* Armonk, N.Y.: M.E. Sharpe, 1992.

Chesneaux, Jean, Francoise Le Barbier, and Marie-Claire Bergere. *China from the 1911 Revolution to Liberation.* New York: Pantheon, 1977.

Chow Tse-tsung. *The May Fourth Movement: Intellectual Revolution in Modern China.* Cambridge, Mass.: Harvard University Press, 1960.

Croll, Elisabeth. *The Women's Movement in China: A Selection of Readings, 1949–1973.* London: Anglo-Chinese Educational Institute, 1974.

Cusack, Dymphna. *Chinese Women Speak.* Sydney: Angus and Robertson, 1958.

De Groot, Gerard, and Corinna Peniston-Bird, eds. *A Soldier and a Woman: Women in the Military up to 1945.* London: Pearson Education, 2000.

Dombrowski, Nicole Ann, ed. *Women and War in the Twentieth Century: Enlisted with or without Consent.* New York: Garland, 1999.

Eastman, Lloyd E., Jerome Ch'en, Suzanne Pepper, and Lyman P. Van Slyke, eds. *The Nationalist Era in China, 1927–1949.* Cambridge: Cambridge University Press, 1990.

Elshtain, Jean Bethke, and Sheila Tobias, eds. *Women, Militarism, and War.* Totowa, N.J.: Roman & Littlefield, 1990.

Garavente, Anthony. "He Long and the Rural Revolution in West-Central China, 1927–1935." Ph.D. dissertation, University of California at Los Angeles, 1978.

Gates, Hill. "On a New Footing: Footbinding and the Coming of Modernity." *Jindai Zhongguo Funu Shiyanjiu* (Research on Women in Modern Chinese History) 5 (August 1997): 115–35.

Gelles, Edith. *Portia: The World of Abigail Adams.* Bloomington: Indiana University Press, 1992.

Gilmartin, Christina Kelley. *Engendering the Chinese Revolution: Radical Women, Communist Politics, and Mass Movements in the 1920s.* Berkeley: University of California Press, 1995.

———. "Gender, Political Culture, and Women's Mobilization in the Chinese Nationalist Revolution, 1924–1927." In *Engendering China: Women, Culture and the State.* Ed. Christina K. Gilmartin, Gail Hershatter, Lisa Rofel, and Tyrene White. Cambridge, Mass.: Harvard University Press, 1994. 195–225.

Gilmartin, Christina K., Gail Hershatter, Lisa Rofel, and Tyrene White, eds. *Engendering China: Women, Culture, and the State.* Cambridge, Mass.: Harvard University Press, 1994.

Guillermaz, Jacques. *A History of the Chinese Communist Party, 1921–1949.* New York: Random House, 1972.

Han Zi, ed. *Nubing Liezhuan* (Biographies of Women Soldiers). Shanghai: Shanghai Wenyi Publishing House, 1986.

Harrison, James Pinckney. *The Long March to Power: A History of the Chinese Communist Party, 1921–72.* London: Macmillan, 1972.

Hershatter, Gail. *Dangerous Pleasures: Prostitution and Modernity in Twentieth-Century Shanghai.* Berkeley: University of California Press, 1997.

Huaxia Composition Committee. *Huaxia Funu Mingren Cidian* (Dictionary of Famous Chinese Women). Beijing: Huaxia Publishing House, 1988.

Jackal, Patricia Stranahan. "Development of Policy for Yenan Women, 1937–1947." Ph.D. dissertation, University of Pennsylvania, 1979.

Johnson, Kay Ann. *Women, the Family, and Peasant Revolution in China.* Chicago: University of Chicago Press, 1983.

Kelly, Joan. *Women, History, Theory: The Essays of Joan Kelly.* Chicago: University of Chicago Press, 1984.

Kerber, Linda. "May All Our Citizens Be Soldiers and All Our Soldiers Citizens: The Ambiguities of Female Citizenship in the New Nation." In *Women, Militarism, and War.* Ed. Jean Bethke Elshtain and Sheila Tobias. Totowa, N.J.: Roman & Littlefield, 1990. 89–103.

Kingston, Maxine Hong. *The Woman Warrior: Memoirs of a Girlhood among Ghosts.* New York: Vintage Books, 1989.

Ko, Dorothy. "Rethinking Sex, Female Agency, and Footbinding." *Jindai Zhongguo Funu Shiyanjiu* (Research on Women in Modern Chinese History) 7 (August 1999): 79–105.

———. *Teachers of the Inner Chambers.* Stanford, Calif.: Stanford University Press, 1994.

Kristoff, Nicholas. "After Half a Century, Japan Is Confronting a Wartime Atrocity." *New York Times,* 27 March 1995.

Li Xiaolin. "Women in the Chinese Military." Ph.D. dissertation, University of Maryland, 1995.

Li Zhisui. *The Private Life of Chairman Mao: The Memoirs of Mao's Personal Physician, Dr. Li Zhisui.* Trans. Tai Hung-chao. New York: Random House, 1994.

Lipman, Jonathan. *Familiar Strangers: A History of Muslims in Northwest China.* Seattle: University of Washington Press, 1997.

Ma Yixiang. *Chaoyang Hua.* Beijing: China Youth Publishing House, 1978.

Malraux, Andre. *Man's Fate/Le Condition Humaine.* New York: Modern Library, 1934.

Mann, Susan. *Precious Records: Women in China's Long Eighteenth Century.* Stanford, Calif.: Stanford University Press, 1997.

Mao Zedong. *Selected Works of Mao Tse-tung.* Volumes 1 and 4. Peking: Foreign Languages Press, 1967.

Meijer, M. J. *Marriage Law and Policy in the Chinese People's Republic.* Hong Kong: Hong Kong University Press, 1971.

Molyneux, Maxine. "Mobilization without Emancipation: Women's Interests, the State, and Revolution in Nicaragua." *Feminist Studies* 11 (Summer 1985): 227–54.

Ono Kazuko. *Chinese Women in a Century of Revolution, 1850–1950.* Stanford, Calif.: Stanford University Press, 1989.

Party History Research Centre of the Central Committee of the Chinese Communist Party. *The History of the Chinese Communist Party: A Chronology of Events, 1919–1990.* Beijing: Foreign Languages Press, 1991.

Pruitt, Ida. *A Daughter of Han: The Autobiography of a Chinese Working Woman.* Stanford, Calif.: Stanford University Press, 1975.

Salisbury, Charlotte. *Long March Diary.* New York: Walker, 1986.

Salisbury, Harrison. *The Long March: The Untold Story.* New York: Harper & Row, 1985.

Semergieff, Kathleen B. *The Changing Roles of Women in the People's Republic of China, 1949–1967.* Ann Arbor, Mich.: University Microfilms International, 1985.

Service, John S. "China Hand: Early Memoirs of John Service." Manuscript in preparation.

Shaffer, Lynda. *Mao and the Workers: The Hunan Labor Movement, 1920–1923.* Armonk, N.Y.: M.E. Sharpe, 1982.

Smedley, Agnes. *The Great Road: The Life and Times of Chu Teh.* New York: Monthly Review Press, 1972.

Snow, Edgar. *Red Star over China.* New York: Random House, 1938.

Snow, Helen Foster. *The Chinese Communists: Sketches and Autobiographies of the Old Guard.* Westport, Conn.: Greenwood, 1952.

Spence, Jonathan. *To Change China.* Boston: Little, Brown, 1969.

Stacey, Judith. *Patriarchy and Socialist Revolution in China.* Berkeley: University of California Press, 1983.

Stockard, Janice. *Daughters of the Canton Delta.* Stanford, Calif.: Stanford University Press, 1989.

Stranahan, Patricia. *Underground: The Shanghai Communist Party and the Politics of Survival, 1927–1937.* Lanham, Md.: Rowman & Littlefield, 1998.

Stree Shakti Sanghatana. *We Were Making History.* London: Zed, 1989.

Topley, Margery. "Marriage Resistance in Rural Kwangtung." In *Women in Chinese Society.* Ed. Margery Wolf and Roxane Witke. Stanford, Calif.: Stanford University Press, 1975. 67–88.

Van Slyke, Lyman. *Enemies and Friends: The United Front in Chinese Communist History.* Stanford, Calif.: Stanford University Press, 1967.

Wang Dingguo. "The Fight to Ban Opium in the Soviet Areas of Sichuan." *Women of China* (October 1997): 43–4.

Wang Fan-hsi. *Chinese Revolutionary: Memoirs, 1919–1949.* Oxford: Oxford University Press, 1980.

Wang Zheng. *Women in the Chinese Enlightenment: Oral and Textual Histories.* Berkeley: University of California Press, 1999.

Watson, Rubie. "The Named and the Nameless: Gender and Person in Chinese Society." *American Ethnologist* 13 (November 1986): 619–31.

Wilson, Dick. *The Long March, 1935: The Epic of Chinese Communism's Survival.* New York: Viking, 1971.

Winchester, Simon. *The River at the Center of the World.* New York: Henry Holt, 1996.

Wolf, Arthur, and Chieh-shan Huang. *Marriage and Adoption in China, 1845–1945.* Stanford, Calif.: Stanford University Press, 1980.

Wolf, Margery. *Revolution Postponed: Women in Contemporary China.* Stanford, Calif.: Stanford University Press, 1985.

Wolf, Margery, and Roxane Witke, eds. *Women in Chinese Society.* Stanford, Calif.: Stanford University Press, 1975.

Yang, Benjamin. *From Revolution to Politics: Chinese Communists on the Long March.* Boulder, Colo.: Westview, 1990.

Yang, Xianyi, and Gladys Yang. *Excerpts from Three Classical Chinese Novels.* Beijing: Zhongguo Guoji Shudian/Panda Books, 1981.

Young, Helen Praeger. "From Soldier to Doctor: A Chinese Woman's Story of the Long March." *Science and Society* 59 (Winter 1995–96): 531–47.

———. "Why We Joined the Revolution: Voices of Chinese Women Soldiers." In *Women and War in the 20th Century: Enlisted with and without Consent.* Ed. Nicole Dombrowski. New York: Garland, 1999. 92–111.

———. "Women at Work: Chinese Soldiers on the Long March, 1934–35." In *A Soldier and a Woman: Women in the Military up to 1945.* Ed. Gerard De Groot and Corinna Peniston-Bird. London: Pearson Education, 2000. 83–99.

Interviews Cited

Chen Zongying, Beijing, June 1987

Deng Liujin, Beijing, June 1986

He Manqiu, Beijing, December 1986 and March 1987

Jian Xianfo, Beijing, September 1988

Jian Xianren, Beijing, December 1988

Kang Keqing, Beijing, January 1987

Li Guiying, Nanjing, February 1989

Li Jianzhen, Guangzhou, January 1988
Li Yanfa, Beijing, June 1988
Liao Siguang, Guangzhou, handwritten material
Lin Yueqin, Beijing, January 1988
Liu Jian, Guangzhou, January 1988
Liu Ying, Beijing, January 1988
Ma Yixiang, Guangzhou, January 1988
Qian Xijun, Beijing, September 1987
Quan Weihua, Beijing, December 1986 and June 1987
Wang Dingguo, Beijing, June 1986
Wang Quanyuan, Taihe, Jiangxi, February 1989
Wei Xiuying, Nanchang, February 1989
Xie Fei, Beijing, October 1988
Xie Xiaomei, Guangzhou, January 1988
Zhang Wen, Beijing, December 1986 and June 1987
Zhong Yuelin, Beijing, February 1989

Additional Interviews

Guo Chen, Beijing, June 1986
Wang Shen, Shigu, Yunnan, June 1997
Yan Jintang, Beijing, March 1986
Zhou Guichuan, Lijiang, Yunnan, June 1997
Zhou Guiying, Lijiang, Yunnan, June 1997

Index

HELEN PRAEGER YOUNG is an associate scholar with the Center for East Asian Studies at Stanford University. Her research interests include Chinese women's modern history and cross-cultural studies.

Composed in 10.5/13 Minion
with Minion display
by Celia Shapland
for the University of Illinois Press
Designed by Paula Newcomb
Manufactured by Thomson-Shore, Inc.

University of Illinois Press
1325 South Oak Street
Champaign, IL 61820-6903
www.press.uillinois.edu